EBELS
AND
IVALS

The Contestive Spirit
in *The Canterbury Tales*

Edited by
Susanna Greer Fein, David Raybin,
and Peter C. Braeger

Foreword by
Derek Pearsall

SMC XXIX
Medieval Institute Publications

WESTERN MICHIGAN UNIVERSITY

Kalamazoo, Michigan, USA—1991

Library of Congress Cataloging-in-Publication Data

Rebels and rivals : the contestive spirit in The Canterbury tales /
   edited by Susanna Greer Fein, David Raybin, and Peter C. Braeger ;
   foreword by Derek Pearsall.
       p.   cm. -- (SMC ; 29)
   Includes bibliographical references and index.
   ISBN 0-918720-41-9. -- ISBN 0-918720-42-7 (pbk.)
   1. Chaucer, Geoffrey, d. 1400.   Canterbury tales.   2. Contests in
literature.   I. Fein, Susanna Greer.   II. Raybin, David.
III. Braeger, Peter C., d. 1988.   IV. Series: Studies in medieval
culture ; 29.
CB351.S83 vol. 29
[PR1875.C65]
821'.1--dc20   90-27626
                                                    CIP

Cover design by Linda K. Judy
Printed in the United States of America

For Elizabeth, Carolyn,

Steven, and Jonathan

CONTENTS

FOREWORD

Another collection of essays on *The Canterbury Tales*, it might be said, stands a chance of being looked at somewhat skeptically by those who are conscious that they have still not read the last two or three such collections. They might prefer it too if such a volume could be readily allocated to its appropriate compartment in the filing cabinet of Chaucer criticism—iconographic analysis, historicism, historical materialism, new historicism, new hermeneutics—and safely forgotten.

There is something about this collection of essays that makes it not so easy to forget. It is not the force and coherence of any common argument to which the contributors subscribe. There is no common argument here, no unanimity of approach: on the contrary, there are a good many unresolved debates between the essays. Nor do the essays have in common a dewy freshness, as of young college teachers recently given money to bathe for the first time in the well of English undefiled. They were not, if my memory serves me aright, all of them very young, and dewy is not their character: something of owl-like sharpness, weasel-like inquisitiveness, mule-like cantankerousness, would be more appropriate. What strikes me again and again about these essays is the very instinctive way in which the authors of them ask new questions, set new agendas, raise new issues. Sometimes it may be because they do not know the old ones, and sometimes the instincts may be those of an unruliness that is determined to give trouble to the authorities. But there is a confidence, too, borne of good close reading and of the sense of closeness to Chaucer, to his poetry at least, that such reading gives.

I have found a lot to disagree with in these essays, and quite a few moments of exasperation. One of the great virtues of the book is that it stimulates this reaction and then offers a rebuke to those who have it. I do not mean in terms of a compulsory pluralism of interpretation: there may be something to be said for letting a thousand flowers bloom (or a thousand points of light twinkle), but what this seems to mean in literary discussion is that one should accept that one's own hard-won opinion on a matter is no more valid than someone else's. There hardly seems any point in putting pen to paper if one's sense of one's own opinion is as feebly relativistic as that. In what frame of mind can a point be argued if it is not to persuade others of its validity? The assertiveness of those who argue that all judgment is relative, and structured in the intersection of social discourse, is a happy absurdity: the unequivocal statement of the inescapability of equivocation is somehow comforting.

It is not, therefore, that this collection of essays persuades one of the interpretative validity of the opinions expressed. Rather, what it gives is a sense of the relish and vigor with which reading is carried on, of the sharpness of response that Chaucer challenges in his readers.

Sometimes this is displayed in the pursuit of some unexpected pattern of imagery or series of associations within a tale, the ups and downs and to-ing and fro-ing that give significant locus of action to The Knight's Tale, for instance (Woods), or the preoccupation with age and senescence in The Reeve's Tale (Fein), or the succession of allusions to the apostolic gifts of the Holy Spirit in The Summoner's Tale and to the house of friars that by contrast will only "inherit the wind" (Ruud). Allusions to Abraham in the same tale set up some piquant contrasts between the place where the faithful find themselves (in his bosom) and the place where the friars, so to speak, "end up."

Sometimes the boldness of innovation is in some twist given to the familiar, some prolonging of attention to the design of a tale that elicits further patterns of meaning, like the suggestion of an opposition between clever John and dull-witted Aleyn in The Reeve's Tale (Cowgill), which makes them, also, part of the nasty adversarial one-upmanship of the tale: the Reeve cannot even imagine *them* as friends. There is something of this boldness too in the argument that Chaucer gives some credit, in The Canon's Yeoman's Tale (Raybin), to the artistic striving that is present in the alchemical enterprise, the desire to assert the human will, the hope of something beyond the limits of the mortal frame, as itself a kind of life of the spirit and not utterly to be condemned.

Elsewhere, it is attention to what Linda Georgianna calls "the forgotten passages," the passages that none of us underlines in preparing our classes, that releases the Chaucerian time-capsule of meaning—the subtle and sensitive "improvisatory rhetoric" of the falcon's complaint in The Squire's Tale (Owen), or the witty putting-down of the friar in the final encounter with the local gentry in The Summoner's Tale (Georgianna). The analysis here of the friar's relationship with the local bourgeoisie (citizen Thomas) as contrasted with his relationship with the lord of the manor and his people is as nice a bit of new historicism as one could wish for, though labels are not the first thing one wants to reach for in reading such witty and alert textual-historical analysis.

Labels would be equally inappropriate elsewhere. Bakhtin swims into one's mind in reading the account of the *Canterbury Tales* pilgrimage as a dialogue of carnivalesque and lenten affinities (Jonassen), but there is much more to this wide-ranging essay than such an association would signify: the pilgrimage rehearses and symbolizes moments of profound change and adaptation in social structure, acting as a bridge to new modes of experience, in which the Host mediates between the Inn and the Cathedral against the threat of the Pardoner, who denies the

legitimacy of both. Nor is there anything of doctrinaire feminism about the vigorous shaking given to those male readers of
The Wife of Bath's Tale (Hagen) who are comforted to find
Chaucer at the end of the tale slipping the cloak of "normality"
back onto the womanhood that has been so aggressively deviant.

Established scholars will enjoy the versatility and incisive-
ness of much of the reading in these essays, even though they
may be heard muttering stifled oaths from time to time. New
readers will relish the combativeness and assurance, the readi-
ness to try out new ideas. No one could miss the vitality and
open-mindedness of approach, or remain uninvigorated by it.

CAMBRIDGE, MASSACHUSETTS   DEREK PEARSALL

PREFACE

Greet was the strif and long bitwix hem tweye,
If that I hadde leyser for to seye. . . .

(I.1187-88)

Once Palamon and Arcite discover that they both have fallen in love with Emily, their rivalrous responses control the rest of the Knight's story. The two men quarrel long and hard, striving, in the words of Arcite, "as dide the houndes for the boon" (line 1177). Not until one cousin is dead does the other win the lady, but then only after years of mourning the lost rival. In a strange way, it seems as though the tale's energy derives more from the rivalry than from the lady's actual favor. As disruptive as this rivalry is, it fuels separate idealistic impulses that drive the young men toward their single cherished goal.

Strife among characters occurs everywhere in *The Canterbury Tales*, in the stories as well as the links. Characters seem always ready to dispute, contradict, declaim, and contend about almost anything. A competitive spirit suffuses the work, from the tale-telling among pilgrims and the personal rivalries that develop on the pilgrimage to the conflicts, beguilings, and one-uppings that go on in the tales.

In fact, once the contest motif is established in the General Prologue and confirmed chaotically by the Miller's insistence that he, not the Monk, tell the second tale, confrontation becomes something of a norm in the development of the poem.

Each narrator, and indeed many a character, insists on the rightness of his or her individual vision, and from quite a few we receive richly cantankerous excursuses upon human behavior. Chaucer's poem exists as a compendium of human comparisons which express life as it is variously lived, holding to perspectives that are individually narrow and collectively focused upon the world in which we all struggle to survive. Conflict among characters—and also among genres, styles, and meanings—is a Chaucerian trademark, a feature of his ever-playful, ever-probing enactment of diverse human affairs.

Conflict does not, however, necessarily require a rivalry among two or more individuals. Often it is the rebel, acting alone or on behalf of a group, who prompts the antagonistic momentum within a Canterbury drama. Perkyn Revelour of The Cook's Tale so mocks the stolid, working-class life to which he is bound that his master must rid his house of the "riotous servaunt" (I.4408). Other typed characters who actively strive to turn the world's values inside-out include not only the intrusive clerks of the fabliaux and the "riotoures thre" of The Pardoner's Tale (VI.661) but also the heroic Christian figures in the tales of the Man of Law and the Second Nun. Chaucer allows readers a glimpse from the pagan perspective, in which acceptance of the Christian faith is an act of rebellion. The Sultan abandons the "lawe sweete" of Mahoun (MLT, II.223) so that he may wed Custance, and Dame Hermengyld adopts Christianity in secret, "Lest that hir housbonde, shortly for to sayn, / Wolde hire for Jhesu Cristes love han slayn" (MLT, II.564-65). In The Second Nun's Tale the religion of Pope Urban and his companions places them well outside the established social order. Urban's existence is in fact much like that of an outlaw; so often has he been "dampned to be deed" (SNT, VIII.310) that he lives covertly in a burial ground.

Rebellious narrators whose social positions suggest anti-hierarchical roles also help to develop the poem's contestive spirit. When the Miller insists on telling the second tale he challenges both Harry Bailly's authority as contest-master and the social rules governing precedence. From this point on, the outlook of an uninhibited drunken man will hold a position in the tale-telling debate as secure as that of a restrained, sober philosopher like the Knight. The prologue of the Wife of Bath offers, in turn, a different challenge, subverting not only patriarchal values but also the storytelling contest itself. Blithely ignoring the interruptive, spluttering reactions of Pardoner, Friar, and Summoner, the Wife weaves a long preamble that undercuts the very notion that the contest will be based exclusively on tales. The Pardoner's Prologue and Tale breaks the bounds of the tale-telling form even further: the demonic rebel attempts to use his tale "for to wynne" (VI.403)—not the contest but his fellow-pilgrims' gold. This challenge opposes the game itself, as proposed by Harry Bailly. In thus probing the limits of his invention, Chaucer highlights the contestive mode in all its pervasiveness, power, and constraints.

Understanding the rebels and rivals of the Canterbury world may well allow us to recognize why Chaucer so insists on the individuality of the characters he creates, why so many characters (rightly or wrongly) resist structures, why they challenge or reject social dogmas, often overturning them. One of Chaucer's favored Boethian images is that of a bird in a cage, well treated but nonetheless seeking desperately to escape:

> Taak any bryd, and put it in a cage,
> And do al thyn entente and thy corage
> To fostre it tendrely with mete and drynke
> Of alle deyntees that thou kanst bithynke,
> And keep it al so clenly as thou may,
> Although his cage of gold be never so gay,
> Yet hath this brid, by twenty thousand foold,
> Levere in a forest that is rude and coold
> Goon ete wormes and swich wrecchednesse.
> For evere this brid wol doon his bisynesse
> To escape out of his cage, yif he may.

PREFACE

His libertee this brid desireth ay.

(MancT, IX.163-74;
see also SqT, V.610-20;
Bo III.m2.21-31)

Alisoun in The Miller's Tale exemplifies such a bird, as does the Merchant's May. The aged husband of each woman, jealous of his young wife's beauty and fearing cuckoldry, "heeld hire narwe in cage" (MilT, I.3224). The willful wives nonetheless break free. The wild spirit that prefers freedom to the luxurious cage symbolizes to no small degree the human inclination toward contrariety, subversion, and contention. In it there is a disruptive waywardness, but there is also the collectively humane voice of individual existence and individual expression.

The essays that make up this collection offer several provocative interpretations of the rivalrous or rebellious spirits that inhabit the worlds of Chaucer's tales. Frederick B. Jonassen's essay, which opens the volume, explores how Chaucer evokes the value systems of the carnivalesque and the lenten to infuse the poem with two diametrically opposed attitudes toward life. Founding his analysis on the socio-historicism of Mikhail Bakhtin and the social anthropology of Victor Turner, Jonassen posits that Inn and Cathedral represent the two symbolic extremes of Chaucer's vision. After the opening in the Tabard establishes a sense of carnival abandon, the subsequent pilgrimage and storytelling connect the two poles of Inn (Carnival) and Cathedral (Lent). The pull between the two intrinsically contentious absolutes epitomizes Chaucer's characteristically pragmatic yet playful focus on the extremes of human belief. The Parson's sober faith and Harry Bailly's tavern humor determine the outside limits within which pilgrims and characters think and act.

The essays of William F. Woods and Bruce Kent Cowgill demonstrate how rivalries among characters who seem almost entirely alike come to motivate or reflect a tale's larger sense of conflict. Woods examines how spatial relationships in The Knight's Tale reinforce the competing values of a generally passive Palamon and a more active Arcite. It is the rivalry between the two fellows—each man's unwillingness to accept that his cousin succeed where he does not—that leads the Thebans to rebel in separate ways against Theseus's will. The characters' axial movements serve to confirm the hierarchical value system that underlies the tale, and a charting of these movements reveals how the two men's different paths corroborate their inner intents.

Bruce Kent Cowgill's study of the clerks in The Reeve's Tale reevaluates a long critical tradition that sees the two Cambridge scholars who get the better of the proud, thievish miller as essentially equivalent characters. While Chaucer's French analogues do indeed treat the pair as interchangeable, Chaucer has created a duo with subtly individuated features. John considers himself the craftier of the two, but it is Aleyn, cast in the role of stupid dolt, who instinctively initiates the bed-switching to get even with the miller. Cowgill's essay demonstrates how the relationship between the two youthful protagonists is itself a competitive contest that reflects in miniature the struggle between miller and students.

This larger conflict between Symkyn and the clerks is the subject of Susanna Greer Fein's analysis of The Reeve's Tale. She examines the tale as a contest between the generations, that is, as a perennial struggle for dominance that always, eventually, topples the old and supplants them with upstart youth. Chaucer portrays the conflict paradigmatically by means of several iconographic props, Symkyn's bald head and the baby's cradle among them. The Reeve's complaint on old age, with its elaborate figure of the cask of life, is seen to provide the central motif of the tale, opening the reader to multiple allusions to life as a cycle. Examining traditional medieval representations of the Wheel of Life, Fein demonstrates how the tale makes life out to be a contestive game where the players grow so embroiled in the spirit of winning and losing—the pleasure or bitterness of it—that they fail to see the overall wheel-turning that unites them all in the passage of time.

The limit of Chaucer's own rebellious vision is the subject of Susan K. Hagen's feminist reading of The Wife of Bath's Prologue and Tale. Hagen sees the Wife's performance as Chaucer's valiant but inevitably unsuccessful experiment in formulating a feminist hermeneutics. The Wife of Bath's Prologue stands as Chaucer's most ambitious creation of an uncompromising feminist voice, but the capitulation to traditional male values implicit in the old woman's final submission to the knight's desires in The Wife of Bath's Tale shows Chaucer ultimately to accept the traditional androcentric hierarchies. Nonetheless, Hagen applauds Chaucer's humanist effort. While the poet's achievements fall short by the standards of twentieth-century feminism, it is inappropriate to condemn him for them. The pervasive fourteenth-century world view simply did not permit that a male poet formulate an authentic gynocentric hermeneutics, or even a truly humanocentric one. To live a life of male privilege necessitated that one be what we would call sexist.

Jay Ruud's and Linda Georgianna's essays on The Summoner's Tale both characterize the friar's place as disruptive and alien in a world governed by appropriate, long-standing rules, whether they be apostolic or feudal. Ruud's essay examines the friar's espoused role as inheritor of the apostolic "spirit," with all the ramifications—both religious and scatalogical—of that wonderfully multiplicitous word. The friar practices his calling by inverting and perverting several Pauline and Franciscan injunctions; and, indeed, the sermon on ire calls in yet another reversal of the gift of the Holy Ghost. Grounded in scriptural and patristic analysis, Ruud's study draws our attention to a previously unexplored allusion to Abraham's bosom that seems to contrast the true inheritors of the Spirit to those false inheritors—the greedy friars—who cluster so graphically in the devil's arse.

Linda Georgianna's interests lie in Friar John's leech-like

intrusion into the social order rather than in his perversion of the religious strictures. Her essay focuses upon the generally ignored court scene toward the end of the tale, reading it as a commentary on the text and observing in the behavior of Friar John toward churl and lord a subtle, symbolic portrayal of the shifting, economy-based class relations that governed fourteenth-century English social life. The tale's conclusion comically restores feudal hierarchy in the face of a rising bourgeois class. It is Friar John, not Thomas, who is the upstart rebel, and the prying, presumptuous confessor is put squarely back in his place by the scatological mockery to which he is subjected in both the peasant and the aristocratic households.

In the essays that close the collection, Charles A. Owen, Jr., and David Raybin examine the critically unpopular tales of the Squire and the Canon's Yeoman by exploring the moral values that underlie Chaucer's attitudes toward rhetoric and art. Owen looks specifically at the lyric convention of complaint, with its own formal rhetoric of discontent and unhappiness, which is in its way another form of contest though one turned inward to self-pity and analysis rather than outward to direct insult. Owen offers a close textual analysis of a neglected passage—the falcon's complaint in the second part of The Squire's Tale. He compares the metrics and structure of the complaint (and especially the forty-line passage that is its thematic heart) to similar passages in *Anelida and Arcite* and The Complaint of Mars, and proposes that Chaucer's experiments with the complaint form grew increasingly refined—and successful—as his career progressed. In the falcon Chaucer creates a betrayed heroine who decries the linguistic duplicity so common in the speech of a wooer; her own language, carefully wrought and powerfully emotive, does not so much avenge the tercelet's deception as transcend it.

In an argument that recalls Jonassen's essay on the mixed duality of Inn and Cathedral, David Raybin reads The Canon's Yeoman's Tale as Chaucer's carefully wrought illustration of two intertwining yet seemingly opposed modes of human knowledge, utterance, and existence: the highest aspirations of art and the lowest reality of matter. Raybin proposes that the meshing of high ideals and sordid reality is a central element in Chaucer's vision of a sturdy human spirit that bends often but shatters only rarely. The key to understanding Chaucer's humane artistry, Raybin concludes, is to recognize that, while the alchemical explosion portrays the human incapacity to comprehend Truth, it is itself a source of wonder and beauty. The composer of *The Canterbury Tales* was a man who saw transcendent beauty residing not in gold alone but also in the more human elements that are "asshes, donge, pisse, and cley" (CYT, VIII.807).

As the foregoing summary suggests, this collection presents not one Chaucer, not one way of reading Chaucer, not even an insistence on the wrong-headedness of any particular way of reading Chaucer. The volume brings together a multiplicity of scholarly approaches, recognizing that critical pluralism offers what is perhaps the best pathway we have toward appreciating the incredible range of Chaucer's mind and accomplishments.

As Chaucer's poem displays the contestive spirit of contrarious human affairs, so the collective spirit of these essays reflects vigorous debate and multi-faceted challenge. They were composed in the aftermath of an intense joint investigation and analysis of Chaucer's *Tales*. The contributors to this volume were among the thirty-three organizers of and participants in a 1987 NEH-sponsored Institute on Chaucer's *Canterbury Tales*. Directed by C. David Benson, with Co-Directors Linda Georgianna and Charles A. Owen, Jr., the six-week Institute united at the University of Connecticut scholars and teachers from throughout the country.

C. David Benson's memoir of the Institute closes this collection. In the midst of what he describes as a kind of self-sustaining institutional frenzy, a cohesive approach to Chaucer was generated by four loosely structured guidelines:

1. Focus on text. The critical assumptions of Institute participants varied, but all accepted the premise that the value in any singular theory lies in its capacity for elucidating the common text.

2. Look anew at what is familiar and at what has been overlooked. Participants explored not only the standard Chaucerian textual problems but also passages, images, and narrative strategies that had not attracted scholarly attention.

3. Be wary of consensus. Participants accepted that single answers are often reductive and thus that two or more responses may well be more accurate than one.

4. Assume Chaucer knew what he was doing. Participants treated the less-acclaimed tales with as much seriousness—and attention—as the often-taught favorites, assuming each tale to possess its own mark of the poet's greatness.

This spirit of open-minded inquiry, with a renewed look at old questions and a posing of many new ones, also guided the preparation of this volume, which features a variety of text-centered critical perspectives.

The essays in this volume offer the sorts of close analyses that teachers use in their college and university classrooms. The reader looking for radical critical stances by brash new scholars ready to topple the citadels of seasoned Chaucerian criticism will not find them here. These essays build on what has been done and suggest, further, that new assessments, based on different strategies and more fine-tuning of one's attention to overlooked details, can lead to greater insights into Chaucer's art.

This is, certainly, the method of fine teachers, and teaching Chaucer well was ever the goal of the Institute endeavors. The 1987 NEH Chaucer Institute has spawned a flock of similar programs for teachers at the high-school level: there have been three descendant programs in two years, one sponsored by the NEH and two sponsored by the Illinois Humanities Council, all designed by participants in the parent Institute who are among the contributors here. Many more are planned and sure to come about. The aim is to bring the teaching of Chaucer back to the foreground of English studies in colleges and in high schools, and to make already fine teachers see both the poet's accessibility to the student and the potential for bringing knowledge of the Middle Ages engagingly to the classroom.

This volume, then, is intended for the dedicated teacher of Chaucer as well as for the specialist in medieval English studies. Our third editor, Peter C. Braeger, was both excellent teacher and accomplished specialist, with an eminence beyond his years. His intended study of The Monk's Tale, in a full synopsis he left behind when he died of cancer in April 1988, is appended to this collection. His study of the variety of Fortune's visitations upon her subjects promised to add depth to our understanding of this technically obscure tale. The contestive human spirit is nowhere more profound than in this tale, where the unchanging life pattern of dominance and demise gets played over and over but with unvarying variety. Admired and loved by his students and colleagues, described once—and before his illness was known— as "the fire that brought life and light" to the Chaucer Institute, Professor Braeger offered the model of an academic: brilliant, kind, dedicated to his profession and to his family. Peter was twenty-eight years old at his death. His co-editors offer this collection in tribute to his memory.

KENT, OHIO
              DAVID RAYBIN
            SUSANNA GREER FEIN

ACKNOWLEDGMENTS

We wish to thank those who supported us in the planning and development of this book. The Director of the 1987 NEH Institute on Chaucer, C. David Benson, and the two Co-Directors, Charles W. Owen, Jr., and Linda Georgianna, offered continuous encouragement and were generous with their Chaucerian expertise. To them and to our other contributors we owe our greatest debt. Others from among the Institute participants offered friendly counsel and skilled readership, most particularly Sr. Mary Clemente Davlin, Michaela Paasche Grudin, John M. Crafton, and Wendy Tibbetts Greene. And for inspiration we must also thank Karen Braeger.

Four principal guest lecturers, Derek Pearsall, Charles Muscatine, Larry D. Benson, and John Fleming, furnished the source of much stimulating talk in the days of the Institute, and the influence of their challenging opinions—whether in reaction against or in support of—may be detected in some of the essays in this volume. The editors are grateful also to their original teachers in medieval matters: Professor Fein, to Larry D. Benson and Morton W. Bloomfield; Professor Raybin, to Joan M. Ferrante, Robert W. Hanning, and W. T. H. Jackson. We also appreciate the support received from our schools. The Faculty Research Council at Eastern Illinois University awarded Professor Raybin a Presidential Summer Research Grant to foster this project. The Research Council of Kent State University provided release time and research travel funds to Professor Fein, and the Department

ACKNOWLEDGMENTS

of English offered generous material support. And we are much indebted to the editorial staff of Medieval Institute Publications, especially Candace P. Woodruff and Thomas H. Seiler, for their knowledgeable and ever-cheerful assistance in seeing the book through production.

HE INN, THE CATHEDRAL, AND THE PILGRIMAGE OF *THE CANTERBURY TALES*

Frederick B. Jonassen

The text of *The Canterbury Tales* begins with the Tabard Inn in Southwark and ends by the Cathedral in Canterbury. The two sites have their respective hosts: the mirthful innkeeper who guides the pilgrims to Canterbury and proposes the storytelling game "to shorte with oure weye" (I.791) and the grave Parson who at the threshold of the Cathedral indicates "the righte wey of Jerusalem celestial" (X.79). If indeed the Inn and the Cathedral are metaphors for the world and the heavenly kingdom, the two sites are then separated by more than the geographical miles that Chaucer's pilgrims traverse on horseback. Another type of distance extends from the Inn to the Cathedral, a symbolic distance between the profane and the sacred that the pilgrims negotiate by telling stories, some sacred and appropriate to the penitential ideal of the pilgrimage, some profane, the stuff of the inn or tavern.[1]

The proximity of sacred and profane would seem to make *The Canterbury Tales* an attractive text for the application of Bakhtinian analysis. To Mikhail Bakhtin, Carnival and Lent

1

served as the most inclusive and convenient terms by which to represent the intense dualism between the material and spiritual ideologies that pervaded the Middle Ages and the Renaissance. Bakhtin associated Lent with official medieval culture that imposed its order and authority by means of rigid social, religious, and political structures justified by a variety of ideological abstractions. This order was temporarily overthrown and degraded during certain holiday periods such as Christmas, Carnival, and the Feast of Fools, and by various forms of medieval satire celebrating the grotesque and material aspects of life. Carnival, in particular, was the quintessential period of festive abandon, "the people's second life, organized on the basis of laughter" (p. 8), in which the popular ideology of the otherwise oppressed masses found expression. During these interludes the abstract values, idealism, and order of the official culture were ridiculed, while the lowly poor and the physical pleasures of the body were exalted. The laughter of Carnival "was linked with the procreating act, with birth, renewal, fertility, abundance . . . food and drink and the people's earthly immortality" (p. 95). In Bakhtin's view, the people loved Carnival, but lenten seriousness was "elementally distrusted" (p. 95). Consequently, carnivalesque abandon and lenten mortification emerge as antitheses informing many cultural artifacts, such as literary texts, with contending and contradictory voices.

When I call *The Canterbury Tales* "carnivalesque," I do not mean that those aspects which celebrate the body and its pleasures are the dominant voices in the work. Indeed, these lose a great deal of their carnivalesque significance without the counterweight of the seriously religious tales. The reign of Zeus evoked the Saturnalia, and Mother Church gave birth to Carnival. The peculiar concepts, forms, and abandon of Carnival would have no meaning, indeed would not exist, were it not for the equally peculiar concepts, forms, and restraint of Lent.[2] The very name of Carnival comes from low Latin, *carnelevarium*, the lifting or removal of meat, referring to the dietary regulations of fasting and abstinence observed by the Church from the early Middle Ages (Ducange, vol. 2, pp. 477-78).

The Inn and the Cathedral, rather than Carnival and Lent, are the symbolic loci with which Chaucer expresses the material/spiritual duality of his time.[3] These two sites stand at opposite ends of his work, defining the limits of the pilgrimage, the storytelling game, and the bawdy and religious tales.

Although it has no obvious counterpart in Bakhtin's schema, the pilgrimage of *The Canterbury Tales*, along with the Inn and the Cathedral, is fundamental to Chaucer's work of art, for it is during the pilgrimage that the poet mixes, combines, and fuses the tendencies of the Inn and the Cathedral so that neither dominates. The pilgrimage is no Carnival, for Harry Bailly maintains more than a modicum of good order. Some pilgrims may drink, tell salacious stories, and enjoy "solaas" on their journey. Others may prefer edifying lessons, religious exempla, or "sentence." It is only at the Inn, however, that the "solaas" of food and drink reigns supreme, and likewise only at the Cathedral that the "sentence" of the deadly sins prevails. During the pilgrimage a dialogue of disagreements, protests, qualifications, insults, and apologies ensues, generating tensions between what might be termed contending carnivalesque and lenten affinities.

The concept of pilgrimage as an ambivalent passage or transition between two states of life is reflected in the work of the cultural anthropologist Victor Turner, whose studies on rituals of reversal in many respects parallel Bakhtin's ideas on Carnival inversion (Stallybrass and White, p. 17). According to Turner, pilgrimage is a cultural compromise between the structural and anti-structural impulses of society. As I shall demonstrate, such a treatment of pilgrimage significantly complements a Bakhtinian approach to Chaucer's work.

The structure of *The Canterbury Tales*, then, is that of a passage from the worldly state of the Inn to the spiritual state of the Cathedral. The pilgrimage acts as an ambivalent, transitional phase. Geographically, the road leads to the shrine at Canterbury, but in the spiritual landscape the stories progress to the celestial Jerusalem of The Parson's Tale.

LIMINALITY AND COMMUNITAS IN CHAUCER'S PILGRIMAGE

For Turner, every society is in a constant process of structuring its hierarchy on the basis of a variety of factors that may be economic, political, hereditary, and so on. The social structure determines how individuals behave toward one another, to whom one shows deference or contempt. The very existence of a structure, however, creates the possibility of denying that structure or the values upon which it is based: "For every structure there is an antistructure" (Turner and Turner, p. 174). Structure limits the members of a society in respect to the roles they play, especially those of superiority and inferiority, creating divisions and tensions within the social organization. On account of this, societies develop a "need" to discard or reverse on occasion the structures upon which they are organized as if to recognize the artificiality of distinctions that determine the high and low: "The structurally inferior aspire to symbolic structural superiority in ritual; the structurally superior aspire to symbolic communitas and undergo penance to achieve it" (*Process*, p. 203).

"Communitas" is the unstructured, egalitarian manner of relationship that often obtains during rituals of reversal: "spontaneous, immediate, concrete—it is not shaped by norms, it is not institutionalized, it is not abstract" (*Dramas*, p. 274). Unlike the camaraderie of everyday life, which remains within a circumscribed area of structure, communitas "tends to ignore, reverse, cut across, or occur outside of structural relationships" and "is frequently affirmed by periodic rituals in which the lowly and the mighty reverse social roles" (pp. 274-75).[4]

"Liminality" describes the state of those undergoing transition in such seasonal feasts and rites of passage. The word comes from the Latin *limen*, or threshold, the area at the en-

4

trance to a room or house, and refers to the peculiar condition of an individual who stands at "the midpoint of transition in a status-sequence between two positions" (*Dramas*, p. 237). Turner extends the term "to refer to any condition outside, or on the peripheries of, everyday life" (p. 53). The state of liminality may be regarded as sacred; it may include an entire society in a state of transition. Although liminality and communitas frequently accompany one another, they are not synonymous. Communitas, like structure, is a "social modality," whereas liminality is a "sphere or domain of action or thought" (p. 52). Indeed, liminality may imply solitude or withdrawal from community.

Religious pilgrimages exhibit aspects of both communitas and liminality, and in this respect are "functional equivalents" of rites of passage (*Dramas*, p. 65). People who go on pilgrimages experience communitas because they share for an extended period of time the pleasures and hardships of the journey with other pilgrims who, but for the pilgrimage, would be perfect strangers to them. Besides this sharing, a unity of purpose prevails since all have as their destination a shrine where, as a group of penitents equal before God, they seek health or blessing.[5] Pilgrimage also exhibits liminality because the pilgrim is one who renounces, at least temporarily, his everyday role or status.

> [W]hen one goes on pilgrimage one is not only moving from profane to sacred space and time . . . one is also moving away from a social life in which one has an institutionalized social status, plays a set of expected roles. . . . One is moving *into* a different kind of social atmosphere . . . stripped of status, role-playing attributes, corporate group affiliations, and the like. ("Pilgrimage," pp. 306-07; italics mine)

During the Middle Ages the pilgrimage routes partook of the communitas and liminality of the shrines to which they led on account of the churches, lodgings, and hospitality that developed along the pilgrim way (Oursel, pp. 45-51). Turner observes that pilgrim shrines were often situated in places remote from major towns and cities, or just beyond the jurisdiction of political or religious administrations, like the remote medieval Marian shrines at Walsingham and Loreto. While Canterbury is not geographically remote, it does present a liminal significance: St. Thomas was martyred for his rebellious refusal to follow the wishes of the secular authority, having placed the Church outside the king's jurisdiction (Finucane, pp. 121-26, 210-11). Symbolic distance, therefore, always separated Becket's shrine from worldly authority, as Henry VIII recognized in his efforts to ban the pilgrimage.

For the person who steps out of his worldly life to become a pilgrim, a shrine is a type of *limen*, a doorway, as it were, to the spiritual realm:

> A pilgrimage center, from the standpoint of the believing actor, also represents a threshold, a place and moment "in and out of time," and such an actor . . . hopes to have there direct experience of the sacred, invisible, or supernatural order. (Turner, *Dramas*, p. 197)

The elements of pilgrimage—the shrine, the route, and the pilgrims themselves—all have liminal status: the pilgrims visit a threshold to the spiritual world in hopes of experiencing a change, one that may involve inward healing of body and spirit or outward healing of relationships with other members of the community (p. 203).

Chaucer's Canterbury pilgrimage is exemplary of others in that "the absolute communitas of unchanneled anarchy does not obtain" (*Dramas*, p. 171). Social distinctions remain, as pilgrimages are, in a variety of respects, within the sphere of social order "a form of institutionalized or symbolic anti-structure" (p. 182).[6] The communitas of pilgrimage, however, is "a means of binding diversities together and overcoming cleavages" (p. 206), for "while the pilgrimage situation does not eliminate structural divisions, it attenuates them, removes their sting"

6

(p. 207). Turner concludes that pilgrimages reflect "a mutually energizing compromise between structure and communitas; in theological language, a forgiveness of sins, where differences are accepted or tolerated rather than aggravated into grounds of aggressive opposition" (pp. 207-08).

In the General Prologue, Chaucer underlines the fact that, while the pilgrims are diverse or "sondry folk," they are also in "felaweshipe" with one another, and that this fellowship occurs by chance or "aventure":

> At nyght was come into that hostelryc
> Wel nyne and twenty in a compaignye
> Of sondry folk, by aventure yfalle
> In felaweshipe, and pilgrimes were they alle,
> That toward Caunterbury wolden ryde.

> (I.23-27)

Two sources of "felaweshipe" unite the heterogeneous group of pilgrims: the Inn where they meet and the Cathedral where they plan to go (Pison, p. 160).

Representing the Inn, Harry Bailly provides a hospitality that unites the pilgrims in the Tabard. He extends this sense of camaraderie out to the road by engaging the pilgrims in his game of storytelling. The communitas that normally obtains on a pilgrimage is thus enhanced by the convivial host and his game. After The Knight's Tale, the Host knowingly states, "unbokeled is the male / . . . / For trewely the game is wel bigonne" (I.3115, 3117). Normal restraints have been loosened; the gaming spirit is free. With the devices of pilgrimage, host, and game, Chaucer creates that relaxation of social and hierarchical distinctions that Turner calls "communitas." On the Canterbury road, where even Harry does not have complete control, all sorts of unusual events will occur. A miller will displace a monk to "quit" a knight while tweaking his occupational rival, a recve. A wife of Bath will articulate her desire for "maistrye" and quote Scripture with minimal interference from the religious pilgrims. A pardoner will show the tricks he uses to fleece his peasant congregations. Chaucer as narrator cautions that "men shal nat maken ernest of game" (I.3186). It is precisely because the pilgrims are acting and speaking not in earnest but in a game, where the social and religious implications of what they do and say have been softened, that they can more truthfully be themselves.

Chaucer also emphasizes the other source of communitas on the pilgrimage, which is the spiritual help, physical well-being, and social harmony that the shrine of St. Thomas Becket offers:

> And specially from every shires ende
> Of Engelond to Caunterbury they wende,
> The hooly blisful martir for to seke,
> That hem hath holpen whan that they were seeke.
>
> (I.15-18)

Chaucer introduces each pilgrim by occupation. But on the pilgrimage they all share the identity of pilgrim, and they make the journey with the belief that the experience at Canterbury will affect them for the better. They are liminal because they are no longer primarily a miller, a man of law, a franklin, a prioress, or a manciple; all are leveled as religious penitents united on a spiritual journey that they hope will improve their lives and perhaps bring them closer to God. They are liminal also in another, more literary sense, for although initially they are known only by their occupations they reveal more by telling their tales. Each pilgrim projects a narrative voice for prologue and tale; this acquaints us with the character apart from its social position. All are in a process of becoming known on the way to Canterbury, where The Parson's Tale reveals that all the stories have been preparatory confessions for the ultimate self-revelation before God, and that, furthermore, the journey from Inn to Cathedral metaphorically represents the ultimate rite of passage from worldly state to "Jerusalem celestial" (X.80).

8

THE INN, THE CATHEDRAL, AND THE PILGRIMAGE

HARRY BAILLY AND THE INN

A painting by Peter Bruegel the Elder, the *Battle of Carnival and Lent*, presents the dichotomy between body and soul as it was symbolized in numerous cultural contexts during the Middle Ages and Renaissance. Although the work was executed in 1559, more than a century and a half after Chaucer put down his pen, and is concerned with town life in Bruegel's native Flanders, it depicts European-wide pastimes that were already ancient in Bruegel's day. The painting may therefore help to illustrate a general pattern in *The Canterbury Tales*. Of particular interest is Bruegel's association of Carnival with an inn and Lent with a cathedral.[7]

The *Battle of Carnival and Lent* portrays a mock joust between figures representing the two seasons. Carnival is a fat man seated on a barrel of wine or ale, brandishing a spit with roast meats impaled upon it. His adversary, Lent, is an emaciated woman whose lance is a baker's paddle with fish on it. In many European towns and cities Shrovetide festivities featured just such a confrontation between groups of revelers who, following the traditional figures, engaged in a mock battle in which the meats and drink of Carnival and the fish and bread of Lent served as weapons and projectiles. Indeed, the arming, assembling, and fighting of the various foods as soldiers is the subject of several literary works: the thirteenth-century French mock romance, *La Bataille de Caresme et de Charnage* (Lozinski); the fourteenth-century Spanish mock epic, "De la pelea que ovo Don Carnal con la Cuaresma," in *El libro de buen amor* by Juan Ruiz; the fifteenth- and sixteenth-century French plays, *La Bataille de Sainct Pensard a l'encontre de Caresme* and Jehan d'Abundance's *Le Testament de Carmentrant* (Aubailly); the sixteenth-century Italian plays, *Il contrasto de Carnevale et de la Quaresima* and *La rappresentazione et festa di Carnesciale et della Quaresima* (Manzoni); and the seventeenth-century English *Jacke-a-Lent* by John Taylor.[8] In the battle itself either Car-

9

nival or Lent might win, and the defeated antagonist might be banished for a year or, particularly in the case of Carnival, for forty days. By allowing the return of the vanquished season the battle effected a compromise between the adversarial representatives of body and spirit in which each was permitted its reign in cyclic succession. Carnival had its rights, privileges, and period of rule licensed by popular custom, as did Lent under the aegis of official religion.

As is typical in Bruegel's work, many smaller scenes fill out the canvas. The whole is set in the town square. To the far left of the viewer, on Carnival's side, is the town inn, the Blue Ship, symbolic of the Ship of Fools and holiday (Gaignebet, p. 334). In another Bruegel painting, *Netherlandish Proverbs*, an inverted globe hangs outside a tavern, signifying the topsy-turvy state of affairs to be found within, the domination of the flesh over the spirit and pleasure over sacrifice. The World Upside Down was, in fact, a common name for English taverns and inns.[9] The Carnival area of the *Battle* also has background scenes of games and customs traditional to the Christmas season, such as a Three Kings' procession and the folk play of Valentin and Ourson. On Lent's side are customs associated with the paschal season, such as the imposition of ashes, a Palm Sunday procession, and confession. To the far right, behind Lent, is found the cathedral, with figures in black going to confession. Thus Bruegel collapses the cycle of several months into a single tableau illuminating the social and cultural map of profane and religious experience in the community.

As Bruegel framed his painting with the Inn to the left and the Cathedral to the right, Chaucer frames his work with the Southwark Inn at the beginning and Canterbury Cathedral at the end. The respective carnivalesque or lenten activities on either side of the painting reflect the matter of the tales, some of which favor the Inn, others the Cathedral. Corresponding to the central joust of Bruegel's painting is the storytelling game of Chaucer's pilgrimage, where profane and religious tales contend in mock combat on the road between Southwark and Canterbury.

Among several scholars who have to varying extents used Bakhtin in their criticism of *The Canterbury Tales*, Carl Lindahl argues that Chaucer shaped his work to reflect medieval festivals (pp. 45-46; see also Andreas, p. 4).[10] Like such holiday customs as the London Pui or court of love, the mystery plays, the Feast of Fools, and Lord of Misrule mummings, Chaucer's work exhibits hierarchical inversion in the election of a mock ruler, the egalitarian inclusion of all the pilgrims in the game, and the mixture of the sacred and profane. Harry Bailly is the mock king or Lord of Misrule, a master of ceremonies who appoints himself judge and governor of the pilgrims during the journey (Lindahl, pp. 47-50).[11] To some extent, Harry's ascendancy over the pilgrims is an inversion of social hierarchy since he assumes some authority over such social superiors as the Knight, the Monk, the Prioress, and the Squire. But the Host also belongs to the upper middle class (Lindahl, p. 22), so that, socially speaking, his rule is not a complete inversion in which the lowest has become the highest—except in respect to Harry's occupation as the proprietor of an inn in Southwark.

With great deliberation Chaucer associates the Tabard Inn with the district of Southwark, even mentioning the name of the district before the name of the inn: "Bifil that in that seson on a day, / In Southwerk at the Tabard as I lay" (I.19-20). He later combines the names again, adding a reference to the nearby "Belle," which was either a tavern or a brothel: "In Southwerk at this gentil hostelrye / That highte the Tabard, faste by the Belle" (I.718-19). The repeated emphasis is an instance of Chaucer's use of topographical proximity to express a moral relation. Southwark was indeed a logical and customary place for pilgrims to gather en route to Canterbury; it did have a Tabard Inn and one Harry Bailly was its proprietor (Manly, *Light*, p. 79). But the choice of an inn in Southwark as the starting point for a religious journey to Canterbury Cathedral also possesses richly ironic thematic considerations, for along with its inns Southwark was notorious for its brothels, taverns, and low-life.

In 1327 Edward III granted Southwark a charter that exempted this district from the jurisdiction of London laws. Southwark became a refuge for craftsmen who were unable to join London guilds or unwilling to submit to their regulations (Myers, p. 11). The victuallers, along with other guilds, constantly complained that craftsmen "repaired to the vill of Southwark" in order to avoid "the punishments of the City" (Tupper, "Quarrels," p. 264; see also Myers, p. 202). Innkeepers like Harry Bailly could serve food and drink and manage their businesses much more freely in Southwark than they could in London. The legal situation also contributed to much lawlessness in the area:

> Prostitutes, driven out of London by the prudish outlook of the city fathers, congregated in Southwark. . . . These dubious taverns were also the haunts of cutthroats and pickpockets, who found the greater laxity of Southwark's government . . . more to their liking than the stricter surveillance of London. (Myers, p. 11)

Southwark's notoriety for taverns and brothels must have made the district a target of the moral excoriation that such establishments proverbially received from preachers during the Middle Ages. A set piece of morality plays was the visit to the tavern where the vices attempt to corrupt the human gull by involving him in the conventional tavern activities.[12] These included not only eating and drinking but also singing, dancing, bawdy joking, swearing, gambling, brawling, and prostitution. "In the literature of the medieval pulpit," writes Gerald R. Owst,

> the tavern and the ale-house, apart from the acknowledged fact that they are the occasion of much gluttony and drunkenness in the ordinary way, stand for a very definite menace to the common weal. They have established themselves as deadly rivals to the ordinances of the Church, to the

keeping of holydays and fast days, and above all to attendance at divine service. (P. 435)

Owst quotes many instances in which medieval preachers contrasted the tavern to the church. Michel of Northgate characterizes the tavern as the Devil's Chapel in his *Aȝenbite of Inwit*. For Michel, the church is where God performs miracles, making the blind to see, the crooked to walk, and the mad to be sane, while in the tavern the glutton falls and the drunk loses his mental powers. These are the miracles of the Devil (Owst, p. 438). Glotoun of *Piers Plowman* is on his way to "holy churche" to "here masse" when he is distracted by the tavern where in the general commotion he eats and drinks himself senseless (C VI.350-441). One preacher describes the Seven Deadly Sins as typical customers of the tavern (Owst, pp. 440-41). Medieval homilists especially complained of those who frequented the tavern rather than the church on holy days. The tavern hinders God's service and cuts short the sermon, and it makes men reluctant "eny thyng to suffre for Godes love, as fastynge or wolwarde goynge, other goynge in pilgrymage, or eny goode werkes." Many a man may "have his tongue in the church, and his soul in the tavern" (Owst, pp. 436-37). Time and again the medieval sermon condemns the tavern as the absolute antithesis of the church.

Harry Bailly runs an inn rather than a tavern, a position that legally and professionally placed him above the taverner or owner of an alehouse. However, the situation was likely one in which the law attempted to impose definitions in an area of commerce where categories were quite fluid. In a recent history of the English alehouse Peter Clark discusses three types of medieval English drinking places. Inns were "usually large, fashionable establishments offering wine, ale and beer, together with quite elaborate food and lodging to well-heeled travellers." Taverns sold "wine to the more prosperous, but without the extensive accommodation of inns," though taverns sometimes did offer food and lodging. Alehouses were "normally smaller premises serving ale or beer (and later spirits) and providing rather basic food and accommodation for the lower orders" (p. 5). These distinctions were not established in statute until the sixteenth century, and Clark points out that there was always a great deal of confusion concerning proper terminology (p. 5). An inn could degenerate into a "mere drinking shop," as the following Tudor decree quoted by F. W. Hackwood implies: "and the master or innkeeper suffer men to sit tippling there in a disorderly manner, it shall be taken to be an ale-house" (pp. 67-68).[13]

Harry Bailly often exhibits a crude sense of humor appropriate for a taverner in Southwark. He likes to eat and drink, and his penchant for swearing is so pronounced that he is scolded by the Parson (II.1170-71). Aside from encouraging the churls' bawdy tales, which properly belong to the tavern, Harry himself demonstrates prurience in his observations on the sexual potency of presumed religious celibates, the Monk and the Nun's Priest, and on the ambiguous sexuality of the Pardoner. Yet Chaucer's description of the Tabard as a "gentil hostelrye" suitable for the likes of the Prioress, the Knight, and the Parson would seem to distinguish Harry from the seamier side of tavern life. The Tabard Inn may adjoin the brothels and taverns of Southwark, and the behavior of the innkeeper himself at times may resemble that of a taverner, but the Tabard is no devil's church, nor is its owner entirely depraved. In this vein, the ambience of the Tabard Inn very much resembles that of the pilgrimage. The journey to Canterbury never becomes an anarchic carnival, nor does Harry's inn succumb to the moral anarchy of its surroundings. It would seem that the Tabard Inn's convivial freedom from strict legal restrictions and stringent social decorum, as well as from the dangerous sports of Southwark taverns, makes it an ideal place for the ambivalence between structure and antistructure that Turner posits as characteristic of pilgrimage.

THE INN, THE CATHEDRAL, AND THE PILGRIMAGE

Harry Bailly is instrumental in negotiating two aspects of the journey to Canterbury, the road and the storytelling game. On the road he constantly announces time and place. The narrator identifies the Host as "oure aller cok" (I.823). Noting the position of the sun, Harry "wiste it was the eightetethe day / Of Aprill" (II.5-6) and warns "The fourthe party of this day is gon" (line 17), urging the pilgrims to continue on their journey. Just before The Parson's Tale, the narrator notes the descent of the sun, "For which oure Hoost, as he was wont to gye, / As in this caas, oure joly compaignye" (X.13-14). In respect to place, the Host often announces the towns: "Lo Depeford, and it is half-wey pryme! / Lo Grenewych" (I.3906-07); "Loo, Rouchestre stant heer faste by!" (VII.1926).

To reach Canterbury one must travel the road. For Harry Bailly, telling stories is the best thing to do while traveling, largely because this diversion makes the road seem shorter and keeps the pilgrims awake so that they do not wander from the path or fall from their horses. His editorial skill parallels his knowledge of the road, as his rebukes, choices of speakers, interruptions, and encouragement match his choices of direction, accommodations, and departures. Harry's service as "horseback editor" and purveyor of "solaas" is evinced by his constant activity to insure the success of his game: he has the Knight tell the first story, stops Chaucer's "drasty" tale of Sir Thopas (VII.923), agrees with the Knight about the insupportability of The Monk's Tale, and persuades the Nun's Priest to pick up the slackened attention of the pilgrims. If indeed the pilgrimage serves as a metaphor for life, Harry Bailly's insistence on telling stories to shorten the way is also a moral assessment that literature generally shortens rather than lengthens the way to the celestial Jerusalem.[14]

There is, however, one danger. The Canterbury pilgrims, having stopped at an inn or tavern, might lose interest in their destination, the tales attracting more interest than the pilgrim shrine; so might the Christian forget the celestial Jerusalem in his care for things of this world (O'Donnell, p. 22). In his classic distinction between *utor* and *fruor*, the use and enjoyment of things, St. Augustine employs a pilgrimage analogy:

> Suppose we were wanderers . . . desiring . . . to return to our native country. We would need vehicles for land and sea which could be used to help us to reach our homeland, which is to be enjoyed. But if the amenities of the journey and the motion of the vehicles itself delighted us, and we were led to enjoy those things which we should use, we should not wish to end our journey quickly, and . . . we should be alienated from our country.[15]

The distractions of stories are not unlike the distractions of the Inn: either might lead the unwary pilgrim to lose sight of his true goal. Here, Harry Bailly's experience as the keeper of a Southwark inn is invaluable. To run a "gentil hostelrye" in Southwark implies an innkeeper who must have been knowledgeable enough in the ways of suburban tavern life to keep its more dangerous and disagreeable manifestations away from his premises, in spite of his own penchant for gustatory delights and swearing. What can be said of the management of Harry's inn might also be said about his guidance of the pilgrims to Canterbury and his governance of the storytelling game. He pushes the pilgrims to tell stories and mentally proceed to Becket's cathedral as effectively as he marks the time and place to push them on the road to Canterbury. Harry Bailly is the guarantor that spiritually, as well as physically, the pilgrims are as safe on the road as they are in his inn.

Nonetheless, Harry demonstrates a pronounced defensiveness about his profession. This reaction occurs not only when the Cook speaks slightingly of innkeeping but also when the Franklin indirectly refers to proverbial tavern activities and when the Pardoner relentlessly attacks them. The exchange between Hogge of Ware and Harry Bailly begins after the Reeve has finished his tale. The Cook, who perhaps regards the inn-

16

keeper as a competitor, needles Harry with a mocking reference to the dangers of lodging strangers in one's house as did the unfortunate miller of The Reeve's Tale:

> "For Cristes passion,
> This millere hadde a sharp conclusion
> Upon his argument of herbergage!
> Wel seyde Salomon in his langage,
> 'Ne bryng nat every man into thyn hous,'
> For herberwynge by nyghte is perilous."
>
> (I.4327-32)

The Host indicates that he recognizes the insult here, for in revenge he proceeds to describe the food available at the Cook's shop in the most unsavory of terms, even implying that the Cook breaks the law in serving reheated meat pies:

> "Now telle on, Roger; looke that it be good,
> For many a pastee hastow laten blood,
> And many a Jakke of Dovere hastow soold
> That hath been twies hoot and twies coold.
> Of many a pilgrym hastow Cristes curs,
> For of thy percely yet they fare the wors,
> That they han eten with thy stubbel goos,
> For in thy shoppe is many a flye loos."
>
> (Lines 4345-52)

Harry claims he is only joking, but Hogge threatens to "quit" him later with a tale about a "hostileer" (lines 4359-62). The Cook's fragment itself concerns a "revelour" (line 4371) who lodges with a friend (lines 4418-19) and enjoys the typical tavern vices of "dys," "riot," and "paramour" (line 4392). It thus anticipates further exchanges in the occupational "flyting" between Harry and Hogge.[16]

Comparing his son unfavorably to the Squire, the Franklin says he has rebuked his boy:

"For he to vertu listeth nat entende;
But for to pleye at dees, and to despende
And lese al that he hath is his usage."

(V.689-91)

The Franklin also dislikes his son's familiarity with those he considers of lower status (lines 692-94). Such profligacy forms the subject matter of many morality plays depicting tavern sins, and the Franklin's lament belongs to a tradition of paternal complaints over sons who waste time in taverns. Another example would be Henry Bullingbrook's complaints about his son, Prince Hal, himself a victim of "that reverend vice," Falstaff (see Shakespeare, *Richard II* V.iii.1-12). The Host's reaction seems rather strong, "Straw for youre gentillesse!" (V.695). This response may evince Harry's intolerance for social affectation. However, an explanation in accord with the Host/Cook dispute would be the Host's touchiness at the disapproving mention of such activities as gambling and prodigal dispense, some of which might well have gone on at or near the Tabard—and even involved the Franklin's son. Given this possibility, Harry is cutting off the Franklin's complaints about the tavern before the connection to his own business is made and his ability to lead the pilgrims is compromised.

Harry's sarcastic manner of addressing the Pardoner, "thou beel amy" (VI.318), provides some provocation for the Pardoner to tell a story in revenge, which, like the Cook's, mocks Harry's profession by displaying the vices of the tavern. But the Pardoner intends to do more. He will challenge the Host's leadership of the group by advancing a puritanical attack on the tavern sins. In accepting the Host's request—

"It shal be doon," quod he, "by Seint Ronyon!
But first" quod he, "heere at this alestake
I wol bothe drynke and eten of a cake"

(Lines 320-22)

—the Pardoner pointedly repeats Harry's peculiar oath; refers to an alestake, the leaf-garlanded sign of Harry's profession;[17] and mimics Harry's professed need for "a draughte of moyste and corny ale" (line 315). Word and action point to the Host as the target of the "honest thyng" (line 328) the Pardoner will tell.

In his Prologue the Pardoner reveals himself to be a thoroughgoing hypocrite of serpentine mendacity: "Thus spitte I out my venym under hewe / Of hoolynesse, to semen hooly and trewe" (VI.421-22). While he preaches against gluttony and lechery, he is himself guilty of these sins:

> "I wol have moneie, wolle, chese, and whete,
> Al were it yeven of the povereste page,
> . . . .
> And have a joly wenche in every toun."
>
> (Lines 448-49, 453)

In spite of this, the Pardoner never ceases to make a distinction between his reprehensible moral nature and the moral efficacy of his story:

> "Thus kan I preche agayn that same vice
> Which that I use, and that is avarice.
> But though myself be gilty in that synne,
> Yet kan I maken oother folk to twynne. . . ."
>
> (Lines 427-30)

Though evil himself, the Pardoner will preach a "moral thyng" (line 325), that is, a moral attack on the Host.[18]

The Pardoner's Tale is set (and possibly told) in a tavern.[19] In the most conventional terms of medieval pulpit oratory, he describes the typical tavern sins, going so far as to identify the tavern as the devil's place of worship:

> In Flaundres whilom was a compaignye
> Of yonge folk that haunteden folye,
> As riot, hasard, stywes, and tavernes,

19

Where as with harpes, lutes, and gyternes,
They daunce and pleyen at dees bothe day and nyght,
And eten also and drynken over hir myght,
Thurgh which they doon the devel sacrifise
Withinne that develes temple in cursed wise
By superfluytee abhomynable.
Hir othes been so grete and so dampnable
That it is grisly for to heere hem swere.

(VI.463-73)

Clearly, the Pardoner sets the tavern in opposition to the church to which the pilgrims are destined. Throughout his prologue and tale he inveighs against the specific sins of the tavern, castigating food, drink, swearing, and convivial game as the antithesis of pilgrimage. He excoriates drunkenness and gluttony, portraying food and the digestive process with terms of disgust (lines 534-35), he blames the worst crimes of lechery on drinking (lines 485-87), and he attacks gambling (lines 590-628). In The Pardoner's Tale the youngest roisterer is murdered when another wrestles with him "as in game" (line 829), and the other two die from a bottle of poisoned wine, a hideous surprise indeed to be found in playing a game and drinking.

This moralizing conspicuously concerns Harry Bailly, who had served the pilgrims food and drink (I.749-50) and proposed a feast at the Tabard as the reward for the best story, sealing this pact with "wyn" (line 819). Harry has just wished for a draft of ale (VI.315) and complimented himself on his swearing: "by Seint Ronyan! / Seyde I nat wel?" (lines 310-11). Though Harry may not be a gambler he loves the mirth of the storytelling game, much of whose intrigue, as in gambling, lies in unpredictability. The Pardoner cleverly associates Harry's food, drink, swearing, and convivial game with the tavern. Those who, like Harry, love to eat and drink, "been enemys of Cristes croys, / Of whiche the ende is deeth; wombe is hir god!" (lines 532-33).

The Pardoner is no less than Harry's greatest rival. In preaching the evil of food and drink the Pardoner wishes to persuade his listeners to give him their money rather than spend it at Harry's inn. But even as he preaches this, the Pardoner reveals his even greater hostility toward religion in his self-admitted hypocrisy, his contempt for credulous faith, and his weakness for the very sins against which he preaches. He hates the spirit as well as the flesh.[20]

If the Pardoner's worldly joylessness implies his spiritual emptiness, likewise his attempt to discredit Harry Bailly and his inn carries with it an implied, but very potent, danger to the religious aspirations of the pilgrims to seek repentance at Canterbury Cathedral. An attack on Harry is, after all, an attack on the reliable guide to Canterbury who represents the communal values that unite the pilgrims on their journey. Indeed, the Pardoner's gambit would put a spiritual end to the pilgrimage by substituting his relics, pardon, and slick preaching for Becket's shrine and the final meditation of the Parson. As Melvin Storm has recently argued, the Pardoner stands "between the Tabard Inn and Becket's shrine as the pivotal figure in the pilgrimage, the meretricious surrogate for what the other pilgrims seek at Becket's shrine" (p. 810). What makes the Pardoner truly pivotal, however, is his malevolence to both Inn and Cathedral, the two sides of Chaucer's overarching dichotomy.

The Pardoner winds up his performance by calling Harry the "moost envoluped in synne" (VI.942), thereby identifying him as the worst sinner in the group and consequently unworthy to lead the pilgrims. The offer to Harry of relics which the Pardoner has revealed to be fake is in effect a mocking request that the Host recognize him as morally superior. If the pilgrims heed what the Pardoner has said, Harry's game and leadership must be abandoned. The Pardoner would become the moral leader of the pilgrimage, and his tale its final word: "I am wont to preche for to wynne" (line 461).

The Host responds by counterattacking the Pardoner where, as it happens, he is most vulnerable, in his relics and his genitals:

21

> "Nay, nay!" quod he, "thanne have I Cristes curs!
> Lat be," quod he, "it shal nat be, so theech!
> Thou woldest make me kisse thyn olde breech,
> And swere it were a relyk of a seint,
> Though it were with thy fundement depeint!
> But, by the croys which that Seint Eleyne fond,
> I wolde I hadde thy coillons in myn hond
> In stide of relikes or of seintuarie.
> Lat kutte hem of, I wol thee helpe hem carie;
> They shal be shryned in an hogges toord!"
>
> (VI.946-55)

The effectiveness of the Host's answer is evident in the silence of the serpent's tongue: "This Pardoner answerde nat a word; / So wrooth he was, no word ne wolde he seye" (lines 956-57). The Host suggests, as he did with the Cook, that his insults were said only in game ("I wol no lenger pleye / With thee, ne with noon oother angry man" [lines 958-59]). It is, however, evident that the anger in the air is in earnest.

This is the one point in *The Canterbury Tales* where the communitas of the pilgrimage is in serious jeopardy of breaking down; the enmity between the Host and the Pardoner exposes the reality of their social roles as rivals and hence comes near to violating the liminality of the pilgrims. By excluding the Pardoner from the game, Harry Bailly almost ruins the communitas he has created. Societal structure intrudes in the person of the Knight, who assumes his social authority while the Host relinquishes his holiday role as master of the revels. The Knight, however, interferes only to save the communitas of the group, to salvage the game and the unity of the pilgrims. He reassures the Pardoner that he is still part of the group and, by making it known that the Pardoner has not ruined the Host's reputation, authorizes Harry to continue as the leader of the pilgrimage:

> "Namoore of this, for it is right ynough!
> Sire Pardoner, be glad and myrie of cheere;

22

THE INN, THE CATHEDRAL, AND THE PILGRIMAGE

And ye, sire Hoost, that been to me so deere,
I prey yow that ye kisse the Pardoner.
And Pardoner, I prey thee, drawe thee neer,
And, as we diden, lat us laughe and pleye."

(Lines 962-67)

In this instance, the communitas of the pilgrimage survives not because of Harry's guidance but because the group's sense of community is no longer dependent on Harry alone. At the Knight's urging, the Host and the Pardoner kiss and the pilgrimage and its stories continue, Harry's game saved by the inter cession of the societal authority that Harry had sought to suspend.

THE PARSON AND THE CATHEDRAL

Among the many points that the Parson makes about sin is his insistence that sin is a reversal of spiritual order, God's world turned upside down: "God sholde have lordshipe over resoun, and resoun over sensualitee, and sensualitee over the body of man./ But soothly, whan man synneth, al this ordre or ordinaunce is turned up-so-doun" (X.262-63). To some extent, the pilgrimage itself has been a world of inversion. The Parson presents his tale as a return to order. Instead of the freely told, unpredictable stories recited earlier, a systematic, structured sermon follows. There is no irony in this hard-bitten penitential tract. The Parson acts in his strict social role of religious counselor.[21] The pilgrims must now decide in earnest and not in game if and in what ways the "ordinaunce" of Harry Bailly may have violated the "ordinaunce" of God.

Turner observes that the theology of several religions implies that man's existence is a rite of passage as he seeks his home in the next life (*Process*, p. 189). In Christian tradition fallen man is indeed a liminal creature, neither beast nor spirit, alienated from God and from the world, struggling with temptation as he seeks his true home. Man is a pilgrim. However, while the heav-

23

enly homeland may be envisioned as an ideal of eternal communitas, in the present world the ideal leads paradoxically to the rigid and narrow bounds of structure that divide rather than unite:

> Communitas is . . . the *fons et origo* of all structures and . . . their critique. . . . The historical fate of communitas whenever it has been manifested in any specific group, seems to have been to pass from openness to closure, from "free" communitas to the solidarity given by bounded structure, from optation to obligation. ("Pilgrimage," pp. 316-17)

The freewheeling communitas and liminality of the pilgrimage come to a natural, if abrupt, end when the pilgrims prepare to receive the sacrament. They must now make serious moral decisions about what to reject as sin from their lives and from the revelatory experience of the tales told on the road to Canterbury.

In Bakhtin's terms, what The Parson's Tale represents is the cyclic succession of Lent after Carnival. Much as Bruegel presents Carnival and Lent as a balanced opposition, Chaucer reflects the same seasonal change of behavior and attitude by placing the Parson's earnest "sentence" after Harry Bailly's playful "solaas." The theories of Turner and Bakhtin, then, provide theoretical justification for Chaucer's radical shift in style from the tales of the road to the Parson's Tale at Canterbury. However, the question remains of whether there is at the heart of Chaucer's work a contradiction between the worlds of the Inn and the Cathedral.[22]

The tavern attracted immense homiletic attention, because it was recognized as the antithesis of the church, the devil's temple where moral order was turned upside down. The tavern symbolized the gratification of bodily pleasures, while the central symbol of the church was one of intense suffering and sacrifice. Nevertheless, apparent opposites can exhibit symmetries: the Inn and the Cathedral are no exceptions. The Communion ritual provided a spiritual counterpart to the food and drink of the tavern. Christ often compared the kingdom of heaven to a feast (Luke 15.25; Delasanta, p. 243). Although the Parson identifies a great deal of the pilgrims' behavior as inversive of order—that is, as sinful—and therefore in conflict with the ethos he represents, his tale nevertheless develops extensive relationships between the realm of the Inn and the spiritual lessons he teaches as they near the Cathedral.

In the prologue to The Parson's Tale, the Host announces that all his "ordinaunce" (X.19) is fulfilled and asks the Parson to "knytte up wel a greet mateere" (line 28), perhaps to tie up that "male" or bag that Harry declares opened at the end of The Knight's Tale (I.3115). Rather than ask permission from Harry Bailly, the Parson appeals to and receives permission from the pilgrims to tell his "meditacioun":

> Upon this word we han assented soone,
> For, as it seemed, it was for to doone—
> To enden in som vertuous sentence,
> And for to yeve hym space and audience,
> And bade oure Hoost he sholde to hym seye
> That alle we to telle his tale hym preye.

(X.61-66)

As the pilgrims had earlier assented to the leadership of the Host on the road to Canterbury, they now accede to the spiritual guidance of the Parson. Whereas the Host and Parson had once contended over Harry's swearing (II.1170-73), the Host now voluntarily relinquishes the group to the religious figure who by common consent is the most worthy to prepare the pilgrims for the visit to the shrine. The differences the merry innkeeper may have had with the religious Parson are now revealed to be minor in comparison to what they have in common. As one critic puts it,

> For Chaucer's pilgrims, their old agreement upon leaving the tavern had promised a free supper as reward for the best-told tale. Their new agreement, through the Parson's guid-

ance, will offer a eucharistic supper available to all who
confess truly and are changed in their hearts. (Peck, p. 98;
see also Delasanta, p. 243)

In this change of guides Chaucer follows Dante. The Host who
has led the pilgrims through the earthly dangers of the road and
its stories now yields to a higher spiritual guide at the threshold
of Canterbury much as Virgil gives way to Beatrice when Dante
reaches Paradise (Wenzel, "ParsT," pp. 94-96).

The Parson emphasizes the complementarity of the journey
on horseback to Canterbury and the journey of the soul to heaven
by beginning his talk with a scriptural verse that maintains the
imagery of pilgrimage:

> *Jer. 6°. State super vias, et videte, et interrogate de viis*
> *antiquis que sit via bona, et ambulate in ea; et invenietis*
> *refrigerium animabus vestris, etc.*
> . . . .
> "Stondeth upon the weyes, and seeth and axeth of olde pathes
> (that is to seyn, of olde sentences) which is the goode wey,/
> and walketh in that wey, and ye shal fynde refresshynge for
> youre soules, etc."/ Manye been the weyes espirituels that
> leden folk to oure Lord Jhesu Crist and to the regne of glorie./
> Of whiche weyes ther is a ful noble wey and a ful convenable,
> which may nat fayle to man ne to womman that thurgh synne
> hath mysgoon fro the righte wey of Jerusalem celestial;/
> and this wey is cleped Penitence. . . . (X.75, 77-81)

Whereas the Pardoner began his sermon by quaffing a draft of ale
only to condemn food and drink later, the Parson begins his meditation by comparing bodily refreshment to the spiritual nourishment of Penance, "refresshynge for youre soules." He equates
"olde pathes" that the pilgrims have traveled with "olde sentences"
that they have heard and speaks of pilgrimage as the life journey to
the heavenly Jerusalem. The Parson indicates that there are many
ways to this goal, but he wishes to present a noble way that will not
fail, much as Harry successfully showed the way to Canterbury.

Sometimes one must look at the world upside down to see what is right side up, and, indeed, the bulk of *The Canterbury Tales* is an examination of the inversive, liminal world as a critique of the world of structure (Klene). Oddly enough, it is the Pardoner, the most inversive and subversive character among the pilgrims, who is the key to this conclusion. Mutual exclusion of body and soul is the way of the Pardoner, not the Parson. In the name of religion the Pardoner offers an uncompromising diatribe against the sins of the flesh. As it turns out, he is the "moost envoluped in synne," being dead to both spirit and flesh, the fate of his revelers very much figuring his own moral state. Whereas the Parson has been the playful antagonist of the Host (but is his ally in reality), the Pardoner is Harry's earnest adversary. He is also the earnest rival of the Parson, proffering himself and his pardons in the moral space that the Parson and his penance later occupy. As the effective negator of both Inn and Cathedral, the antithesis of the Host in his condemnation of tavern sins to which he is addicted and the antithesis of the Parson in his contempt for the spiritual values that he hypocritically professes, the Pardoner is the most perfectly upside-down character Chaucer creates.[23]

The Parson offers no quick fix for penance. Instead, he presents the way to penance as a continuation of the pilgrimage that Harry Bailly has led. Nor does the Parson utter any absolute condemnation of the flesh. This can be seen most clearly in the way the Parson speaks about one of the Pardoner's subjects, gluttony. While it is true that the Parson frequently praises fasting and abstinence, he also points out that "a man hath nede of thise thinges generally: he hath nede of foode, he hath nede of clothyng and herberwe" (X.1031). In contrast to the Pardoner, the Parson describes hell not as indulgence in food, drink, and friendship but as the deprivation of these wholesome offerings of the Inn: "And moorcover the myscyse of helle shal been in defaute of mete and drinke./ . . . / And forther over, hir myseyse shal been in defaute of freendes" (lines 194, 199). Just as the

Parson begins his talk with a reference to spiritual refreshment, he ends it with a description of heaven, where "ther as ne is neither hunger, thurst, ne coold, but every soule replenyssed" (line 1079). If one were to regard "mete and drinke" and "freendes" with contempt, as the Pardoner urged, how could one understand the Parson for whom the food, drink, and conviviality typical of Harry's inn provide a meaningful worldly image of the heavenly kingdom?

The Inn not only foreshadows the heavenly homeland; in patristic tradition it is the means to that end. St. Augustine and St. Gregory the Great, both of whom the Parson frequently quotes, use the figure of the Inn when they discuss the pilgrimage of life. St. Gregory, for example, develops this idea in the *Moralia in Job*: "But just men thus are refreshed by temporal assistance, as a traveler makes use of a bed in an inn: he stops and hastens to retire; he rests his body, but his mind is on something else."[24] Although Augustine, as I noted earlier, perceives the road and its accommodations as a potentially distracting threat to the pilgrim, he nevertheless recognizes that these means are worthy of love because of the end to which they lead:

> We are to use the world, not with the love and delight we would show to our true home, but only with the passing love we would give a highway or the vehicles of travel. We love the things that carry us only because we love the place to which they carry us.[25]

One must love the things of this world if one loves heaven. Life at the Inn is not spiritual death in the Church when that inn is the "gentil hostelrye" of Harry Bailly.[26]

The Parson's Tale does not constitute a rejection of all that went before but rather a complement to it, a fulfillment of the celestial Jerusalem dimly and imperfectly perceived in the Inn and approached with difficulty through traveling the road and telling stories. *The Canterbury Tales* is an emphatic reconciliation of the Inn and the Cathedral, which are united in the idea

28

of pilgrimage.[27] Chaucer's Christianity recognizes that the flesh often strives with the spirit, but its central mystery is that the Word was made Flesh. Love of the spirit must imply love of the world. A reader may take what he wishes of the "solaas" and the "sentence" that Chaucer offers. As for the pilgrims, the poet leaves them at Canterbury, where they may enjoy the type of banquet for which the poet himself was preparing, not at the Tabard Inn but in eternity.[28]

NOTES

[1] I am interpreting the text as it stands, though there are indications that Chaucer originally intended to end the CT back in Southwark (I.790-801). See Root; Manly, "Tales"; Owen, *Pilgrimage*; and Howard, pp. 21-28, on this question. Peck, examining the Pauline quotations in the CT, perceives the pilgrimage to be a dual spatial/spiritual journey, "one on horseback and another in the mind. The two journeys merge in the *Parson's Tale*" (pp. 97-98)

[2] See Caro Baroja, p. 26: "For Carnival (that is, our Carnival), whether one wishes to admit it or not, is the offspring (although a prodigal son) of Christianity; in other words, without the idea of Lent ('Quadragesima'), Carnival would not exist in the exact form in which it has existed since the obscure times of the European Middle Ages" (my translation).

[3] To be sure, Chaucer's work does not present many direct references to Shrovetide or its customs, but the pilgrimage to Canterbury does take place about mid-April, which is a period with lenten affinities.

[4] Turner's "communitas" reads like an objective expression of Bakhtin's more colorful description of holiday activities. As Bakhtin describes it, "carnival celebrated temporary liberation from the prevailing truth and from the established order; it marked the suspension of all hierarchical rank, privileges, norms, and prohibitions. . . . All were considered equal during carnival. . . . People were, so to speak, reborn for new, purely human relations. These truly human relations were not only a fruit of imagination or abstract thought, they were experienced. The utopian ideal and the realistic merged in this carnival experience, unique of its kind" (p. 10).

29

A parallel to Turner's idea that the structurally superior undergo penance in communitas is Bakhtin's concept of the "uncrowning" (pp. 197-99) or categorical degrading of the serious or abstract through the ridicule, obscenity, and laughter of Carnival: "The essential principle of grotesque realism is degradation, that is, the lowering of all that is high, spiritual, ideal, abstract; it is a transfer to the material level, to the sphere of earth and body in their indissoluable unity" (pp. 19-20).

[5]Particularly poignant is the testimony of the Black Muslim, Malcolm X, concerning his pilgrimage to Mecca: "Love, humility, and true brotherhood was almost a physical feeling wherever I turned. . . . All *ate* as One, and slept as One. Everything about the pilgrimage atmosphere accented the Oneness of Man under One God. . . . Never have I witnessed such sincere hospitality and the overwhelming spirit of true brotherhood as is practised by people of all colors and races, here in this Ancient, Holy Land, the home of Abraham, Muhammad, and all the other prophets of the Holy Scriptures" (qtd. Turner, *Dramas*, p. 204).

This account invites comparison with a medieval verse describing a pilgrimage to the shrine of St. James of Compostella:

> This was the whole of Christendom in one single being
> Advancing up the bedrock pavement
> In one irresistible Body
> To the place that love and the vow of its heart had centered
>   on.
>
> (qtd. Turner, *Dramas*, p. 181)

[6]See Turner, *Dramas*, p. 182; "Pilgrimage," passim; and *Process*, pp. 131-33. Pison applies the concept of liminality to the CT as a whole and to the FranT; Bloomfield does so for the FrT. See also Andreas.

[7]My comments on the painting are based on the analysis of Gaignebet, pp. 313-45.

[8]Chaucer may have become familiar with the folk customs as well as the literature of the battle of Carnival and Lent through his travels on the continent. It is known, for example, that he visited Spain, and parallels between the CT and *El libro de buen amor*, in which his near contemporary, Juan Ruiz, portrays the battle, are numerous and have been noted for more than a century. See L. D. Benson, p. 795.

THE INN, THE CATHEDRAL, AND THE PILGRIMAGE

[9]Larwood and Camden, pp. 462-63, find records of "The World Upside Down" tavern signs in England as far back as the eighteenth century. That the idea is much older is suggested by a passage written by Thomas Nashe: "it is no maruaile if euery Alehouse vaunt the table of the world turned vpside downe, since the child beateth his father, and the Asse whippeth his Master" (*To the Gentlemen Students* III.315). See Shakespeare's *1HenIV* in reference to a Rochester inn: "This house is turn'd upside down since Robin ostler died" (II.i.10-11).

[10]Other Bakhtinian treatments of the CT include David, *Strumpet*, pp. 93-94; F. A. Payne, pp. 3-9; J. Cook; Kern, pp. 40-46; Andreas; and Ganim, "Voices" and "Bakhtin." Note Muscatine, *Fabliaux*, pp. 163-66, for a dissent to Bakhtinian analysis of the CT. I would add the caution that, though it may be desirable to identify the carnivalesque or lenten characteristics of each pilgrim, there is a danger, reminiscent of Tupper's attempt to identify the pilgrims with the Seven Deadly Sins, of reducing these highly complex, ironic, and even paradoxical characters to fit a theoretical scheme. (See Tupper, "Chaucer"; Lowes's critical response; and Tupper's little-noted response to Lowes ["Sinners"]).

[11]On the customary election and reign of a mock ruler and the accompanying parody of legal verbiage in the English Inns of Court, though from a later period, see the *Gesta Grayorum* in Nichols, vol. 3, pp. 262-352, and *The Christmas Prince*. Chaucer may have witnessed such a custom. But see also Hornsby, who argues that although Chaucer may have had a legal education he could not have gotten it at the Inns of Court, which in his days probably housed lawyers rather than law students.

[12]Scattergood provides examples of tavern revelry resembling Perkyn's activities from the fifteenth-century morality *Mankind*, Skelton's morality *Magnyficence*, the *Bowge of Courte*, the Digby *Mary Magdalene*, and several lyrics. These examples could easily be multiplied.

[13]One of the definitions the *MED* provides for *inn* is indeed "tavern." In the prologue to *The Tale of Beryn* one finds, aside from the carousing of the pilgrims, the Pardoner's attempt to arrange a tryst with the tapster Kitt, which leads to a raucous fight. All of this typical tavern activity takes place at an *inn* called the Checker of the Hope (lines 13-14).

[14]On the Host's relation to time and place, see Page, p. 8, C. Richardson, pp. 333-39; on his editorial policies, see Gaylord; for his views on "sentence" and "solaas," see Leitch; for his commentary on the tales, see Scheps.

[15]Trans. Robertson, *Augustine*, pp. 9-10. The Latin text reads: "Quomodo ergo, si essemus peregrini . . . in patriam redire vellemus, opus esset vel terrestribus vel marinis vehiculis quibus utendum esset ut ad patriam, qua fruendum erat, pervenire valeremus; quod si amoenitates itineris, et ipsa gestatio vehiculorum nos delectaret, et conversi ad fruendum his quibus uti debuimus, nollemus cito viam finire, et . . . alienaremur a patria" (*De doctrina christiana* I.4.4, *PL* 34, cols. 20-21).

[16]On the occupational quarrel between the Host and the Cook, see Tupper, "Quarrels," p. 264, and Lumiansky, p. 61.

[17]See Hilary's discussion of CT VI.321-22 (p. 904). Gerould, pp. 57-59, speculates that the alestake and cake may refer to the Summoner and the piece of bread he carries as a buckler. See also Jusserand, pp. 132-33.

[18]The question of the Pardoner's motivations has evoked a great variety of conjectures. Sedgewick surveys the criticism to 1940, Halverson covers the period 1940-70 ("Pardoner"), and Hilary presents more recent developments (pp. 904-06). Several critics have previously suggested that the Pardoner is attacking the Host: see Tupper, "Tavern," p. 563; Mitchell, p. 443; Elliott, p. 23; and Fritz, p. 353. I do not accept Lumiansky's idea that the Pardoner hopes to sell his relics after revealing they are false (pp. 204-05). Rather, after attacking the Host in his tale, he continues to humiliate him. Kean also sees this as a "personal attack" on the Host (2:104).

[19]This is argued by Tupper in "Tavern" but rejected by Sedgewick, pp. 441-42.

[20]Pearsall argues that Death haunts the Pardoner: "The smoothness of his performance . . . is all the more shocking in relation to his reptilian deadness to all that he says" ("Pardoner," pp. 363-64). This idea is stressed by Stevens and Falvey: "The *Pardoner's Tale* projects a curious feeling that the whole world is in the process . . . of organic decay. . . . Everywhere life is turned to death and spirit and flesh into hollow bones" (pp. 148-49).

[21]See the emphasis upon social hierarchy in the following passage from the ParsT: "But certes, sith the time of grace cam, God ordeyned that som folk sholde be moore heigh in estaat and in degree, and som folk moore lough, and that everich sholde be served in his estaat and in his degree" (X.771).

[22]The most eloquent statement of the Parson's pre-eminence in the CT is that of Baldwin, who has been followed by many others: "This very pilgrimage to Canterbury is to be the spiritual, that is, anagogical, figure for the pilgrimage to the heavenly Jerusalem. . . . The pilgrims, wayfarers in time, become *potius mystice quam chronice*, wayfarers to eternity. . . . The Parson replaces the Host . . . because this is the function of a priest, not an innkeeper, and all the pilgrims to Canterbury in becoming pilgrims to the Heavenly Jerusalem must take the *wey* or *via* of Penitence" (*Unity*, pp. 91-92).

Owen, "Development," argues that the ParsT was never meant by Chaucer to be part of the CT. Finlayson, p. 100, and Allen offer ironic readings of the tale. Dissent to these views has been registered by both Delasanta and Wenzel ("ParsT"). See Patterson ("ParsT") for an argument that the ParsT departs from its sources to provide specific comment on the previous tales, and Finke for a recent expression of skepticism on the significance of the tale: "What distinguishes the Parson from the Pardoner is his Platonic and patristic horror of role-playing in which the Pardoner seems to revel. . . . Chaucer's ironies, not the Parson's certainties reflect the paradox of the Christian mystery" (pp. 102-04).

[23]The Pardoner is also liminal in his ambiguous sexuality, his supposed effeminacy also setting him in contrast to the Host, who "of manhod hym lakkede right naught" (I.756). The sexuality of the Pardoner has of course received much attention: see Hilary's discussion of the Pardoner's portrait (pp. 823-24). The dispute suggests that modern sexual categories may not adequately fit Chaucer's Pardoner, but it is in any event clear that he is not in proper control of his libido.

[24]My translation. The Latin text reads: "At contra justi . . . sic . . . temporali refoventur subsidio, sicut viator in stabulo utitur lecto: pausat et recedere festinat; quiescit corpore, sed ad aliud tendit mente" (*PL* 75, col. 857; qtd. Ladner, p. 236 n. 11). Also see Augustine, *Sermo XIV*, *PL* 38, col. 114; qtd. Ladner, p. 236: "He knows that he is on a journey, and he treats

these riches just as one treats a room at an inn. He may refresh himself, he is after all a traveler; he may refresh himself and move on; he does not take with him anything he finds in the room. Another traveler will come along, and he will have the room, but he will not take anything away with him" (my translation) [*Sciat se viam ambulare, et in has divitias tanquam in stabulum intrasse. Reficiat, viator est: reficiat se, et transeat; non secum tollit quod in stabulo invenit. Alius viator erit, et ipse habebit, sed non auferet*].

[25]Trans. O'Donnell, p. 21. The Latin text reads: "Debemus uti, non quasi mansoria quadam dilectione atque delectatione, sed transitoria potius, tanquam viae, tanquam vehiculorum, vel aliorum quorumlibet instrumentorum, aut si quid congruentius dici potest; ut ea quibus ferimur, propter illud ad quod ferimur, diligamus" (*De doctrina christiana* I.35.39, *PL* 34, col. 34).

[26]In exegetical tradition the Inn can be a figure for the Church and the heavenly homeland. Consider the following commentary from Bede's *Expositio in Lucae evangelium* on Lk 10.34, from the story of the Good Samaritan, "And setting him on his own beast, he brought him to an inn and took care of him": "But the inn is the present Church, where travelers, returning to the eternal homeland from the pilgrimage here, are refreshed (my translation) [*Stabulum autem est Ecclesia praesens, ubi reficiuntur viatores, de peregrinatione hac in aeternam patriam redueuntes* (*PL* 92, col. 469)].

Also note Bede's comments on *diversorium* in Lk 2.7, "And she brought forth her first son, and wrapped him in swaddling clothes, and laid him in a manger, because there was no room for them in the inn": "He who sits at the right hand of the Father, took a place in the inn, so that he could prepare many mansions for us in the home of his Father. Although he was born not in the house of his parents but in an inn and on the way, this can be interpreted in a higher sense. For he himself said, 'I am the way, the truth and the life' (John XIV). Therefore, he who through his divine essence remains the truth and the life, through the mystery of the Incarnation was made the way by which he might lead us to the fatherland where we may enjoy the truth and the life" (my translation) [*Qui ad dexteram Patris sedet, in diversorio loco eget, ut nobis in domo Patris sui multas mansiones praepararet. Quamvis hoc quod non in parentum domo, sed in diversorio et in via nascitur per significationem intelligi altius potest. Ipse namque ait: Ego sum via, et veritas et vita (Joan. xiv). Qui ergo per divinitatis essentiam veritas et vita permanet, per Incarnationis mysterium via factus est qua nos ad patriam ubi veritate et vita frueremur adduceret* (*PL* 92, col. 231)].

THE INN, THE CATHEDRAL, AND THE PILGRIMAGE

[27]Bruegel's painting also evinces an element of unification in the central figure sitting above the battleground and dressed as a fool or clown. Gaignebet, p. 342, identifies this figure as Christ, relying on 1 Cor 1.20, "Has not God turned to foolishness the 'wisdom' of this world?" and 3.19, "For the wisdom of this world is foolishness with God." The figure sits above the painting much as Christ sits in judgment above the souls in traditional paintings of the Last Judgment. There is, however, a carnivalesque twist. In Bruegel's painting the Carnival revelers are on the Christ/Fool's right, where the saved are traditionally placed in Last Judgment paintings, and the lenten figures are at the left of the Christ/Fool, where one expects the damned: another Carnival inversion, perhaps, but one that places all under Christ, the wise fool. Ladner, in his discussion of *homo viator* (p. 257), suggests that the fool of the Renaissance festival replaced the pilgrim of the Middle Ages as the essential figure of ambivalent status. See also Kaiser, p. 3.

[28]Poets have since echoed the theme (Rendle, p. 8). Consider, for example, Spenser's "death is an equal doom / To good and bad, the common inn of rest," and Dryden's "The world's an inn and death the journey's end." Note especially Archbishop Leighton (1611-84): "Were I to choose a place to die in, it should be an inn. It looks like a pilgrim going home to whom the world was all an inn, who was weary of the noise and confusion of it."

P AND DOWN, TO AND FRO: SPATIAL RELATIONSHIPS IN THE KNIGHT'S TALE

William F. Woods

This essay will discuss some ways in which spatial relationships contribute to the structural patterning of The Knight's Tale, thereby reflecting its social background and thematic content.[1] "Spatial relationships," in this discussion, refers to: (1) vertical relationships that organize and endow with a larger, cosmic significance the action of the tale—e.g., the burial of the dead Thebans, followed by the "resurrection" of Palamon and Arcite; (2) horizontal relationships that also organize the tale and give it meaning, not by suggesting ultimate goals and values but by typifying the movement, the restless passage to and fro of the characters, which creates their presence and develops their roles within the chivalric world of the tale; (3) progressive changes in the loci for action—e.g., the prison cell, the glade, the temples, the amphitheater—that reflect the characters' inner intents and trace their diverging paths as they pursue their destinies under the constraints of chivalric custom and natural law.

Chaucer uses these three configurations of narrative space to frame the world of The Knight's Tale and, perhaps more important, to dignify it with a world view. Arcite's agonized deathbed question, "What is this world? What asketh men to have?" (I.2777), implies at least that such a world view is needed. What the world is in this tale and what men can ask of it are implicit in the bonds between man, nature, and the First Mover; in the ties that bind men in the world; and in the ways in which men are drawn by their ideals to their separate destinies.

UP AND DOWN

Vertical relationships in The Knight's Tale are numerous and central to the action. The phrase "up and doun" occurs eleven times in this narrative, but "up and doun" is only one example of many: vertical relationships of all kinds reflect the characters' fortunes at various levels of the text—sometimes grandly, as in the raising of Palamon and Arcite from among the fallen in battle, and sometimes in minor ways, such as lovers' moods going up and down as a bucket in a well or Arcite's dying because neither vomit upward nor laxative downward can save him. The many ups and downs in this tale reflect, in fact, the fundamental relationship between heaven, which is "hool," "parfit," and "stable," and earthly life, which is a succession of parts, derived from that whole but "corrumpable" and transient. Connecting the parts with the whole—their origin and destiny— is Theseus's great chain of love, the golden and thus imperishable link between the Creator and His world. But our immediate concern here is not the Chain of Being, that profound neoplatonic idea, but rather the cycles, relations, and mannered gestures which embody that idea in The Knight's Tale, helping to create the dimensions of its narrative space.

The frame of The Knight's Tale is created by Theseus's war with the Scythians, or Amazons, and his marriage to Hippolyta, their queen. His exemplary progress from war to marriage is reversed by a war and funeral at the beginning of the long

Theban narrative but reaffirmed at its end by a combat, a funeral, and a marriage that unites Thebes and Athens. But within this cyclic movement from division to union are other balances and symmetries, many of them figured by vertical relationships. We begin the narrative as Theseus does, confronting the Theban queens, kneeling "in the heighe weye" (line 897). This public abasement reflects their fall from high place and contrasts with the unnatural tyranny of Creon, who has left the queens' dead husbands above ground, unburied. Quickly, Theseus restores the queens to their former estate, slaying Creon and razing the town. At the same time he restores a moral, or natural, balance by burying the dead and disinterring Palamon and Arcite, who are wounded but living men buried in a heap of dead. This deed is prophetic, in that it matches analogous events that close the tale. Arcite is reburied with full honors, which ful fills a destiny predicted throughout the narrative by fire images and other details that anticipate his funeral. Palamon, meanwhile, mourns for Arcite until Theseus "resurrects" him to create the marriage of state with Emelye.[2]

These alternations between up and down, high and low, signify the fluctuations of men's fortunes and the fortunes of cities like Thebes and Athens. But they are also in symmetry with the eternal alternation of life and death, the cycle of nature, which seems in this tale to be correspondent to the influences of the planets, so that the apparent vacillations and inconstancies of human life are actually, if obscurely, in phase with the cosmic rhythms set in motion by the First Mover. One way in which mundane rhythms reflect cosmic ones is through the mythic patterns that Chaucer weaves into the tale. Thebes is, of course, the city founded by Cadmus and Amphioun. Amphioun made music that charmed the very stones, dancing them into place to create the walls of Thebes. Cadmus, for his part, was married to Harmonia, the daughter of Venus and Mars and a symbol of compromise between radically different natures. Both Amphioun and Harmonia suggest the ideal of harmony, then, but

Cadmus's rule was a cycle of discordant reality: having slain the dragon, he planted its teeth, only to have them spring up as armed men who fought each other and then served Cadmus for the eight years (one Pythagorean "year," or cycle) that he needed to atone for killing a serpent sacred to Zeus (Tripp, pp. 140, 259). A parallel appears when Theseus slays Creon, "Fulfild of ire and of iniquitee" (line 940) and then buries the dead Thebans, at which point Palamon and Arcite (Creon's kinsmen) rise up to struggle over Emelye for the next eight years. At the end of this time Palamon will be defeated and lose Emelye in the tournament, and Arcite will die, having fallen from his horse during his victory lap around the theater. Thus at the end of this "life cycle" both boys return to the earth, as it were, so that the next cycle—a marriage suggesting both domestic and civil harmony—can begin with Theseus's retrieval of Palamon from the ashes of his grief.

Such grand cycles frame the narrative and help to create its authority, its apparent symmetry with higher truths and the outlines of legend. But the majority of vertical figures in The Knight's Tale are brief reminders of chivalric ideals that comment on the varying fortunes of Palamon and Arcite. The sun, for instance, rises four times in The Knight's Tale, once in each part of the tale, and each time to accompany one of the four major figures as he or she "rises up" to greet the day. In the first part, the sun is bright for Palamon (lines 1062-65); then Arcite (lines 1493-99) and Emelye (lines 2273-74) have their turns, while Theseus, "Arrayed right as he were a god in trone" (line 2529), seems almost to provide a second dawn as he emerges, like a sun of chivalry, at his palace window. But there are also sunsets in The Knight's Tale, one at midpoint, the other at the end of the tale. Both times the sun sets on a field of combat. In Part II Theseus looks "under the sonne" (line 1697) to make out Palamon and Arcite after they have fought each other all day; in Part IV, "er the sonne unto the reste wente" (line 2637), Palamon is defeated, brought to the stake. At that point, as far as

Theseus and the rest of the chivalric world are concerned, the day of the tournament is over, Arcite is still horsed, and the destiny of Emelye is "darreyne[d]" (line 2097).

But another cosmic rhythm overarches the sun's course: the influence of Saturn, announced in Parts I and III (lines 1328, 2443-78) and promising a different end to the "strif" between the two boys as well as that between Venus and Mars. The result of Saturn's intervention is, of course, Arcite's sudden fall and consequent death. Fire images and other verbal clues embedded in Emelye's prayer (Part III) foreshadow Arcite's death, but the central and climactic figure that links Saturn, Diana, and Emelye with Arcite's necessary fall is a vertical relationship that appears in Part IV. When the victorious Arcite looks up at Emelye seated in the stands, she looks down at him—just as on the walls of the temple where Emelye prayed a portrait of Diana looks down toward her kingdom of the dead. When Arcite lies "as he were deed" (line 2690), black as coal[3] with the blood run to his face, another sun of chivalry has set, and there is nothing in this world that can help him: neither "vomyt upward, ne dounward laxatif" (line 2756) can alter his condition, and, as the cold of death rises up from his feet, the strength of his arms "is lost and al ago" (line 2802). At this point "Nature wol nat wirche" (line 2759); Arcite's wound is mortal, but there is also the implication, later reinforced by Theseus, that his death is the end of a natural cycle of events that runs back to his very first sight of Emelye, the "endere" of his life.

Indeed, love and combat (the primal impulses of attraction and aggression) are interdependent in The Knight's Tale and might be described as functions of each other. Consequently, it is not surprising that the unstable love relationships of this tale are also conveyed by vertical figures, which are analogous to the ups and downs of chivalric combat and help to predict the ultimate destinies of both boys. In Part II, for instance, we find Arcite safe in Thebes, but so low in spirits that he is hardly recognizable. Returning to Athens disguised as a laborer, he

41

worships Emelye as Philostratus ("lover of heights") and rises to the heights of royal favor as one of Theseus's retainers. Thus good fortune brings low spirits, while humble service (and innate nobility) brings good fortune.

Arcite's being turned "up so doun" in both habit and disposition (lines 1377-78) anticipates his final upset in the arena in Part IV and also introduces the conflict with Palamon in the glade. In one of the splendid ornamental pieces that decorate The Knight's Tale, Arcite rises with "firy Phebus" (line 1493) and rides out into the field to greet "the myrie day" (line 1499). But suddenly, having enjoyed the morning like any lover, he falls into a pensive mood,

> As doon thise loveres in hir queynte geres,
> Now in the crope, now doun in the breres,
> Now up, now doun, as boket in a welle.
>
> (Lines 1531-33)

He sits down, and after complaining about the gods' will and his despairing love for Emelye ("Ye sleen me with youre eyen, Emelye!" [line 1567]), falls down in a long trance (a little death), and then gets up again (lines 1572-73). At this moment—an interval blurred by the trance, just as Arcite's death will later delay the marriage—Palamon leaps up from under a bush to assert his claim to Emelye. This episode, with all its ups and downs, emphasizes the reciprocal alternations of men's fortunes as well as the unsteadiness of lovers' moods. It also reflects the causality of the tale, for these impulses of love and aggression both underlie human relationships and signify man's immersion in nature.

The Knight's Tale ends when Arcite is laid low by Saturn, who thereby stabilizes the shifting fortunes that have become characteristic of this tale (see Elbow, pp. 89-90). The problem is how to account for the finality (the permanent downturn) of Arcite's death in a narrative dedicated to the balance of high and low, good and evil. In fact, the real difficulty is the presence of death itself—"'Why woldestow be deed,' thise wommen crye, / 'And haddest gold ynough, and Emelye?'" (lines 2835-36)—in a narrative that celebrates life and does not speculate about matters of the spirit ("Of soules fynde I nat in this registre" [line 2812]). The answer is provided in four parts, each in its way a summary of the whole of life: Egeus's funereal wisdom; the ritual of Arcite's funeral; Theseus's Boethian speech on divine necessity; and the marriage, which makes "of sorwes two / O parfit joye" (lines 3071-72). It is not surprising, given the summarizing function of these episodes, that the four parts divide into two halves that mark a progression from death to life. The funeral serves as exemplum for Egeus's speech, the marriage for the speech of Theseus. This four-part sequence restates, in an abbreviated, dialectical form, the opposition between life and death, or up and down, which the four sections of The Knight's Tale have dramatized at some length.

Theseus's "olde fader Egeus" (line 2838) is the human counterpart of Saturn, "That knew so manye of aventures olde" (line 2444); both of them draw upon "olde experience" (line 2445), either to create the necessity of misfortune or to rationalize it. For our purposes, it is crucial that Egeus describes "this worldes transmutacioun" (line 2839)—the world's inconstancy—in terms of changes "up and doun, / Joye after wo, and wo after gladnesse" (lines 2840-41). These are the perennial changes of Fortune's Wheel, their only pattern the constant alternation of high and low. It is only reasonable to describe such a madly changeable world as "a thurghfare ful of wo" (line 2847).

Egeus's speech appropriately introduces the long funeral episode in which all the elements of chivalric life either surround the pyre or are thrown into it. Arcite has come full circle, in both chivalric and natural terms: having entered the story in a heap of dead soldiers, he leaves it in a heap of trees, the remains of "that selve grove, swoote and grene" (line 2860) where he had fought so savagely for the love of Emelye.[4] This funeral pyre is itself a figure of change. As a catalog—or chain—of

43

burning trees, it represents nature's cycle of "transmutaciouns." It is also, of course, a summative figure of life, and of the life of Arcite. Notice that this pyre is very nearly an allegorical entity: it has a head ("his grene top" [line 2915]) and arms ("And twenty fadme of brede the armes straughte" [line 2916]), as though the pyre were one great tree containing within it a multitude of trees, hence symbolizing "treeness," greenness, the essence of life. The arms of the pyre stretch out 120 feet—as broad, exactly, as the amphitheater was high—so that the glory of Arcite's victory is balanced by the grandeur of his death.[5] The fire that consumes Arcite is carried to the pyre by Emelye, the source of his desire and thus the ender of his life. When this green pyre burns, we have, in effect, seen Arcite's life passing in review, topped with green youth but ending in ashes.[6] Indeed, the flames climb toward the top of the pyre in much the same way that earlier the coldness of death crept up toward Arcite's head.

Theseus's speech reverses Egeus's "fire sermon," acknowledging the necessity of change and death for living things but balancing it with the golden chain of love, which represents the further necessity for all things to complete their cycle by returning to their eternal source and destination. "Every part" of creation is derived from its "hool" (line 3006), runs its limited course in the "corrumpable" (line 3010) world, and then returns "by successiouns" (line 3014) to the "propre welle" (line 3037) of the Creator, "From which it is dirryved, sooth to telle" (line 3038). So saying, Theseus concludes "this long serye" (line 3067)—his argument, but also the lengthy chain of events that makes up The Knight's Tale—by raising the two most sorrowful characters to joy by uniting them in marriage. Just as he had pitied the suffering of the Theban queens, raising them to their feet and then restoring them to high estate, he now raises Emelye from her "swownynge" (lines 2819, 2943) and Palamon from his mourning and unites them in a marriage that balances the "wo" of the funeral pyre by transmuting both their sorrows

44

into "blisse," "richesse," and "heele" (line 3102).

This balanced, metamorphic ending is neat but somehow unsatisfying. After all, Arcite has to die to create the marriage. And, indeed, the shadow of Arcite's demise is present ("et in Arcadia ego") even within the formulaic, fairytale ending:

> For now is Palamon in alle wele,
> Lyvynge in blisse, in richesse, and in heele,
> And Emelye hym loveth so tendrely,
> And he hire serveth so gentilly,
> That nevere was ther no word hem bitwene
> Of jalousie or any oother teene.

> (Lines 3101-06)

"Jalousie" was precisely what Arcite conquered on his deathbed (line 2785) by giving up his life and yielding his place to Palamon. But, satisfying or not, it is the wisdom of The Knight's Tale that nature requires a balance: there must be woe in the world—there must be a descent from paradise—for otherwise there can be no ascent to joy. The fortunes of love and war, the fall of cities, and the cycles of nature are all, at various removes from the center of the narrative, reflective of this one capacious but uncompromising truth. The chain of love, binding the varied elements of the world together, is balanced by the chain of green trees—the entire grove—dissolving in flame. So, too, the divine stasis of the Prime Mover ("stable . . . and eterne" [line 3004]) is necessarily balanced by the chaotic, divisive natural impulses figured in the temple wall paintings and by the destructively chaotic influence of Saturn. Indeed, Saturn's influence is necessary to the dynamic unity (*coincidentia oppositorum*) of creation (McAlindon, pp. 52-53; Barkan, pp. 122-24). Order and chaos, bright and dark, up and down, are essential to The Knight's Tale; for despite Theseus's or anyone else's attempts to preserve order, stable harmony cannot exist without its polar opposite, discordant change, any more than divine wholeness can cease to issue forth in the plenitude of earthly "divisioun."

WILLIAM F. WOODS

TO AND FRO

Devices such as the golden chain of love give the pagan world of The Knight's Tale a neoplatonic, Christian framework, despite the fact that God's name is hidden in a trope ("Firste Moevere") and heaven is yet to be explored. But even in a tale where vertical relationships often have demonstrable thematic significance, there are times when "up and doun" simply means "here, there, everywhere." For instance, when Theseus rides forth toward Thebes, his red-and-white banner shining in the sun, all the fields around him "glyteren up and doun" (line 977). Here, the function of "up and doun" is to create space that will frame Theseus, his flags, and "his hoost of chivalrie the flour" (line 982). The surrounding fields lend coherence to the central figures and create a vivid heraldic tableau with a distribution of colors (red, white, gold, and green) that will later acquire their own significance. But there is more to this image than symmetry. These fields that glitter bear witness to Theseus's chivalric splendor; they stand for the assumed background world within which chivalry performs its routines and has its meaning. This background contains the furniture of chivalric romance— the minor, class-connected details that nevertheless sustain the tale's moral and social ambience. Even indefinite formulaic phrases such as "up and doun" or "to and fro" can suggest a representative largeness or grandness of scope or create loci for typical activities that identify the characters as belonging within the chivalric purview.

What a "typical activity" might be is exemplified by Emelye's walking in the garden at sunrise in Part I:

> And in the gardyn, at the sonne upriste,
> She walketh up and doun, and as hire liste
> She gadereth floures, party white and rede. . . .
>
> (Line 1051-53)

A few lines later Palamon sees her roaming up and down (line

1069), as if she shares in the restlessness of the spring morning. He then describes her in terms of his own "romynge" (lines 1071, 1099), and in Part II, as Arcite rises with the sun, *he* roams up and down in the green grove, thinking of Emelye. All this "roaming" suggests that strong natural bonds are being formed (see Kolve, *Imagery*, pp. 88-91), but it also has a social significance. Emelye's walking to and fro in the garden implies an area and a duration of activity, thus creating for her a characteristic behavioral presence in the narrative. Indeed, her walking has no real purpose: it is "idling," a class-related activity that identifies these aristocratic characters just as surely as do their family trees. In The Knight's Tale "up and doun" or "to and fro" is repeatedly used to display characteristic behavior— that of the armorers (line 2508), for instance, or the heralds "prikyng up and doun" (line 2599), or the wood gods "Disherited of hire habitacioun" (line 2926). Palamon, in praying to Venus, describes fame as "veyne glorie / Of pris of armes blowen up and doun" (lines 2240-41), fame being the *extent* of one's reputation, voiced again and again while it endures.

These typical activities are part of the chivalric tapestry, fixed permanently by the static, traditional society of the tale. To call this world "static" is not to imply that nothing happens or that such a world is confining. Like any romance, The Knight's Tale thrives on action—it is *about* the typical liveliness of young men bleeding for love—and extensiveness in time and space is one of its generic features. For years the story swings back and forth between Athens and Thebes, and, when the day of tournament arrives, we sense the profundity of the event in the expansiveness of its details, from the height of Theseus's window (lines 2528-29), to the shouting of the people, which "touchede the hevene" (line 2561), to the vast amphitheater where the nobles take their places "in degrees aboute" (line 2579), high above the crowd in the lower "seetes" (line 2580). What is static is the social hierarchy, as the theater itself implies. In such a world the fortunes of lovers may fluctuate "up and doun," cities may fall and be raised again, and Arcite may stoop to being Philostratus before he "chaunge[s] hous" (line 2809) to become a glorious memory. But none of these metamorphoses reflects a change in social role, nor is there ever an intent to become someone higher or better than oneself.

The traditional society does not exclude ambition, of course. It is in the nature of this narrative that raw youths such as Palamon and Arcite should rise (from a heap of dead) to marry a princess and be king, or fall in battle and die well. But even though this cyclic rise and fall, as reflected in various spatial images, may have a natural or ethical significance, it is never socially meaningful.[7] Theseus the noble duke and Creon the debased ruler are two sides of a coin, opposing halves of the same social round. There is no such thing as "upward mobility" in The Knight's Tale, just as there is no possibility of moving even one link up or down the Chain of Being that provides this tale with its metaphoric structure.

In effect, the social space of The Knight's Tale is two-dimensional—a flat area, infinitely extendable, where there is freedom to roam but nowhere to climb. As in other aristocratic romances, the action is discursive and cyclical, looping out and returning home (to Thebes) at last because its true subject is not self-transcendence (as in tragedy or bourgeois romance) but *extension*: a gradual revelation of character through the varied adventures of an essentially unchanging literary type. In romances this revelation is usually effected by engaging the hero with a succession of similar types—mirror figures—and that is the formal reason why Palamon and Arcite are so much alike: driven out into the "wyde world" by passion, they confront each other recurrently, and their very similarity forces attention to the mysterious causality of their different intents and fates. Appropriately, Palamon and Arcite are themselves central examples of the extensive, timeless activities of this traditional society, as their fitful passions lead them back and forth between Thebes and Athens, the polar extremes of decayed and upright chivalry, which sum up between them the entire chivalric world.

In contrast to these compulsive journeyings is the stability of Theseus, whose every action seems fraught with purpose. This noble duke may act, as when he raises the queens to their feet, slays Creon, passes judgment, or gives way to mercy, but he is never characterized by "activity": even his recreation, hunting, is purposeful, as befits one who is an earthly counterpart to the First Mover. Theseus is, in effect, the still center of The Knight's Tale, making judgments for the world "as he were a god in trone" (line 2529). His centrality and authority are especially evident at the end of the tale, when Arcite has died and some kind of rationale, or summation, seems necessary. As suggested above, Egeus introduces the funeral, Theseus the marriage; their speeches offer the dark and bright sides of the same truth. For our purposes, it is noteworthy that both Egeus and Theseus sum up the world and its changes by framing its vast extension in space.

Egeus knows the world's "transmutacioun," as he has seen it "chaunge bothe up and doun, / Joye after wo, and wo after gladnesse" (lines 2839-41), and indeed we have seen it change in the course of The Knight's Tale. "This world," he continues, "nys but a thurghfare ful of wo, / And we been pilgrymes, passynge to and fro" (lines 2847-48). The ceaseless, characteristic activities of lovers (and rivals), ladies, soldiers, heralds, and armorers—these too have been part of the tale, described frequently as movement here and there, "to and fro." In Egeus's schematic yet grimly appropriate summary, it seems as though nature's changes—vicissitudes of fortune, birth, death—are oriented to a vertical axis, a series of ups and downs, while the activities of men who endure these changes seem to have a horizontal, here-and-there quality that ultimately leads nowhere but does serve to place them, to give them their brief presence in space and time. These two axes represent man's ambiguous relationship with change and time, which imprison but also in a larger sense sustain him, offering a share in eternity, which is the only salvation this tale can offer. The vertical axis, nature's metamorphoses, reflects the endless ups and downs, but it also implies the constancy of change: it reminds us that change is eternal, cyclical, and thus timeless, the "eternity of nature." The horizontal axis, social change, reflects the limited durations of men's journeys, loves, customs ("gyses"), ambitions. Yet these brief, repetitive, and thus typical presences in time also imply a social continuity, the aristocratic "social eternity" we sense when, like Charles Muscatine, we say that the characters and events of The Knight's Tale resemble figures in a tapestry ("Form").

Theseus's hopeful speech both amplifies and reverses Egeus's funeral remarks: he reaffirms the necessity of death while reinterpreting it as a necessary return to the wholeness of the Creator (here, Jupiter). But the spatial orientation, or "deep structure," is the same in both speeches. Theseus also begins with the vertical axis, represented here by the "faire cheyne of love"; the chain sets "in certeyn boundes" the four elements, "The fyr, the eyr, the water, and the lond" (lines 2991-93), implying the ancient model of concentric spheres, which is a vertical hierarchy. Then he proceeds to the "Certeyne dayes and duracioun" (line 2996) of every earthly part that is derived from the incorruptible "hool" (line 3006), duration in time suggesting horizontal extension in space. In a similar way Theseus's following remarks, which illustrate the truism that "all must die," suggest both vertical and horizontal space, thereby recreating the dimensions of the world as a means of summarizing it. The oak is tall and the stone is low, worn down by those who pass to and fro; the broad river is also long, and the "grete tounes" are high (lines 3017-25). Having framed the dying world, extending it upon its two axes, and having summed up the variety of its mortal creatures in every degree (another pair of axes), Theseus reaches his concluding "sentence," his fundamental precept for those who would live in such a world: "Thanne is it wysdom, as it thynketh me, / To maken vertu of necessitee" (lines 3041-42).

This final wisdom provides for the compromises by which the stable, though narrow and limited, customs of chivalry may be brought into accord with nature's uncompromising law of eternal change (see Halverson, "Aspects"; Elbow, pp. 92-94). Thus it is also his rationale for the upcoming marriage, which, like the marriage of Cadmus and Harmonia or of Theseus and Hippolyta, represents yet another compromise by warring social elements, another union made from scattered human remnants.

LOCI FOR CHIVALRIC ACTION

At the very end of The Knight's Tale, when the Knight calls upon God to bless Palamon and Emelye's marriage, he opens his benediction with a final summary statement about the world, God's creation: "And God, that al this wyde world hath wroght, / Sende hym his love that hath it deere aboght" (lines 3099-3100). "Al this wyde world" combines neatly with his final line—"And God save al this faire compaignye! Amen" (line 3108)—to bracket, and in a sense protect, this paradisal vision of matrimony, which has no more in common with reality than did Palamon's love vision of Emelye in the garden so many years before. In effect, one ideal has replaced another. We assume that life in the world of the tale will go on, perhaps as painfully as before, but the charmed circle of the marriage is presented as free from pain and beyond change. This contrast between the outer world and the inner landscape of the ideal represents a third way in which spatial relationships are significant to the Knight's Tale.[8] As Palamon and Arcite are drawn toward their ideals of love and victory, their progress is reflected by two kinds of relative movement in narrative space. They come increasingly to share the same locus with Emelye, the object of their desire; but as they come nearer to her, and to their separate fates, their positions diverge—they become increasingly separated from each other in space.

51

These two spatial developments begin early in the tale, when Palamon and Arcite catch sight of Emelye from their prison window and acutely sense their separation from her. Palamon sees her "thurgh a wyndow, thikke of many a barre / Of iren greet and square as any sparre" (lines 1075-76), and after their first quarrel Arcite sadly concludes that, despite their love, "Heere in this prisoun moote we endure" (line 1185). Their prison cell, where they wrangle fruitlessly, isolates them from the fresh, green garden and the "hevenyssh" object of their love, just as any real life is remote from its ideals. In each major section of the tale, these two loci—one signifying love's lack and the other its promise—are reasserted; but as the narrative progresses the separation between them narrows, then eventually disappears. At the same time, however, Palamon and Arcite are increasingly separated from each other. Beginning as sworn brothers united in death (buried in the same heap of dead), they occupy progressively divergent loci as each moves toward the realization of his separate ideal. Their love debate turns to dueling for love, then mounted combat, and finally permanent separation by death and by marriage. What is thus created is the story of how Palamon and Arcite enter the world and are progressively assimilated to their ideals of love and glory through nature's metamorphoses.

In the glade episode the two boys and Emelye now occupy the same locus, the fresh, green grove, while she becomes aware for the first time of their existence. The theme of natural balance, reflected in the garden scene by floral patterns of white, red, and green, is now expressed by Palamon and Arcite themselves, who serve Venus and Mars while trying to get some "grene" (love), in the words of Arcite's song (line 1512). Nonetheless, they are far from being in harmony with their pleasant surroundings, having taken the opportunity of their freedom to turn their earlier debate into a death duel, reddening the green grass with blood up to the ankle. By contrast, Emelye is riding with Theseus and Hippolyta, all of them dressed in green for the hunt, a kind of natural compromise between the pursuit of love and the pursuit of arms. The hunt is a reminder that while Theseus, by serving Diana and marrying Hippolyta, has made his peace with the impulses of Venus and Mars, Palamon and Arcite are still struggling in blind passion over Emelye. Freed from the isolated frustration of their prison cell, they come closer to Emelye, and to death, by turning their love debate into an equally fruitless armed combat.

In the third main episode Palamon and Arcite are further divided from one another by separate loci, the temples. But each has come proportionally closer to his heart's desire and has more fully revealed his own inner nature, his intent (cf. Elbow, pp. 75-79), by choosing his place within the world-figure of the great theater: Palamon enlists the aid of Venus and Arcite prays to Mars, while Emelye visits the temple between them, which represents for her the neutral protection of Diana. In the prison cell they looked out upon a paradisal vision of Emelye in the garden, but now that ideal seems to have been internalized, and therefore compromised. The paintings on the temple walls are lurid and tragic, more like projections of the human heart and of human desires than remote visions of paradise.

Finally, in the fourth episode, the pattern of change completes itself. When Palamon and Arcite enter at opposite sides of the vast amphitheater, each heads a body of one hundred picked knights—small armies, reminiscent of small nations, and led by two kings magnificently opposed in their astrological significance and chivalric pride. This formal separation becomes final when Arcite is mortally injured at the peak moment of his victory. Yet his departure from the world is, paradoxically, the flowering of his destiny. Arcite has been identified throughout the narrative with freedom from earthly bonds and also with exile: to pursue Emelye, he sets aside his sworn brotherhood with Palamon; freed from prison at Perotheus's request, he is exiled by Theseus on pain of death; he breaks Theseus's command by returning to Athens, where he serves under a false name; he prays to Mars, Venus's adulterous lover; and in death (a "coold" death, reminiscent of Mars's temple in frosty Thrace [lines 2800, 2815]), his body goes to a lonely grave (line 2779), while "his spirit chaunge[s] hous" for unknown regions (line 2809). His death sends him beyond the confines of the narrative ("Of soules fynde I nat in this registre" [line 2812]), where both freedom and separation from earthly concerns become his permanent condition. In contrast, Palamon, who spent so much time in prison, is now consigned to a marriage of state, bound most willingly to the woman who captured his heart. If Arcite, having chosen victory, has escaped the world-prison of The Knight's Tale, Palamon has entered its enclosed garden of matrimonial delight. He has joined Emelye "in blisse, in richesse, and in heele" (line 3102)—a timeless vision of aristocratic "wele" (line 3101) that the tale projects indefinitely into the future.

In fact, the pattern of episodes that we have just observed—a movement from the envisioning of an ideal to its realization—occurs in each half of the tale. Palamon and Arcite move from cell to glade, then from temple to theater, and these changes in locus create a steady expansion of scope. When in Part IV Palamon and Arcite for the last time occupy the same space (the huge theater), separate temples and then separate armies provide them with places of their own within the containing walls. The walls themselves, lined by the "degrees" (line 1890) of the spectators' seats, reflect the confines of their chivalric world and of the aristocratic social structure. After the combat Arcite has his own place, the funeral pyre, which is among other things an emblem of dispersion: its "armes" (line 2916) stretch out, broad as the containing walls of the theater "world" are high, and its top reaches toward heaven. By contrast, Palamon's final locus is within the marriage, a matrimonial variation on the ancient *topos* of the earthly paradise. Like his cousin, Palamon comes full circle, from union with Arcite in the heap of dead to the mile-round ring of the theater to the union of marriage. The

Knight-narrator (but not the pragmatic Theseus) describes this marriage as a timeless ideal (lines 3101-07) not unlike Palamon's original vision of Emelye in the garden. Timeless, indeed, and yet questionable, given its presence in such a changeable world. In its way this description of the marriage is as unsatisfying as Theseus's remarks on the glorious death of Arcite. Both the marriage and the death are extreme expressions of opposed ideals; they reflect the apotheoses of two essential chivalric activities, love and combat. Individually, neither of these two endings is convincing or even satisfying. Yet, to be fair, it is probably unrealistic to remove any ideal from its worldly context or to deprive it of the company of other ideals. For in combination the fates of Palamon and Arcite demonstrate a compromise between the polarities of love and war, and life and death, that constitutes the realism peculiar to this tale.

The pattern of spatial relationships we have traced here develops in two ways, then. As the boys move apart in space and in identity, each of them follows his heart, and thus his destiny, toward either the periphery or the center of the chivalric world. In the beginning the two young and nameless knights lie together in a heap of dead, having fought as blood brothers under the same coat of arms. In the course of the tale these aristocratic twins are progressively individuated: their essentially different visions of Emelye, the symbol of chivalric grace, send them out along divergent lines of development, one ending in the boundless otherworld of fame (the martial heaven),[9] the other in the innocent, inner heaven of earthly love.

In this schematic balancing of aristocratic ideals, The Knight's Tale usefully leaves itself open to contrary readings from other points of view, while its inclusive, world-framing dimensions make an extravagant, class constrained claim to truth, an appropriately provocative opening for that great fabric of world views, *The Canterbury Tales* (see Siegel). Its strong vertical orientation, focused by the chain of love but elaborated throughout the tale by vertical relationships and movement up and down, provides physical (as well as metaphysical) referents for ethical and natural values in this tale and subsequent tales. The corresponding horizontal orientation, the recurrent imagery of "to and fro" (sometimes merged with "up and down" in its general sense of "here and there") creates an indefinite and thus typifying extension in space that frames the movements and journeyings of the characters, giving them the solidity of types. More generally, such horizontal imagery forms an axis of reference for the impulses and actions of chivalric activity, the life of the world as seen by the aristocratic eye. Finally, the diverging loci of Palamon and Arcite undergo their own spatial transformations as one youth is assimilated to the remote freedom of immortal fame and the other to the close, timeless union of earthly love. Thus each hero is finally placed in terms of his inner intent as it relates to the complex of ethical and societal values implicit in the tale; and since each "place" represents the culmination of a development, the realization of an ideal, both boys become, like Theseus, chivalric icons worthy to "drawen to memorie" (line 2074).

NOTES

[1]As Stanbury observes in a recent article, "There has been curiously little discussion of space in medieval narrative in general" (p. 488 n. 2). Kolve, *Imagery*, ch. 3, does provide a major treatment of narrative space in the KnT, but our treatments are substantially different. Other relevant sources are Blodgett and Joseph. Suggestive, though not referring to the KnT, are Peter Brown and Boklund.

[2]This aid to Palamon parallels Theseus's earlier attempt to retrieve his good friend and sworn brother, Perotheus, from hell. See also DiMarco's discussion on CT I.1132 (p. 830).

[3]Arcite's face is actually dark red, as if the red of Mars had combined with the darkness of Saturn to produce this deep sunset effect.

[4]On the grove, see McAlindon, pp. 50-51.

[5]On the height of the amphitheater, see line 1890, "of sixty pas." I am assuming that one pace measures two feet, and that Chaucer also assumed this, so as to make the dimensions of theater and funeral pyre match each other.

[6]Emelye is garlanded in the garden scene, and Arcite later rides to the grove to pick greenery for a garland. Other garlands, sustaining what is ultimately a sacrificial motif, belong to Daphne, in Diana's temple painting "yturned til a tree" (line 2062); Emetreus, Arcite's champion (lines 2175-76); Emelye, praying in Diana's temple (line 2290-91); Arcite again, as he lies on the pyre (line 2875); and the pyre itself, "with his grene top" (line 2915).

[7]By contrast, the spatial imagery of the houses in the MilT and RvT points unambiguously to the class differences that separate peasants and townsmen from clerks, and the action of these tales derives in part from attempts by the characters to maintain or subvert that separation.

[8]For a more extensive treatment of the following material, see Woods.

[9]Although the narrator declines to speculate about Arcite's final destination (lines 2809-10), his necessary fate is to dwell in the underworld, the "memory" of the classical world, which was, like the ecstasy of love, an answer to the threat posed by mortality and the heedless flux of nature's eternal changes.

LERKLY RIVALRY IN
THE REEVE'S TALE

Bruce Kent Cowgill

Much recent criticism of The Reeve's Tale and its place in Fragment I has focused on its sustained imagery of ill-tempered diminution—a combative sense of "quitting" as "getting even" (R. Payne, p. 115) that marks the reductive vindictiveness of the tale and its climactic position within the fragment's "deliberate descent into disorder" (Traversi, p. 62).[1] Within this context of human values scaled ever downward toward the domineering and mean-spirited, where all mutuality of thought and feeling has been pared like the Reeve's beard, "as ny as ever he kan" (I.588), Edward Vasta has drawn attention to Oswald's "adversitive" aggressiveness, arguing that "as a literary character the Reeve is virtually a domesticated, hence comic, personification of the Adversary" (p. 8).

In the following pages I wish to explore one extended example of this thematic focus on rivalry in The Reeve's Tale, hitherto largely unattended to by critics, including Vasta. Specifically, close attention to Chaucer's description of the Aleyn-John relationship reveals just how deeply embedded is the narrator's adversarial world view—extending even to figures whom virtually all critics (including Vasta) have seen in essentially undifferentiated terms.[2] V. A. Kolve, for example, describes the clerks' character as "generic" (*Imagery*, p. 235), while Charles A. Owen, Jr., speaks in passing of the Reeve's imagined world as one in which the old are trampled by the young, who are "indistinguishable from one another except by name" (*Pilgrimage*, p. 109). The view is shared by Robert Worth Frank, Jr., who sees the clerks as "scarcely distinguishable one from the other" (p. 58), and by C. David Benson, who contrasts the two Cambridge clerks with their Oxford counterparts to illuminate The Reeve's Tale's diminished world view: "Instead of clever Nicholas or flamboyant Absalon, we have the bumpkins Aleyn and John" (*Drama*, p. 92). In short, virtually all recent critics would seem to agree with Murray Copland's neat encapsulation: "Alan and John—they are as inseparable as a comedy team" (p. 24).

Yet such generic views of the clerks' homogeneity ignore an important contrast that Chaucer has taken considerable pains to develop. Aleyn and John are not only distinguished from all other fabliau students through the clarity with which the narrative "particularizes" their status within the university class, as Copland argues (p. 23); they are subtly differentiated one from another as well. Briefly stated, the students' relationship forms a comic subplot that sharpens the tale's central theme—its vivid evocation of domineering one-upmanship—by playing John as cleverer clerk off against his more brazen but slower-witted companion.

The initial evidence for this interpretation emerges from a comparison of The Reeve's Tale to its two closest analogues: the late twelfth-century *De Gombert et les II clercs* by Jean Bodel and the anonymous thirteenth-century *Le Meunier et les II clers*. It is likely that Chaucer knew at least the latter version (Benson and Andersson, p. 100).

In both French versions of the story the clerks are so little differentiated that neither is ever named, nor is there any attempt to establish which clerk is speaking at a particular moment. Thus, while *Le Meunier et les II clers* is considerably more detailed than Bodel's version, its author's total unconcern for differentiating the two youths appears in the recurrent use of interchangeable speech markers, such as "Li uns dist a l'autre," "Li uns clers a l'autre parla," and "Li autres a lors respondu" (Benson and Andersson, pp. 100-15). So closely are the two clerks identified throughout that they consistently speak with a single voice, as in their plea that the miller grant them lodging for the night: "'Munier,' font il, 'Deus soit o vos! / Por amor Deu, avanciez nos'" (p. 104). In The Reeve's Tale, by contrast, with but a single exception—the mutual outcry "Keep! Keep! Stand! Stand!" (line 4101)—it is clear which of the two clerks is speaking.

Far more significant is what the analogues reveal about Chaucer's handling of the tale's two seduction scenes. It will suffice for purposes of illustration to concentrate only on *Le Meunier et les II clers* (the later and more detailed work) both because it better illuminates Chaucer's alterations and because virtually identical conclusions emerge from a similar analysis of the fabliau by Bodel. For clarity I will refer to the youth Chaucer calls Aleyn as the "girl's clerk," the John-counterpart as the "wife's clerk."

The distinction is a crucial one. For viewed *together*—in the way critics have traditionally perceived them—both John and Aleyn illustrate the kind of reduced intellect so consistent with the pervasive diminution that is the tale's governing aesthetic principle. As is appropriate to the Reeve's world of sour mean-spiritedness, neither Cambridge clerk is as clever as his counterpart in the analogues. Viewed *separately*, however, Aleyn's and John's roles reveal a telling differentiation from those in the French fabliaux, a distinction that leaves Aleyn with not a glimmer of the fabliau tradition's clerkly cleverness while John's light at least faintly flickers.

In *Le Meunier et les II clers*, for example, the girl's clerk is able to seduce the miller's daughter only after first gaining entry to the cupboard where she has been locked, then presenting her with a ring stolen from an andiron as a miraculous golden band guaranteed to preserve her chastity. Chaucer, by contrast, describes Aleyn's seduction of Malyne as involving merely a daredevil's brazen disregard for the perilous miller, whom he views as worth no more than "a flye" (line 4192):

> And up he rist, and by the wenche he crepte.
> This wenche lay uprighte and faste slepte,
> Til he so ny was, er she myghte espie,
> That it had been to late for to crie,
> And shortly for to seyn, they were aton.
>
> (Lines 4193-97)

In the case of John, however, the diminution is not nearly as pronounced. His cradle trick, performed "softely" (line 4211) as he bears the instrument of deception "softe unto his beddes feet" (line 4213), differs from that in *Le Meunier et les II clers* in but a single significant detail: unlike the wife's clerk in the analogue, John does not pull the baby's ear to make it cry.

This background of the French versions offers a base from which to pursue a more detailed analysis of the Aleyn-John characterizations, for the changes Chaucer has made—and *not* made—provide initial grounds for suspecting a hierarchical distinction between Aleyn and his slightly brighter companion. Such an analysis will substantiate the critical assumption that "the most dramatic change Chaucer has made in the plot of his original" is the omission of the cupboard and miraculous ring, while it strongly challenges the subsequent inference that he did so only because the scene is "cumbersome and inappropriate" (Frank, p. 60). It will, moreover, illuminate an increasingly competitive differentiation between the two clerks—sustained throughout as a comic subplot—that both counterpoints and delineates the more obviously combative rivalry between the Cambridge youths and Symkyn.

It is Aleyn who is assigned nearly all the menial tasks mentioned as the story progresses—chores strongly suggestive of a subservient status. As the two clerks prepare to set off for the mill, for example, "This Aleyn maketh redy al his gere, / And on an hors the sak he caste anon" (lines 4016-17). The reference here to "an hors," coupled with the later explicitness of line 4071 ("This John goth out and fynt his hors away"), leaves little doubt that the warden's palfrey is in John's charge—a further intimation of his more dominant stature. It is also clear from John's reaction after their discovery of the horse's escape that Aleyn is the one held responsible for tending it badly: "Why ne had thow pit the capul in the lathe?" (line 4088).

Such indications of John's intellectual dominance are reinforced through additional details, some of which would seem to have little function other than character differentiation. The tale makes explicit, for example, not only that it is he who leads the pair to the mill ("John knew the wey—hem nedede no gyde" [line 4020]),[3] but also, after the horse's recapture, that he holds what is presumably the clerks' single purse:

> "But specially I pray thee, hooste deere,
> Get us some mete and drynke, and make us cheere,
> . . . .
> Loo, heere *oure* silver, redy for to spende."
> > (Lines 4131-32, 4135; italics mine)

While it is the less calculating, more direct Aleyn who first addresses Symkyn upon the clerks' arrival at the mill ("Al hayl, Symond, y-fayth! / Hou fares thy faire doghter and thy wyf?" [lines 4022-23]), it is John—in a much longer speech—who explains to the miller *why* the two have come. Especially notable are the aphorisms that throughout the tale serve to differentiate John's speech from Aleyn's,[4] ultimately giving it, in relative terms at least, a patina of rustic wisdom:

> "Symond," quod John, "by God, nede has na peer.
> Hym boes serve hymself that has na swayn,

Or elles he is a fool, as clerkes sayn.
Oure manciple, I hope he wil be deed,
Swa werkes ay the wanges in his heed;
And forthy is I come, and eek Alayn,
To grynde oure corn and carie it ham agayn;
I pray yow spede us heythen that ye may."

(Lines 4026-33)

After Symkyn agrees at once to grind the grain, John again takes the lead, this time as creator of the deceptive explanation to account for watching Symkyn at the mill:

"By God, right by the hopur wil I stand,"
Quod John, "and se howgates the corn gas in.
Yet saugh I nevere, by my fader kyn,
How that the hopur wagges til and fra."

(Lines 4036-39)

Comically consistent with both his impulsiveness and his lesser stature of subservience, Aleyn immediately follows John's lead with a response that offers a perfect visual image of his role: "John, and wiltow swa? / Thanne wil I be bynethe, by my croun" (lines 4040-41). In a single deft stroke, Chaucer captures both Aleyn's position "bynethe" his fellow clerk and the "croun" deficiencies that make his role inevitable.[5]

In the tale's next scene, after Symkyn has loosed the horse and the two students have discovered its loss, John's reaction extends our awareness of these relative positions in the hierarchy. Urging his slower-witted fellow to action, he

gan to crie "Harrow!" and "Weylaway!
Oure hors is lorn, Alayn, for Goddes banes,
Step on thy feet! Com of, man, al atanes!"

(Lines 4072-74)

The greater befuddlement of Aleyn is implicit both in his immediate reaction ("Al was out of his mynde his housbondrie. /

64

'What, whilk way is he geen?' he gan to crie" [lines 4077-78])
and in John's instructions following the wife's exclamation that
the horse is in the fen ("Aleyn, for Cristes peyne / Lay doun thy
swerd, and I wil myn alswa" [lines 4084-85]). John's disdain for
his companion's dullness then intensifies in an outcry that re-
sounds with colloquial notes of intracollegiate rivalry: "Why ne
had thow pit the capul in the lathe? / Ilhayl! By God, Alayn,
thou is a fonne!" (lines 4088-89).

John's dominance in the pecking order of the subplot continues through the following scene of the clerks' bedraggled
return, "wery and weet" (line 4107), to the mill. Implicit in both
the word order and the rhythm of line 4108—"Comth sely John,
and with him comth Aleyn"—is the suggestion of a field com-
mander trailed by the hapless private who has mucked things up
intolerably, an image reinforced by Aleyn's silence even after
John's outburst swells to its crescendo:

> "Allas," quod John, "the day that I was born!
> Now are we dryve til hethyng and til scorn.
> Oure corn is stoln; men wil us fooles calle,
> Bathe the wardeyn and oure felawes alle,
> And namely the millere, weylaway!"
>
> (Lines 4109-13)

John's concern for his reputation as he leads the horse toward
the mill, his acute awareness of how much contempt will be
heaped upon the clerks by their Soler Hall peers, will be easily
understood by anyone who has spent an hour in a college pub or
fraternity house. Chaucer has further demonstrated John's
authority through the long speech in which he arranges for the
night's food and lodging (lines 4127-35). These details suggesting John's dominance set up perfectly the comic humiliation
toward which virtually everything in the tale's subplot has been
pointing: the sudden role reversal in which the downtrodden
Aleyn, the "fonne" so sharply tongue-lashed for his stupidity,
suddenly rises from his bed of woe to gain the solace the miller's

"wel ygrowen" (line 3973) daughter lies ready to provide.

When it is thus Aleyn, not John, who resolves to avenge himself through his brazen plan to "swyve" the miller's daughter, the tale's comic subplot has fallen into perfect alignment with the main plot's imminent climax—the toppling of the domineering character in the Reeve's hierarchical world of crude one-upmanship. Like the humiliated Symkyn, whom we will soon see knocked "bakward" (line 4281) onto the dishonored womb of his wife, John is forced to lie in his own bed of humiliation while his bumbling, slower-witted companion finds "somwhat for his harm" (line 4203). That Aleyn has done so with nary a hint of cleverness or guile, with nothing more than a bullheaded bravado that has made a mockery of his own cautious restraint (lines 4188-91), serves only to deepen John's disgrace:

> This John lith stille a furlong wey or two,
> And to hymself he maketh routhe and wo.
> "Allas!" quod he, "this is a wikked jape;
> Now may I seyn that I is but an ape."

> (Lines 4199-4202)

In a tale celebrated for its evocation of naturalistic detail,[6] Chaucer creates few scenes as comically vivid as this one—the once cocksure clerk, ever "lusty" like his fellow "for to pleye" (line 4004), lying now in the solitary awareness of what it truly means to be an "ape." Like legions of scholars across the ages, John draws from his sorry situation the bitter lesson no lecture hall is needed to provide. His conclusion pays grudging tribute to his dumber but infinitely luckier companion:

> "He auntred hym, and has his nedes sped,
> And I lye as a draf-sak in my bed;
> And when this jape is tald another day,
> I sal been halde a daf, a cokenay!"

> (Lines 4205-08)

Then, acting with a decisiveness that alone can re-establish his dominance, John vows, "I wil arise and auntre it, by my fayth!" (line 4209). The action—performed, as we have seen, so "softely" the word is repeated for emphasis—simultaneously proves both his own courage and his larger claim to clerkly cleverness through the deceptive transfer of the crib. It reinforces our sense not only of John's greater craftiness but also of his prudent caution, a caution Chaucer subtly underscores in his description of the seduction act itself:

> But faire and wel she creep in to the clerk,
> And lith ful stille, and wolde han caught a sleep.
> Withinne a while this John the clerk up leep,
> And on this goode wyf he leith on soore.
>
> (Lines 4226-29)

Set against the earlier image of his forlorn humiliation in an unshared bed, the brief "while" that precedes his daring "leep" hints at a wiser man's caution still not fully abandoned. Yet John's culminating act ("He priketh harde and depe as he were mad" [line 4231]) suggests a desperate need for dominance that edges the subplot away from comedy toward the darker psychic levels to which the tale's main plot has also been pushed.

The climactic scene at which we have thus arrived—the fusion of the subplot's comic evocation of student rivalry with the main plot's similar but far more bitter emphasis on the total humiliation of Symkyn—is a consummate example of Chaucer's skill at sustaining a parallel for the ultimate purpose of sharpening a contrast. For with an irony that immeasurably deepens Symkyn's disgrace, John the humiliated clerk—his Symkyn-like position echoed in his own self-condemnation through the milling image of a "draf-sak"[7]—has turned the tables and salvaged both his future reputation and his accustomed role of dominance in an aggressive act that serves simultaneously as Symkyn's crowning humiliation—the "swyving" of his "noble" wife (line 3942). This union of the two plots in reciprocal climax is reminiscent of the similar fusion at "Help! Water! Water!" in The Miller's Tale (line 3815), suggestive of both the tight interconnecton and comparable artistry of the two tales.

Aleyn's actions at this climactic juncture conform to his lesser role as the dumber but more brazen lover. In a comic reminder of his subservient status as the more menial laborer, he waxes "wery in the dawenynge, / For he had swonken al the longe nyght" (lines 4234-35). Then, "toty of [his] swynk" (line 4253), he dull-wittedly enters the bed of an occupant whose "rowtyng" is loud enough to be heard "two furlong[s]" away (line 4166), and immediately seizes his neck (line 4261) and maligns him as a "swynes-heed" (line 4262). It is a term of pungent irony, illuminated by Beryl Rowland's note that a probable meaning of "swynes-heed" is "sluggard" (*Beasts*, p. 76). The term strikes a universal chord as the swinking man's timeless epithet of revilement for his intellectual superior: "So much for brains," it says, "in the face of a man willing to work his rear off." That the Aleyn we have seen to this point in the tale has said so little—that he has simply taken in silence John's verbal lashes while the clerks' horse runs wild after mares in the fen— dramatizes the adversarial sting of both his night's sexual labors and his triumphant insult.[8]

Chaucer leaves ambiguous the exact amount of physical suffering Aleyn experiences in the tale's explosive denouement, as he and Symkyn wallow through a mélange of smashed faces and a clutched "throte-bolle" (line 4273), but it is clear that his fellow clerk emerges scot-free. As John has earlier borne the intellectual humiliation of an officer overrun by plans that have hopelessly backfired, Aleyn shoulders as best he can the foot soldier's lot of hard knocks. When the tale is done, the narrator surveys the battleground he has created and offers a final distillation of its meaning; the stark, adversarial imagery of top-dog domination culminates with grim, relentless inevitability:

CLERKLY RIVALRY IN THE REEVE'S TALE

And God, that sitteth *heighe* in magestee,
Save al this compaignye, *grete and smale*!
Thus have I *quyt* the Millere in my tale.
(Lines 4322-24; italics mine)

The broader implications of this reading of the Aleyn-John relationship are pronounced. First, through the clerks' collegiate combativeness, their largely unspoken rivalry set as ironic backdrop to their boisterous mutual combat with Symkyn, Chaucer links his world to our own through an unchanging universality of scholastic contentiousness. Second, given the intense youthful rivalries in the preceding tales of Fragment I and The Reeve's Tale's culminating place in the reductive sequence, a student relationship that is essentially adversarial rather than co-operative is surely what we would expect Chaucer to have produced: we have moved from The Knight's Tale's epic struggle of Palamon and Arcite, replete with echoes of Eteocles and Polynices (Haller, "KnT"; Cowgill), through The Miller's Tale's thunderous mock-epic war of fart and plowshare, to the pettiest of sophomoric conflicts in the Reeve's shrunken domestic universe. Finally, the nuances of the Aleyn-John rivalry show further just how carefully calibrated are the poem's "social relationships and pressures" (C. D. Benson, *Drama*, p. 102). That The Reeve's Tale "demonstrates more obviously than any of Chaucer's other fabliaux his peculiar genius for characterization" (Benson and Andersson, p. 86) makes it most unlikely that the poet would have intended us to see two of the tale's three central characters as collegiate clones.

And yet the fact remains that Aleyn and John have traditionally been viewed as doubles. Can Chaucer possibly have drawn such sharp character distinctions as those explored above when so many readers have seen little differentiation? The best evidence for an affirmative answer, I think, lies in the fact that we come to Chaucer's art primarily as silent readers, ill attuned to features that emerge distinctly only when the poetry is read aloud. This distinction relates particularly to the fabliau, a genre Charles Muscatine contends that Chaucer likely experienced more through oral tradition than through literary sources. Given this probable context of "postprandial conviviality" and "orally transmitted jokes,"[9] one can easily imagine what a narrator with a flair for gesture and intonation would have done with the roles of Aleyn and John. That such speculation is especially applicable to The Reeve's Tale—indeed, that in the clerks' characterizations Chaucer insists upon a close attention to auditory nuance—his precise rendering of their speech in Northern dialect amply testifies.

NOTES

[1]On the personal animosity of the Reeve, see also Siegel, p. 18, and P. Olson, *CT*, pp. 80-84. On the tale's reductiveness, see Pearsall, *CT*, pp. 183-92, and "Comedy," pp. 133-35; Donaldson, pp. 1070-71.

[2]Vasta, for example, explores the scholars' combativeness only as it applies to Symkyn, not to one another: "The young scholars from the North reflect the spirit of the Reeve's remembered youth: the spirit of the adversary" (p. 9).

[3]That the original reading (as in the Hengwrt manuscript) may have been "hym," not "hem," suggests that Chaucer intended an even sharper emphasis than is reflected in many modern editions. See Manly and Rickert, p. 443. Bennett, pp. 94-101, offers useful social background on the two clerks.

[4]John's habitual use of maxim and metaphor is also apparent in lines 4086, 4129-30, 4134, 4206, and 4210—a consistent if crude verbal facility that Aleyn approaches only in his brief farewell to Malyne. On the function of proverbs in the tale, see Whiting, pp. 86-87.

[5]"Croun" may here refer to the clerk's tonsure; see Spearing and Spearing, p. 102. That the term more broadly suggests "head" or mental capacity, however, seems clear from Symkyn's later application of "by my croun" to

himself (line 4099). That it also connotes a literal crown, or secular lordship, further underscores the power game that lies at the heart of the hierarchical relationships in the tale.

[6]Kolve, to offer one recent example of this widespread view, notes the tale's "obsessive concern with literal fact" (*Imagery*, p. 235).

[7]Chaucer reinforces the John-Symkyn parallel in the climactic passage through another metaphor of deprecation: John's indictment of himself as an "ape" (line 4202). The image of simian stupidity resonates against its counterpart in the tale's opening portrait of the Trumpington miller: "As piled as an ape was his skulle" (line 3935).

[8]John is the speaker of thirty-six of the forty-five lines of clerical dialogue prior to Aleyn's sudden turning of the tables at line 4168. This verbal imbalance reinforces such indicators of social gradation as John's guardianship of the horse, his leading of the pair to the mill, and his offering of "oure silver" (line 4135). On vindictiveness rather than healthy pleasure as the primary motivation for both clerks' sexual aggressiveness, see Howard, p. 240.

[9]Derived from a formal address by Professor Muscatine at the NEH Institute on *The Canterbury Tales* (Storrs, Conn., July 1987). See also Muscatine, *Fabliaux*, pp. 5-12, and Heist, pp. 251-58.

# AT THE CHILDREN PLEYE":
THE GAME BETWIXT THE
AGES IN THE REEVE'S TALE

Susanna Greer Fein

In what amounts to a lyric moralization upon death, the Reeve characterizes the "tappe of lyf" as a stream of ale drawn by Death, starting its flow at birth and continually decreasing until there is "namoore" (I.3891-98). In this mood of complaint the Reeve declares himself too old to "pley" (line 3867), too soured to laugh with the others at the "jape" of the injured carpenter. From his perspective time is lost with every moment; the flow cannot be stopped. While old age is a cooling of physical strength, the vices of the will remain hot. Harry Bailly interrupts this moaning over ebbing vitality with a brusque command to "tarie nat the tyme" (line 3905), thus presenting another perspective: time is to be used fruitfully—in the tale-telling—not bemoaned uselessly by an old man who sees only rottenness.

This much-praised passage has taxed critical attempts to find a link between the old man's lament and the ensuing tale of thievish trickery.[1] Glending Olson states flatly that "there is nothing in the tale which develops the morbid concern with aging that dominates the Reeve's prologue or even points to an

73

old man as its teller" ("RvT," p. 228). Paul G. Ruggiers declares
the speech an "aside" that is beyond the concern of the tale, an
outgrowth of old John's plight in the preceding tale (p. 69).
Derek Traversi struggles to see how a theme of aging might
operate in a tale where both young and old are defeated in turn:
"the Reeve, for reasons which perhaps have to do with his own
resentful awareness of age, needs to show that the old are not less
vulnerable than the young to deception and exposure" (p. 86).
Suggesting a likeness between the Reeve and Death, Alfred David
finds The Reeve's Tale a fabliau overcast by decay (*Strumpet*,
p. 111), while Derek Pearsall contrasts The Miller's Tale's
"youthful vitality" with The Reeve's Tale's "obscene senescence"
(*CT*, p. 185).

Despite varied attempts to find—or deny—a correspondence
between teller and tale,[2] the issue of aging, which the Reeve explicitly raises, has yet to be explored closely within the tale. If
the prologue does indeed provide a rhetorical stance that enriches
the tale, as suggested by Robert Worth Frank, Jr. (p. 54), then the
Reeve's morbidly conventional moralizing is more than a side-
track. In this essay I examine the Reeve's prologue and tale for
their common concern over aging, or, more precisely, over the
full cycle of life. The old man's densely figurative lament com-
mences a motif that reverberates in the tale through symbols,
images, and wordplay: the perennial contest between age and
youth whereby age possesses what youth desires until, inevitably
losing strength with time, age must cede to acquisitive youth all
its holdings, youth now supplanting—but in the process becoming—age.[3] Such contest is the stuff of fabliau, as the Miller
reminds us, "For youthe and elde is often at debaat" (line 3230).
The conflict has just been enacted in The Miller's Tale, where
John began as foregone loser,[4] and it is now to be reenacted in
The Reeve's Tale, where Symkyn enters armed and ready to
defend his rights, even if he is certainly doomed to lose.

What is remarkable about the manifestations of the ages
theme in The Reeve's Tale is how the story elements persis-

tently allude to, without overtly presenting, the medieval iconographic conception of the life process that was evidently in
Chaucer's mind's eye. Chaucer hangs the props and details of
his tale upon an unstated structure that he must have assumed
his audience would apprehend in some way, either consciously
or subliminally. In this conception life is a cycle enacted upon a
wheel (a formulation widespread in medieval art); time is a
flowing stream (an ancient commonplace); and each person's
mortal frame contains a fluid allocation of vital spirits that gradually dries as one proceeds from cradle to grave (a generalized
medical theory open to widespread metaphorical expression).
Both the vessel and the wheel motifs link the sites of origin and
demise; the womb (later, the cradle) and the coffin similarly
house the body (as body houses soul), and the loci of birth and
death meet on a representational wheel: from dust, to dust. The
Reeve's tapped-cask figure, a vessel, becomes one expression of
this larger conception. The Reeve's self-portrait forms another,
largely by paradoxically mixing up traits traditional to *puer* and
senex and by reinforcing the paradoxes with scriptural allusion;
the Reeve-narrator shows himself to be a man whose process of
maturation has diverged from the natural course. The tale bor-
rows freely, also, from the iconography of the life cycle, placing
the characters implicitly upon a wheel, where they vie for dominance at the topmost position. Chaucer need not have had specific
illustrations or sources before him; he needed only to be a person
of his time. The discovery of these patterns within the tale allows
us a glimpse into mental habits different from our own, while it
also grants us insight into Chaucer's literary artistry.

THE REEVE: PREACHER, *PUER SENEX*, AND *PUERILITAS*

The youthful perspective of The Miller's Tale sanctions
laughter at the old and foolish. The ending of The Miller's Tale,
with its ridicule of John, now held "wood in al the toun"

(I.3846), is a "jape" at the expense of an old carpenter's "harm" (line 3842). The laughter extends into the company of pilgrims ("they loughe and pleyde" [line 3858]), where the only one who cannot smile is the old Reeve. It is this laughter that compels Oswald the Reeve to speak on the misery of old age. The Reeve identifies with the Miller's character, sharing John's carpentry skills, advanced age, and perhaps also his fear of cuckoldry. Carpentry, the first link, provides transition into the prologue, but it is the Reeve's identifying with John's old age that motivates his complaint. Perhaps Oswald speaks for all the offended old men who make the mistake of not turning the leaf to pass over The Miller's Tale. The world at large, however, leans toward the genial good humor of the Miller and away from jealous, old carpenters.[5]

Left out and ostracized, Oswald does not want to play because "playing" when one is old invariably means losing to the young. This high-spirited audience does not care about his knowledge of willful desires made impotent by passing time. When finally, at Harry's prodding, he does agree to tell his tale, he justifies the vengeful story of a proud miller with a legalistic proverb: "For leveful is with force force of-showve" (line 3912). The aggressive law here expressed is one that permeates the tale: meet force with force; use your utmost strength to prevent rivals from taking what is yours. Accordingly, Oswald explains his own motives:

> "This dronke Millere hath ytoold us heer
> How that bigyled was a carpenter,
> Peraventure in scorn, for I am oon.
> And, by youre leve, I shal hym quite anoon. . . ."
>
> (Lines 3913-16)

The disgruntled Reeve speaks out to avenge a personal affront: the tale of the thieving Miller has deprived the old carpenter of his dignity.

While it is thus dramatically plausible, the established voice of the Reeve is also rhetorically apt, unfolding multiple complexities of symbol and paradox. Millers are not the only thieves abroad in the world. The Reeve also is a thief, as is intimated in the General Prologue (lines 597-612). He embezzles and loans back his youthful lord's possessions, privately enriching himself and joining forces with old men like Symkyn (and not like John) who deceive their younger clientele in order to lengthen their age of dominance. The Reeve's name is itself a pun upon the verb *reven*, "to rob,"[6] a verb that appears with this sense in the tale, echoing Oswald's own maxim on meeting force with force:

> And hardily they dorste leye hir nekke
> The millere sholde not stele hem half a pekke
> Of corn by sleighte, ne by force hem reve. . . .
>
> (Lines 4009-11)

The cunning Reeve seems somehow to exemplify—in his professional name, his practices, and the tenor of his tale—the concept of Thievery, much as the Pardoner in his character and tale represents antithetically the idea of Christian pardon. The issue of his character and his role extends, then, beyond dramatic realism: the Reeve comes to symbolize an aspect of human nature, the instinctive will to steal what we can before Death steals us from life.

Such an outlook begets defensive self-assertion. Accordingly, this character depicts himself not as the reaver but as the bereaved: not only has the Miller maligned him, but Time—in the figure of Death—is also a thief, robbing him of strength, but not will, to carry on his sorry life:

> "For sikerly, whan I was bore, anon
> Deeth drough the tappe of lyf and leet it gon,
> And ever sithe hath so the tappe yronne
> Til that almoost al empty is the tonne.
> The streem of lyf now droppeth on the chymbe.
> The sely tonge may wel rynge and chymbe

Of wrecchednesse that passed is ful yoore;
With olde folk, save dotage, is namoore!"

(Lines 3891-98)

The poetry records life's passage in protracted yet concentrated details that mimic the methodical process of time passing. Each image figures a progressive drying toward death: the dripping tap is like a tongue chiming, which in turn is like the clapper of a bell tolling a death knell that ends hollowly on "namoore." The Host's reprimand brings us sharply back to life, into the world of objective time and practical goals:

"Sey forth thy tale, and tarie nat the tyme.
Lo Depeford, and it is half-wey pryme!
Lo Grenewych, ther many a shrewe is inne!
It were al tyme thy tale to bigynne."

(Lines 3905-08)

Harry Bailly's message is clear and brusque: "You are not dead yet, Oswald, so make good use of your time." Chaucer beckons us to contemplate a theme not merely of old age but one of larger dimension: how one perceives and uses such time as is allotted between infancy and senescence. In the words of both Reeve and Host there is a metaphor of speaking to represent life lived, time used or misused. Groans squander time; tale-telling brings profit and indicates good living.

By morbidly complaining, however, the Reeve refuses to accept gracefully his time-bound experience in the world and hence lives a kind of death in life: "Til we be roten, kan we nat be rype" (line 3875). Chaucer plants many indicators that the Reeve is a man out of sync with time, a person whose life has not adhered to the due course of maturation. His old man's lament marks him as a traditional type within medieval ideas on aging: he is *puerilitas*, the old man who remains boyish, foolish, and lustful, not advancing, as is proper, to a wisdom that transcends worldly desires (Burrow, pp. 150-51). Instead of bearing the seasoned acumen of an elder, as does the Knight, the Reeve exemplifies rotten, vice-ridden senescence.[7] Even the Christian name Chaucer assigns to the Reeve alludes to how the character is at odds with time. On the surface, the name Oswald is plausible enough: it commemorates an English saint who shares the Reeve's northern provenance, whose life was written in Cambridgeshire (Bennett, p. 87). The name's chief importance for Chaucer, however, would seem to derive from a venerable hagiographic tradition of precocious virtue, to which belonged St. Oswald, a *puer senex* ripe in wisdom before his natural time (Burrow, pp. 100-01; Curtius, pp. 98-101).[8] Comic in its inverted applicability to this "preaching" Reeve, the name Oswald calls attention to the Reeve's morbid obsession with time, which did not ripen him to early saintliness but left him, with his "olde lemes" and "coltes tooth," decrepit in his veniality.

Whether or not Reeve Oswald's self-righteous tendency to "speke alday of hooly writ" is motivated by the devil, as Harry claims (lines 3902-03), it also is perversely and selectively inverted.[9] The nexus of images for a "hoor heed" atop a moldy heart, a rotted fruit, a lusty "grene tayl" (lines 3869-78) reverses a familiar scriptural aphorism on the wisdom brought by gray hairs: "For venerable old age is not that of a long time, nor counted by the number of years: but the understanding of a man is gray hairs, and a spotless life is old age" (Wisdom 4.8-9; see Curtius, pp. 98-101, Burrow, pp. 95-101). From the Reeve's vantage point, gray hair denotes not unspotted wisdom but necessary rottenness: "Myn herte is also mowled as myne heris" (line 3870). Here is not the wisdom of Egeus, who sees order in the unfailing cycles of transient life (lines 2839-46); here is a half-wisdom that stops with the material world, acknowledging only, like Shakespeare's Jaques, that growth is a form of decay (*As You Like It,* II.vii.26-27).

Another scriptural allusion in the Reeve's prologue bears close examination as well, especially as its central idea—life as "hopping"—seems a probable verbal play upon the hopper of

Symkyn's mill (a point to which I will return); for the present purpose, one need only see how the allusion reaffirms the Reeve's puerile condition. In the phrase Oswald chooses to describe the incessant urgings of the flesh, "We hoppen alwey whil that the world wol pype" (line 3876), he alludes to Christ's words to the disbelieving Pharisees and lawyers:

> "To what shall I compare the men of this generation, and what are
> they like? They are like children sitting in the market place and
> calling to one another, 'We piped to you, and you did not dance;
> we wailed and you did not weep.'" (Luke 7.32; see Spearing and
> Spearing, p. 92; Kolve, *Imagery*, pp. 224-25, 451)

The Reeve identifies himself with the children of the market, that is, the "hoppers" who respond only to the piping of the world and lack the wisdom of a maturer vision; they can only perceive dimly that Christ turned another, inscrutable way. Again, the allusion joins the Reeve to the theme of age. As follower of the world, he is a child. His sour lament reveals him, moreover, as aged child, a puerile old man, who ironically possesses a name denoting saintly precociousness. In name and in person Chaucer's portrait of the Reeve entirely violates Horace's maxim: "To avoid giving the role of an old man to youth, or that of a mature man to a boy, we must always adhere to what is suitable to each age."[10]

THE WHEEL OF LIFE: SYMKYN *VIR* AND CLERKS *JUVENES*

Despite the Reeve's decrepit humorlessness, he does enter the tale-telling game of performing before his fellows, an act of life from this voice of *memento mori*. The paradoxes of the situation become intense, especially as the tale is to be a comic fabliau, where the young inevitably best their elders. Nonetheless, the truth behind the Reeve's defeatist spirit is borne out by the generational conflict found in the tale. The prologue asserts a basic, invariable philosophy: in the game of life the odds go to the young; the older the player, the less chance he has, and so, the Reeve states, the aged may as well not play at all. The best the old can do is compensate for their age handicap by exercising their wits. One rages against the "dying of the light" by trying to cheat time—and other men—of the losses it imposes.[11]

The game of life operates, then, according to rules that the crafty old have learned by experience but have mastered all too late, as they unfortunately fail in strength. In the order of things, the old pass on those rules, by example, to the young, who with their superior vitality topple their elders from dominance. The comic chaos of The Reeve's Tale lies in the nature of the rules: to survive and prosper, one must learn to cheat. As John tells his fellow before initiating the bedroom farce, "Man sal taa of twa thynges: / Slyk as he fyndes, or taa slyk as he brynges" (lines 4129-30). Such as he brings—his bare existence, his body, his willful desires—and such as he finds—whatever belongs to his neighbor that he can acquire for himself. It is a philosophy of survival through taking (that is, "reaving"), of maintaining a precarious advantage so long as Fortune allows, knowing full well that the advantage will end with enfeebled age. The philosophy of the tale is thus fatalistic (because time runs out, youth supplants age), cynical (because cheating is essential to winning), and profoundly comic (because confusion is generated in a world where humans strive perpetually against others to subvert laws for their own gain).[12]

Embedded within the village scene that opens The Reeve's Tale is the image that reflects the tale's central metaphors for life: the mill—which must be imagined with its wheel—upon the brook:

> At Trumpyngtoun, nat fer fro Cantebrigge,
> Ther gooth a brook, and over that a brigge,
> Upon the whiche brook ther stant a melle.
>
> (Lines 3921-23)

To Trumpington go the two young clerks Aleyn and John, "testif" and "lusty for to pleye" (line 4004). The mill is operated by Symkyn, proud "as any pecok" (line 3926), defined by his possessions ("a wyf he hadde," "a doghter hadde they," "greet sokene hath this millere" [lines 3942, 3969, 3987]), and dangerously jealous of any encroachment upon his territory ("Ther was no man, for peril, dorste hym touche" [line 3932]). The narrative situation, stated in these elementary terms, evokes, in a way directly accessible to a literate medieval audience, the familiar motif of Fortune's Wheel. As in the Middle English poem *Somer Soneday*, the young men go out to test themselves in the game of life, come to a water boundary marking passage into the next stage of experience, cross the bridge, and try their luck at the wheel, where they learn their place in a fickle world.[13] Instead of Lady Fortune, the wheel-turner is a crafty miller, known to be a thief. And instead of witnessing four kingly riders upon the wheel, each representing an age of man (Smallwood, pp. 238-45; Dove, pp. 67-73), the clerks watch a movement set within the turning millwheel, the to-and-fro wagging of the hopper that passes the grain to the trough below (line 4039), a motional image that anticipates, in mechanistic terms, the copulative acts later to occur in the bedroom.[14] While the image is thus altered, the subject is always the continuity of life. The miller's wheel is not overt in The Reeve's Tale, but it is omnipresent: the miller, a wily "King World,"[15] controls the mill (indeed holds regional monopoly), protects his possessions, increases himself through theft, and tolerates with amusement these "children" come to outsmart him. He represents the world's challenge, and in mastering him the clerks successfully cross the line from innocence to experience.

The depiction of the life cycle as a wheel, with *infans* and *decrepitas* at the bottom (its beginning and end, entering and exiting the mortal time frame), and *juvenes* or *vir* at the apex, occurs often in medieval art (Sandler, pp. 38-41, 124-25; Sears, pp. 145-51), with the number of ages ranging anywhere from four to twelve. In presenting the figures for each age the artists strove for symmetry, so that young aspirants to the top of the wheel (upon the left side of the rim) correspond visually, or verbally in verses assigned to each, to the descending older figures (upon the right side of the rim). The motif of Life's Wheel often merged imperceptibly with Fortune's Wheel; both represent man's precarious, ever-changing position in time (Dove, pp. 75-76; Sandler, figs. 44-45). Sometimes, instead of a wheel, artists represented life as a tree; the figures appear in symmetrically paired medallions that ascend and descend in two vertical lines upon the branchtips (Sears, figs. 93-96). However presented, the figures themselves display consistent demeanors and accoutrements. The popular seven-age scheme, for example, usually divides life into *infans, puer, adolescens, juvenes, vir, senex,* and *decrepitas* (or *corruptio*). *Infans* typically lies in a cradle; *puer* rides a stick horse; *adolescens* holds a falcon; *juvenes* carries a sword; *vir* clutches a moneybag; *senex,* somnolent and bearded, leans on a staff; and *decrepitas* lies upon his deathbed, an attending physician examining a urine bottle. If the last figure is *corruptio*, he is a decaying corpse, with coffin and spade near at hand (Sears, fig. 92). Sometimes *juvenes* is a falconer upon horseback and *vir* holds the sword as well as his moneybag (see Sears, fig. 85). In most sevenfold representations *juvenes* is the central figure, rising to the topmost position within a wheel design. In other schemes, such as the ten-spoked wheel of the De Lisle Psalter (fol. 126^v; Sandler, pp. 40-41), *vir*, sceptered and crowned as a king, holds the topmost position and is flanked by *juvenes* (jaunty upon a horse) and *senex* (walking with a staff). Many of the props are obviously phallic (stick horse, sword, scepter, staff, spade), and often the linear shape of these objects adds to the symmetry of the pictorial design (stick horse opposite staff, sword ascendant). While names and specific objects vary, the recognizable assemblage and order of items render the iconographical language readily decipherable. In other words, the props belong to the motif, and as a known collection of signs they were as available to a medieval artist of words as to an artist of paints.

What interests the reader is how frequently Chaucer embeds the props of the motif into his story. The net result is an illustrated contest between the strongest ages—*juvenes* toppling *vir*—while the extremes of birth and death remain at the edges of the narrative. In Symkyn are combined attributes of *vir* (his swords, his greed) and, in the second half of the tale, *senex* (his sleeping soundly, his bald pate, a staff against the wall). The "yonge povre scolers two" (line 4002) represent inexperienced and empty-handed youth (*adolescens* on horseback or *juvenes* with a sword).[16] The clerks carry swords, which they lay aside (line 4085) when Symkyn's strategem with the horse succeeds in destroying their "housbondrie" (line 4077); later in the night, however, their prowess succeeds in destroying his. Two references to beards and crowns carry similar iconographical innuendo. When Symkyn brags,

> "Yet kan a millere make a clerkes berd,
> For al his art; now lat hem goon hir weye!
> Lo, wher he gooth! Ye, lat the children pleye.
> They gete hym nat so lightly, by my croun"
>
> (Lines 4096-99),

he unconsciously alludes to both his status and theirs. As *vir* he is defending his privileged, "crowned" position, but unwittingly he is bringing the clerks to maturity, hence "making their beards." At the same time, the speech depicts his pride in his wisdom—the chief and most desirable attribute of seasoned age (as Symkyn elsewhere asserts, "The gretteste clerkes been noght wisest men" [line 4054])—and how he, with his wiser arts, has made fools of these children-clerks. An earlier asseveration by Aleyn, "by my croun" (line 4041), also hints at how the tale is a contest within the tradition in which "the flower of man's life is represented as a king among the ages" (Dove, p. 89). And John's oath "by Seint Cutberd" (line 4127), while naming another northern saint of venerable wisdom in youth (like Oswald), seems primarily to pun upon the emasculation that the clerks will soon inflict upon Symkyn.[17]

THE CASK OF LIFE: CRADLE, COFFIN, AND TIME-STREAM

Even as Frank identified a tone of *memento mori* in the Reeve's voice (p. 55), a tone which, if there, exists in a soured, disharmonious way,[18] a true *memento mori* figure exists within the tale. The manciple lies upon his deathbed, and King's Hall must now suffer the outrageous thievery of the miller (lines 3994-99). An earlier contest between the ages had been played and lost by the manciple, whose supine figure, suffering a probably fatal dental malady (lines 4029-30), lies in the tale's background and motivates the newest contest, as John asserts: "And forthy is I come, and eek Alayn" (line 4031). *Infans* exists in the tale as well, in the six-month-old baby, which, like the manciple, is introduced quietly so as to keep the theme of the ages subtly buried beneath the high antics of the fabliau plot. The narrative focus is upon the daughter so valued for her potential inheritance:

> A doghter hadde they bitwixe hem two
> Of twenty yeer, *withouten any mo,*
> *Savynge* a child that was of half yeer age;
> In cradel it lay and was a propre page.
> This wenche thikke and wel ygrowen was. . . .
> (Lines 3969-73; italics mine)

They have a daughter, and *that is all, except* for a mere baby. The baby remains a faceless character, never even crying (as it does in one analogue, when a clerk tugs at its ear[19]); it is the baby's cradle, not the baby itself, that takes a crucial position in the lively bedroom farce.[20]

The baby, at an age where it cannot yet walk, does, however, provide balance to the dying, bedridden manciple. His deathbed and its cradle are both familiar images in the Wheel of Life schemes. The cradle traditionally counterpoints the coffin, *infans* versus *corruptio* (Sears, fig. 91). In some depictions of the ages the mother's bed, in which she nurses the newborn (*nascens*), substitutes for the cradle but still supplies the opposing visual complement to the deathbed of *moriens* or the casket of *mortuus* (Sears, figs. 94, 95). It must be no coincidence that Chaucer rhymes the placing of the cradle, where Symkyn's wife may "yeve the child to sowke," with the emptied cask of ale, "dronken al was in the crowke" (lines 4157-58). The cradled baby's instinct for nourishment plays against the snoring Symkyn's state of drunkenness described in terms of the emptied container, hence echoing the Reeve's metaphor for old age, "almoost al empty is the tonne" (line 3894). The empty "crowke" has entirely established Symkyn's fated impotency and corporeal decline: "This millere hath so wisely bibbed ale / That as an hors he fnorteth in his sleep" (lines 4162-63). The crock is empty, the "wise" miller has drunk himself senseless, and time robs the slumbering man in his bed as stealthily as it fosters the growing infant in its cradle.

The metaphor of life as a fluid, of time passing as a stream, warrants close examination, for Chaucer inserts it into the tale with great variety. The baby is a tiny vessel to be filled with a nourishing liquid, milk, while its father is a senescent vessel futilely filling himself with the life-robbing (that is, crock-emptying) potation, ale. The Reeve's metaphor is certainly present here: the tun is full at birth but it empties as life declines, until "save dotage, [there] is namoore!" (line 3898). In suggesting that the basic constituent of bodily life is moisture, the Reeve's tap-of-life image fits with an ancient physiological theory, dating at least from Galen (2nd century A.D.), that life begins with heat and moisture and ends with cold and dryness, moisture being a kind of fuel consumed to give the body heat (Burrow, p. 21). A Middle English medical treatise shows this tradition preserved in Chaucer's time:

> What is age? Age is spase of þe life of a best whenne it
> begynnys for to encrese as in youthe, or for to stonde as in
> myddil age, or for to lesse prively as in helde, or for to be
> lesse opynly as in olde age. As Galen seyþ *in libro de com-
> plexionibus*, whe be made in þe uttermost limosite and
> humidite, and þe hete of our bodi sesþ not for to ete or
> waste his moistenes unto þat deþ come, which is disteyned
> to every man.[21]

Human life consumes bodily moisture until finally one dries up
and grows cold in death. The Reeve has simply restated the
theory in metaphoric language.

There is, moreover, in the image of life as a stream another
specifically physiological meaning, the flow of semen. The
Reeve's metaphor depicts male potency as strong in youth, increasingly dry in old age (Heffernan, pp. 40-41; David, *Strumpet*, p. 111; Pearsall, *CT*, p. 184). Bernardus Silvestris explains
how the procreative principle of Nature relies upon fluids, and
thus he speaks of Nature itself "flowing" through time:

> Blood sent forth from the seat of the brain flows down to the
> loins, bearing the image of the shining sperm. Artful Nature
> molds and shapes the fluid, that in conceiving it may repro-
> duce the forms of ancestors.
>
> The nature of the universe outlives itself, for it flows back into
> itself, and so survives and is nourished by its very flowing away.
> For whatever is lost only merges again with the sum of things,
> and that it may die perpetually, never dies wholly. But man,
> ever liable to affliction by forces far less harmonious, passes
> wholly out of existence with the failure of his body. (P. 126)

The fluid of life enables "perpetual death," that is, the perpetual
recurrence of the life cycle, even though each person within the
scheme must fade out of existence.

Chaucer elsewhere echoes Bernardus's notion of successive
change as the natural means to perpetual life. According to
Theseus's famous explanation of universal order, the Prime Mover

> "hath so wel biset his ordinaunce
> That speces of thynges and progressiouns
> Shullen enduren by successiouns,
> And nat eterne, withouten any lye."
>
> (Lines 3012-15)

In the philosophic perspective of The Knight's Tale all human existence accords to timed cycles of growth and decay. In a line that might be applied tellingly to Symkyn, crowned *vir*, and his son, the "propre page," Theseus explains how all mortals meet the same end: "He moot be deed, the kyng as shal a page" (line 3030).

To put the phenomenon of life's perpetuation into the Reeve's terms, every sexual coupling combines both a coital "boring" and a potential birth:

> "For sikerly, whan I was bore, anon
> Deeth drough the tappe of lyf and leet it gon,
> And ever sithe hath so the tappe yronne. . . . "
>
> (Lines 3891-93)

The Reeve's pun upon "bore" conflates the moment of conception with the moment of birth. With the tapping of the keg comes the immediate emission of the lifestream.[22] The sexual act thus embodies both life and death, as a person on the continuum to death moves according to the instinct that may create a new life to replace his own. The tap-of-life image does indeed anticipate the sexual energies that animate the miller's bedroom. Youth's bed is alive with generative vitality, flanked on either side by the cradle of slumbering infancy and the torpid bed of snoring age. The bed-hopping melee delivers in fact a variant version of the old motif of three ages (that is, past, present, future). This version comically relocates the familiar motif to its domestic site of perpetual renewal (the bedroom) and figures each age not astride horses (as they appear elsewhere) but sleeping in their respectively appropriate beds, with only youth carrying on the procreative ride.[23]

ASCENDANT YOUTH: FLOUR, HOPPER, AND BEDROOM

Time perforce must pass. In the Reeve's metaphor it is a stream of flowing liquid, an image that metamorphoses subtly into the millstream that opens the tale. With remarkable aptness Chaucer implicitly allows the brook and the millwheel to recede into a background figure for Time advancing the Wheel of Life.[24] Traditionally linked to the notion of time, the visual image of a wheel well conveys a sense of perpetual movement and cyclical recurrence. In artistic depictions, moreover, it invites one to see within its spoked outline, in reversed silhouette, the flourishing rose, symbol of youth and transient beauty (Howard, pp. 199-209; Leyerle, "Design," pp. 281-305). The verses set inside the *rota/rosa*-shaped diagram of *Duodecim proprietates condicionis humane* in the De Lisle Psalter (fol. 126) liken the growth of man to the blossoming and withering of a flower:

> Reason: O flower, soon to wither away, what gives
> you grounds for being cheerful?
> Adolescent: The flower of life, bringing virtuous habits
> into being in me, promises sweet scents.
> Reason: You are more contemptible than withered
> grass—surely you are not proud of yourself?
> Young man: I rejoice in the flower of youth, in the beauty
> of my appearance.[25]

Here the Wheel of Life is linked directly to a blossoming flower, specifically in reference to the younger ages. In *Somer Soneday* as well, the youngest of the four wheel-riders is "bryȝt as þe blostme."

Chaucer, too, denotes the prime of a man's life his "flower." It adds to Arcite's honor that he die "in his excellence and flour" (lines 3047-48). In The Reeve's Tale the usage is suited to the milling metaphors. The object of the contest is to gain the "flour." Many have noted the multiple imports of the phrase "flour of il endyng" (line 4174). It literally means the best outcome of a bad end, but in the milling context it evokes a play upon the milled corn stolen from the clerks by Symkyn, and in the bedroom where the phrase is uttered it suggests Malyne's soon-to-be deflowered virginity (see Spearing and Spearing, p. 40). Within the nexus of allusions to a patterned contest between the ages, the prized "flour" takes on another possible meaning: the prime of life, which, like the stolen meal and Malyne's favors, goes to the youthful clerks. However one views the situation, they gain the "flour."

Many elements basic to the Trumpington setting—the mill-wheel, the stream, the ground flour—thus serve to connect this world of milling to traditional symbols for transitory life. The hopper also partakes of the symbolism. The Reeve's succinct "We hoppen alwey whil that the world wol pype" rivals the tapped-cask image in dense allusiveness. Taken as a generalization about mankind, the biblical reference declares us all children who follow the way of the world, blind to mature truths. We are "hoppers," that is, dancers to the world's pipe, or in the Wife of Bath's parlance, participants in "the olde daunce" (I.476) that created us and continues the future ages.[26] Hopping to the world thus implies the perpetual movement,[27] the sexual activity, the everyday worldly dealings that carry on our temporal business. As a transformed likeness of this figure in the Prologue, the mechanical image of the hopper that shakes grain into the trough (lines 4039-43) becomes a potent symbol of worldly activity, specifically of male mastery in the world. When the clerks first enter the contest, released by their "wardeyn" (line 4012)[28] and "lusty for to pleye" (line 4004), they naively observe the vigorous shaking motions of the hopper and find their innocent tricks, which are far too feeble and obvious, no match for the practiced deceptions of Symkyn.[29] They joke about what "ille . . . millere[s]" they are (line 4045). But after experiencing the humiliation of the miller's tricks, they too learn to "hop" to the same tune as Symkyn, who "pipen . . . koude" (line 3927). The sexual suggestiveness of the mechanical hopper becomes explicitly human as Aleyn and John imitate in the bedroom what they have learned in the mill, taking control now of Symkyn's "stable."[30]

Once the clerks have regarded Symkyn's way of foul playing, they catch onto this world of rule by the fittest and craftiest, and they cheat him of wife, daughter, stolen flour, and cake, as well as a night's lodging. Part of the story's humor lies in seeing the clerks educated not in their Cambridge world but in the "real world" (as students now phrase it), the school of experience or hard knocks. An archaic meaning for the verb *trump* is "cheat, deceive" (*OED*). Trumpington is literally "Cheatingtown," the place for young clerks to learn the rules necessary for survival and increase, a process that lasts until the next generation takes charge and one's own generative process has turned the corner to corruption and extinction.

In Chaucer's tale, however, the wheel is as much symbol of life as it is reminder of death. Those not yet at the apex ascend and grow, and the sight of the clerks chasing after their horses and mixing up the beds abounds with a chaotic and adventurous zest for life. As Murray Copland has observed, each half of the tale contains a subdued section dominated by Symkyn followed by vigorous clerkly antics, giving rise to a tale of "aesthetic shapeliness and moral coherence, however arrived at" (p. 24). The game has high stakes, being no less than the game of life, but the youths approach it playfully, with Chaucer comically inserting a true idea of the risks. To prevent the miller's stealing, "they dorste leye hir nekke" (line 4009), a promise later echoed in the final neck-throttling and even bloodletting between Symkyn and Aleyn (lines 4273, 4276). Other oaths reveal the nature of the contest: John swearing "by [his] fader kyn" (line 4038) that he never before had opportunity to watch a hopper in action, and later, bested by the miller and feeling a fool, John cursing the day that he was born (line 4109). Despite such reminders that this game is about survival, the only penalty feared seriously by these fabliau characters is the threat of becoming known as a simpleton; death is remote and taken lightly, as in John's offhand remark, "Oure manciple, I hope he wil be deed, / Swa werkes ay the wanges in his heed" (lines 4029-30).

Playfulness also pervades the bedroom farce. The day's victory having gone to Symkyn, the narrative pauses for what Glending Olson calls a "half-time" intermission ("RvT," p. 225), during which the players share bread, ale, and shelter, the basics of life. At midnight, however, the players retire to the bedroom; this precise time, as represented on a clock face, may possibly signify the apex of a wheel, with *juvenes* and *vir* in a precariously balanced struggle for the top position. As soon as the clock hands pass twelve, Symkyn's decline begins. By night, the "strong ale" most affects the older man, who snores away, oblivious to the dangers in his own bedroom. Here in the night youth prevails and wins back all the losses, and more.

Aleyn is first to seize opportunity. Reiterating the Reeve's "use force against force" maxim, Aleyn complains that they have "had an il fit al this day" (line 4184) and looks for "esement" (line 4186) to compensate their losses. Despite the risk (John timidly warns, "The millere is a perilous man" [line 4189]), Aleyn perseveres, appearing, in his way, positively heroic. The narrator soon leaves Aleyn preoccupied with "pley" (line 4198) and turns to John's cradle trick. Inspired by Aleyn's daring ("He auntred hym, and has his nedes sped" [line 4205]), John too is soon engaged in "this joly lyf" (line 4232).[31] The "il fit" of the day meets its comic, and no doubt punning, reversal in the "myrie . . . fit" enjoyed by Symkyn's wife (line 4230).[32] Success in this perilous world clearly involves more than simply waiting out the natural course of time, and more than random chance;[33] it entails young men "auntering," that is, taking a risk and seizing their chance before it slips away.

The feebleness of aged desires, meanwhile, is well portrayed by the miller snoring in the midst of his losses. The final trump in Trumpington may be played, albeit innocently, by the baby:

the moved cradle deceives Aleyn and leads to the pandemonium
of the closing scene. While Chaucer has gone out of his way to
make the baby negligible as a character, one must remember the
sleeping infant to see the full depiction of the ages in this very
active bedroom. The two extremes, *infans* and *vir senex*, sleep
passively while *juvenes* actively engages in procreative pleasure. Chaucer did, of course, inherit the cradle trick with the
story, but the way he makes it serve the theme of the ages seems
nonetheless ingenious and appropriate. In regarding the baby as
an innocent accomplice to the betrayal of Aleyn, one can perhaps detect a foreshadowing of the future doom of the youths:
they too will succumb to the passage of time when the baby's
generation comes into its own.

Into the pandemonium of the bedroom fray Chaucer un-
leashes the furious competitive energy that has perpetually
spurred the contest between old and young. Symkyn learns that
his daughter's prized virginity is gone, his family treasure stolen
by this base, upstart clerk. His astonished exclamation "hast?"
(line 4268) encapsulates the finality of the theft: what he once
had is now utterly lost, entirely in the past. As Harry Bailly
platitudinously asserts, in a statement no doubt inspired by The
Reeve's Tale,

> "'. . . los of tyme shendeth us,' . . .
> It wol nat come agayn, withouten drede,
> Namoore than wole Malkynes maydenhede. . . ."
>
> (II.28-30)

The miller's angry reaction is to declare the soon-to-come
mortality of this false clerk: "Thow shalt be deed, by Goddes
dignitee!" (line 4270). Next ensues the famous fracas in the dark
bedchamber, which the startled wife ends abruptly by singling
out the props that go with Symkyn *senex*. She seizes the staff
and "crowns" her husband, her choice between whom to strike
going, naturally, to the disadvantage of age, whose bald pate
shines in the moonlight. The confusion of the characters renders

the deliberateness of the artistic details—staff, bald head, maimed crown—all the more comic. The game ends fittingly with the vanquished miller stretched out on the floor—now like the manciple—and thoroughly cheated of his winnings.

The Reeve, who "list not pley for age," has "quite" the Miller just as he had sworn to (line 3916), displaying in the crude yet comic violence of the characters and in his vengeful spirit the vices of "avauntyng" and "anger" to which he said his old, ashen flesh was prone (line 3884). He has also proven, through his tale, the validity of his moan that age perpetually weakens and loses to youth. While it conveys the expected outcome, his fabliau is edged with truths that are the privilege of age: that youth's victory is fleeting and that the final, inevitable loss is a bitter one. With such fatalism in the message, it is perhaps fitting that while the company laughs at the Miller's tale of youthful high spirits, The Reeve's Tale ends only with the vulgar cackle of the isolated Cook. The good-humored Miller's Tale wins after all, as the joyless Reeve knew it would, but he nonetheless departs from his moment of literary life by displaying a "quited" old miller knocked out cold, force "of-showved" with force, the perpetual youthfulness of the Miller's idyllic world exposed for the illusion that it is, if anyone cares to look. The tale-telling, as a metaphor of time well used, allows the Reeve himself momentarily to halt time: the tale as art freezes his perspective on life, preserving it as one among various individual views in *The Canterbury Tales*. Tale-telling does not hold off that thief Death, but its duration does represent the Reeve's poetic life—as fictional character the only life he has. As with Elde at Death's door in another Middle English poem,[34] a character's being old does not prevent him from having his full say. Nearness to death can grant a privileged awareness to the narrative, despite a cynical bias in the decrepit speaker.

The tale's moral, if "moral" it may be called, goes beyond the evident fact of mortality in time, a fact which is, however disruptive to human lives, a natural principle of order. The world of The Reeve's Tale is gloriously disordered: Trumpington is a place where wily, greedy humans take whatever they can succeed in taking, where predictability is lost amidst the deliberate scheming, the displacement of other people's objects, the accidents of cross purposes, and the mistakes of perception created in a place where everyone is out for himself. Horses do not stay tied; watched millers cheat anyway; cradles move; beds fail to contain their proper occupants; and wives mistake clerks for husbands and husbands for clerks. The Reeve's Tale presents the mutable world from within an immediate, connivingly mortal perspective, where humans seem to create their own mixed-up universe, acting entirely upon survival instincts and bowing unwillingly to only one law the natural sequence of growth, decline, and eventual death.

In the rich tap-of-life metaphor the fictional Reeve has supplied readers with the key to Chaucer's creation of The Reeve's Tale. Within the everyday world of Trumpington are the symbols of aging, the characters never seeing in their riotous activities the whole pattern of the wheel upon which they ride. The symbol of worldly activity, the hopper, is contained within the wheel of the mill. The bored cask suggests a similar design, the circle with the straight tap. The phallic symbols accompanying the figures upon the Wheel of Life ascend and descend with the uppermost ages, *adolescens*, *juvenes*, *vir*, and *senex*; the lowermost figures recline in their wooden receptacles, cradle or coffin. The tapped cask emblematizes, then, the full range of ages iconography: it is the casket of life and death, that is, the mortal bodily frame, the "soul-house" that encloses the fluids of our existence, carrying each of us from womb and then cradle to deathbed and then grave, propelled upon the natural course of growth and acquisition of worldly goods followed by decay and abandonment of all that we have won.

NOTES

An earlier version of this essay was presented to the Harvard Graduate Medieval Colloquium, March 1988. I am indebted to the members of this group, especially to Larry D. Benson, for many helpful comments that influenced my revisions. I am also grateful to M. Teresa Tavormina, who delivered a provocative response to this essay at the meeting of the Midwest MLA, November 1988, and to Charles Muscatine, whose probing comments had an effect on the final version.

[1]The passage on old age has been praised soaringly by Coffman, pp. 272-75, and its richness analyzed by Kolve, *Imagery*, pp. 129-31; Heffernan, pp. 36-43; and David, *Strumpet*, pp. 110-11. Its sexual overtones have often been noted: see esp. Heffernan, pp. 40-41; and Pearsall, *CT*, p. 184, who finds that the image "disturbingly associates life, being alive, with sexual potency." Vasta calls the metaphor of the barrel merely "obscene" (p. 9). Heffernan also sees in it an allusion to the baptismal Fountain of Life, but this argument is not persuasive. For Kolve the image is troubling precisely because it *omits* the Christian belief in the afterlife: "it is an image that ends in depletion rather than completion, drawing no strength from any system of meaning larger than itself" (p. 231). Forehand looks at the passage for evidence that Chaucer gave to the Reeve, in the General Prologue portrait, symbols of old age; while the Reeve's "rusty blade" (line 618) does suggest the impotency of the tap-of-life image, Forehand's discussion of the symbolism is largely unconvincing.

Heffernan's speculation upon the contents of the cask (wine, beer, cider, or water) is not particularly relevant to the passage. Along with Kolve, I assume the content to be an alcoholic tavern drink such as ale, in association with the ale consumed in the tale. Regardless of the cask's content, the generalized notion of a liquid streaming out of a container has metaphoric significance, as outlined in this essay.

[2]Those who believe that the Reeve's outlook dominates the tale usually find it bitter, dark, and savagely realistic (see, for example, P. Olson, "RvT," pp. 1-17; Vasta, p. 10; Muscatine, *Chaucer*, pp. 201-02; David, *Strumpet*, pp. 109-15; Ruggiers, p. 74; Owen, *Pilgrimage*, p. 107; Traversi, pp. 84-88). Even those who resist a dramatic reading may find that the tale's morals are harsh, presenting the "cruel realities of the fallen world" (C. D. Benson, *Drama*, p. 103; see also Kolve, *Imagery*, p. 255). Other scholars have countered these views by asserting the tale's essentially comic, fabliau nature. Craik hears the Reeve's voice only in the prologue and the concluding anti-Miller benediction; the tale, he says, is in

Chaucer's voice, and comedy dominates (p. 47). Finding most critics too serious, G. Olson stresses the tale's prevailing atmosphere of game and contest ("RvT," p. 224), and Frank, in an important article, finds in the tale a "comedy of pride and desire" (p. 55). Indeed, recent studies have convincingly demonstrated how Chaucer's upper-class satiric wit overshadows the fictive voice of the Reeve (see, for example, Brewer, p. 81; Frank, pp. 54-63; G. Olson, "RvT," p. 229). Surveying both sides of the question, Pearsall believes that Chaucer has openly encouraged the dramatic reading by shaping the tale as requital of the Miller, even as the tale sharply displays his humane literary intelligence (*CT*, p. 190).

[3]While most critics have focused upon the contest as one of wits rather than of age (e.g., G. Olson, "RvT," p. 224), this attitude has ignored the traditional connection between wisdom and advanced years (see Burrow, pp. 107-09, 150-51). Indeed, the two themes operate together. Virtually no one has mentioned the contest of ages outside of the controversy created by the Reeve's voice. Owen, for example, finds the old Reeve's choice of a tale favoring the young to be "unconscious" (*Pilgrimage*, p. 108; see also Spearing and Spearing, pp. 20-22, 28-29). Brewer's recent essay is the chief exception. In showing the folkloric aspects of the plot, Brewer describes the primal generational pattern underlying the RvT: "It illustrates the aggressiveness of young men towards the established order of possession and protection, authority and convention. . . . When the children destroy the parents (metaphorically, of course) the result is invariably comedy—or romance. That must obviously be the case for biological reasons, for the very continuation of the race. That is why we are, willy-nilly, on the side of the young. . . . In the most general terms this story is about killing the father, winning the mother, and getting away with it, as everyone wants to do" (pp. 72-73).

[4]As Kolve comments, "We are shown a world of the 'wylde and yong,' through which old John wanders at some risk" (*Imagery*, p. 170); see his fine analysis of the spirit of youth in the MilT (ibid., pp. 166-73).

[5]As Brewer asserts, it is natural for us to be on the side of the young: such is the pattern of comedy; tragedy occurs when the old destroy the young (pp. 72-73). Moreover, the tradition of the unsympathetic *senex amans* was deep-seated. Burrow demonstrates how the elderly were thought incapable of love and unnatural as sexual partners, an outlook that justified their ruthless treatment by writers of courtly literature (pp. 157-62). By yoking oldness, carpentry, and cuckoldry, both in the MilT and here in the RvT, Chaucer must

have intended a faint allusion to St. Joseph, who was popularly portrayed in mystery cycles as a jealous, old husband (see Burrow, pp. 158-59).

[6]*Reven* in this sense is a common ME verb, deriving from OE *rēafian* (*MED*, s.v. *rēven* v.; *OED*, s.v. *reave* v.[1]). On the pun on "reve" (line 4011), see also Tkacz, p. 131, and Vasta, p. 2. Mann cites the proverbial saying "Thefe is reve" and documents the tradition associating reeves with cunning and fraudulence (pp. 163-67, 283-84).

[7]Copland points out the childish sulking of the Reeve in lines 3861-63 ("He gan to grucche, and blamed it a lite."). This contest between the Knight and the Reeve deserves attention. While their tales adopt differing perspectives of the old, the intervening Miller offers a wholly youthful view.

Critics have written a good deal upon the Reeve's self-portrait, that is, upon how he reveals himself in his prologue and his tale; see, for example, Copland, pp. 25-26 ("a man pared to the quick," exhibiting "a kind of obscure excess"); P. Olson, "RvT," pp. 2-3, 7 (a thief and a blackmailer, employing "the rhetoric of ingratiation"); Vasta, pp. 2-4 (a character "constructed out of privations"); David, *Strumpet*, p. 115 (a "voice of the establishment"); and Kolve, *Imagery*, pp. 220-29, 254-56 (a portrait "of moral kind, capable of ending the pilgrimage fun and games altogether"). Frank, however, argues that while Oswald is not admirable his is primarily a comic portrait (p. 55). Whether we see Oswald as a comic or malicious hypocrite, there is little doubt that his portrait and world view invert the Miller's: his reflects a jaded sparseness, a deathly perspective; the Miller's fulsome robustness, a world of God's "foyson," a life-filled perspective (see Muscatine, *Chaucer*, p. 200; Copland, pp. 30-31; Kolve, *Imagery*, pp. 225, 255).

[8]Indeed, the wording of Eadmer's *Life of Oswald*, by contrasting the young saint to impure older men, uses an imagery similar to the details found in the RvPro (cf. lines 3869-70): "When he was made dean, a young man was preferred to old ones, so that the gray-hairedness of his mind and his spotless life might serve to purify the impure life of the old men and overcome their puerile minds by dint of spiritual discipline" [*Decanus factus, adolescens praeponitur senibus; quatinus canities sensus illius et immaculata vita illius maculatem senum vitam emacularet, ac pueriles sensus illorum studio disciplinae caelestis evacuaret*] (qtd. and trans. Burrow, pp. 100-01). William de Brailles illustrated the contrast between the worldly life and the saintly life by drawing an inner ring in a Wheel of Life. The outer circumference carries the traditional figures

of the ages in a clockwise motion, to the apex (man's kingly peak) and down again (to the grave). The inner ring depicts scenes from the life of St. Theophilus, with his death at the apex and his worldly temptation by devils at the bottom, a reversal of the ordinary mortal sequence: see Sears, p. 146 and fig. 86.

[9]Curiously, in finding the preacher in the Reeve critics have focused upon his sermonish moralizing and his friarish appearance but have neglected his use of Scripture. Muscatine writes of the "vagary" of the sermon (*Chaucer*, p. 200), and Vasta sees the preacherly demeanor as hypocritical ploy: "The Reeve's tone is so strongly sermon-like as to obscure, at least for Harry Bailly, the stupidity of the Reeve's self-conflicting defense" (p. 9). David declares that "the Reeve's 'sermonyng' . . . has nothing to do with scripture" (*Strumpet*, p. 110). The Reeve's biblical response to Harry's outburst against speaking "alday of holy writ" has, however, attracted critical notice; on the Reeve's "mote in the eye" speech (alluding to Mt 7.1-4), see esp. P. Olson, "RvT," p. 14, and Baird, pp. 679-83. For a scholarly discussion of the idiom of preaching in the RvT and elsewhere in CT, see Wenzel, "Chaucer," pp. 138-44.

[10]*Ars poetica*, lines 176-78, qtd. and trans. Burrow, p. 195. The Latin text reads:

Ne forte seniles
Mandentur iuveni partes pueroque viriles,
Semper in adiunctis aevoque morabimur aptis.

[11]The wisdom in this view is not idealistic. It is a materialistic vision that sees life as a span designed for acquisition. Some have commented upon the Reeve's particular vision of life. Copland states that "the Reeve is comfortably aware of his own superior insight into the true appallingness of human nature" (p. 31), and Frank notes that "The 'old man' topos, given the proper emphasis, can serve as a kind of *memento mori*. It does so here: not so broodingly as to cause a chill, only enough to cast a cool, ironic air over the tale of comic pride and comic sexuality that follows. . . . In the old man's mouth, the narrative becomes a wry celebration of desire, certainly not a condemnation of it" (p. 55). Thus, while the tone of *memento mori* brings an awareness of life's limitations, the prologue and tale assert how one deals with a bad situation. The resultant philosophy becomes, in a sense, a "wry celebration," but it also harbors an edge of grasping, last-ditch expediency.

[12]On the essential comedy of the plot, see Brewer (n. 3 above). That the tale does have a philosophy is important to note. Siegel proposes that the "accidental judgments and purposes mistook" (p. 18) of the RvT amount to no operating philosophy at all: "The tale lacks what the *Miller's* and *Knight's Tales* provide, a systematic and implicitly prescriptive account of the world and human affairs" (p. 17); it contains no "large explanatory principles or . . . statement of values" (p. 19). Spearing and Spearing note a valueless, natural philosophy that unfairly favors youth: "life is amoral, and . . . on the whole those who are young, attractive and cunning stand a better chance of success than those who are not" (p. 20).

[13]The narrator in *Somer Soneday* departs from a hunting party, crosses a river, and encounters his own fortune in the figure of Lady Fortune's Wheel:

> And als I sat beside, I say, soþ forto sey,
> A wifman wiþ a wonder whel weue with þe wynde
> > And wond.
> > Opon þe whel were, I wene,
> > Merye men and madde imene;
> > To hire I gan gon in grene,
> > And fortune yfond.
>
> > > (Lines 33-39)

[14]Lancashire discusses the sexual jokes implicit in the milling action ("Innuendo," pp. 164-67). On the hopper, he comments that "Chaucer's description of the mill's inner workings is apparently superfluous unless it is an off-color prefiguration of the students' nocturnal activities" (p. 166). Cf. also the Wife of Bath's metaphor of sexuality as milling: "Whoso that first to mille comth, first grynt" (III.389).

[15]See Dove, p. 74: the manual of iconography by the eighteenth-century Byzantine Dionysius of Fourna was drawn from "centuries-old conventions," perhaps directly from writings by the fourteenth-century Byzantine master Manuel Panselinos. In it are instructions for creating a Wheel of Life with "the 'vain and seductive and wily' King World" at its center. Cf. also the morality play *Mundus et Infans* (early sixteenth century), in which "newly born Infans immediately enters the service of Mundus, who gives him fine clothes and confers upon him the name of Wanton" (Houle, p. 104).

[16]The adjective "povre" thus adds importantly to the ages theme. Others have not recognized the figurative meaning of this detail. David (*Strumpet*, p. 113) notes the incongruity of the adjective against the students' ability to pay in silver (line 4135); Spearing and Spearing, finding no significance attached to the clerks' poverty, state that the phrase "poor scholars" is formulaic (p. 100). For a detailed discussion of the clerks' probable material state, see Bennett, p. 99. Concerning the adjective "yonge," Bennett, p. 98, offers evidence that the clerks may have been as young as fourteen. In the tradition that each of the seven ages lasts seven years (see Burrow, pp. 38-54; Bartholomaeus Anglicus, pp. 291-93), this age would put the clerks precisely upon the threshold between *adolescens* and *juvenes*. That Chaucer was aware of and used this scheme is apparent in the age of the boy in PrT (seven) and the age of Virginia in PhyT (fourteen).

[17]On the form "Cutberd" and the saint's traditions, see Bennett, p. 101, and Burrow, pp. 105-06. The tales of Cuthbert's precocious youth apparently included one of his seeing "the soul of a reeve carried up to the sky on his death" (Colgrave, p. 73). Unfortunately, the story has been lost except for this reference to it by an anonymous twelfth-century biographer, but it may have been known to Chaucer. See Tkacz, pp. 127-33, for a good discussion of the puns upon Cutberd, to which should be added the play upon the idea of aging. Beards commonly distinguish age from youth. Eight beardless men clamber up the left side of the thirteenth-century rose-wheel window at Amiens Cathedral; a kingly figure is enthroned at the top, and eight more figures, all bearded, tumble down the right side of the rim (Sears, p. 145). The tale also includes an allusion to hawking, the attribute of youth (line 4134).

[18]Kolve characterizes this distinctive paradoxical voice as "the merriness of an unmerry man, the obsessively moral vision of a man whose own life is not good" (*Imagery*, p. 255). See also nn. 7 and 11 above.

[19]*Le Meunier et les II clers*, lines 247-48 (Benson and Andersson, pp. 112-13).

[20]Critics tend to ignore the baby. Craik considers the cradle "a shifting landmark" that is "more important than the baby it contains" (p. 35), and Copland comments that the baby is a mere "narrative 'plant'" that is "cursorily dismissed, being morally neutral" (p. 18). Patterson suggests that the baby, a moral reference point, "serves as the guiltless and so all the more telling mechanism by which the clerks exact their revenge" ("Man," p. 161).

That the baby is male seems essential to the ages iconography here outlined, because the Wheel of Life motif traditionally depicted men in growth and decline. The place of women within this scheme is a provocative topic that is, unfortunately, outside the scope of this essay. M. Teresa Tavormina has drawn my attention to the possible role of the grandfather priest as another elder figure, with a generational line of women depicted in Symkyn's wife and daughter. In terms of the male-oriented iconography dominating the tale, however, women play a subsidiary role as merely the physical means by which men propagate and prosper. One can note, in passing, how both women, through natural instinct, seem to cooperate with and benefit from the desires of youth. The tapped-cask image suggests, moreover, both the womb and the phallus.

[21]Gonville and Caius MS. 176/97, p. 19 (qtd. Burrow, p. 28). Burrow adds this note: "Galen explains the heat and humidity (*lumosite*: slimyness) of the new-born by their origins in sperm and blood, both moist and hot substances" (p. 28). He distinguishes this tradition from the later and more prevalent four-part system based upon the seasons and the humors. Cf. also Bartholomaeus Anglicus, pp. 137-45, under the headings *De siccitate* ("drynes hastiþ elde" [p. 140]) and *De humiditate*.

[22]On the pun in general, see MacLaine, pp. 129-31. An imagery of wetness, which is widespread in the tale, gravitates toward such sexual innuendo. The world outside of Symkyn's narrow house contains not just a brook but a damp fen and a waterlogged ditch from which the clerks retrieve their errant stallion (lines 4106-07). The ditch recalls the unflattering simile given to Symkyn's wife, "as digne as water in a dich" (line 3964). There is a salacious scatology at work here: women become ditches, and the clerks "wery and weet" in their labors.

[23]For the traditional Three Ages upon horseback, see *The Parlement of the Thre Ages*. For the motif in the KnT, see Tristram, pp. 88-91. It probably exists in the MilT as well, since Absolon's epithet "child" would seem to place his age—or at least his maturity—below that of Nicholas; see Cowen.

[24]Time as a flowing river is of course a literary commonplace (see Meyerhoff, pp. 14-30), occurring, for example, in Ovid (p. 339) and elsewhere in Chaucer (CT II.20-24).

"LAT THE CHILDREN PLEYE"

[25]Trans. Dove, pp. 89-92. The De Lisle text reads:

Racio:	O flos, o fenum, que te dat causa serenus?
Adolescens:	Informans mores, in me flos promit odores.
Racio:	Tu sublimatus, in quo sis, quaero, beatus?
Vir:	Viribus ornatus, in mundo vivo beatus.

[26]Indeed, idiomatic Middle English phrases include *hoppen in a ring*, "dance in a circle," and *hoppen on love's ring*, "fall in love" with apparent sexual meaning (*MED*). Kolve comments upon how this scriptural metaphor for life is "inimical to fabliau, a genre that cannot flourish in the presence of long perspectives, continuing pain, or the reality of death. In his self-portrait the Reeve implicitly rebukes the Miller's celebration of young people in a green and growing natural world, ever at odds with the cares and labors of age" (*Imagery*, pp. 224-25). While it is true that the perspective reverses the traditional close focus of fabliau, one must also note how appropriate is the image of "hopping" to describe the animated quality of Chaucer's fabliau characters.

[27]On the traditional notion of the living world being in constant motion, see, for example, Bartholomaeus Anglicus: "Remigius seiþ þat þe age of a man is nouȝt elles but . . . mene bitwene contrary meuyng, or elles mene bitwene quiete and reste. For hereby men passen and dyen, and neuere abyden in þe same state" (p. 291). See also pp. 516-17, on generation and corruption as two of the six principal "meovingis."

[28]Like the detail "povre" (see n. 16 above), the release of the clerks by their college warden seems figurative in meaning: youth on the threshold of maturity. Bennett discusses the relative rarity of the term *warden* for the head of a Cambridge college (pp. 97-98). Bartholomaeus Anglicus uses the term to describe a father's diligent keeping of his sons: "A man loueþ his childe, and fediþ and norischith him, and . . . puttiþ him to lore vndir warde and kepinge of wardeynes and tutours" (p. 310). Horace defines youth in part by its unsupervised freedom: "The beardless youth, at last free of his guardian [*tandem custode remoto*], rejoices in horses and dogs and the grass of the sunny sports field" (*Ars poetica*, lines 161-62, qtd. and trans. Burrow, p. 195).

A figurative meaning derived from the ages theme may explain another textual crux. The name "Soler Halle" (line 3990) does not survive as the name of any fourteenth-century Cambridge college, but it may refer to King's Hall, which had many upper rooms known as "solars" (Bennett, pp. 93-97). The term may be introduced by Chaucer, however, as another indication of the clerks' existence upon life's continuum, perhaps with a suggestion of "strong youth in his middle age" at the sun's zenith (Shakespeare, Sonnet VII). By analogy to the span of a day, the sun's movement typically represented the progress of a human life; see Burrow, pp. 55-57. In the Ptolemaic system a planet controlled each of the seven ages. The sun ruled the middle age, the period of "change from playful, ingenuous error to seriousness, decorum, and ambition" (Ptolemy, *Tetrabiblos* IV.10, qtd. Burrow, p. 198).

[29]Ruggiers delineates how precisely Chaucer uses northern dialect to play up the scholars' naiveté as they try to work a "childish and transparent stratagem" upon the craftier miller (pp. 74-75). The clerks' gullibility enboldens the miller. See also Muscatine, *Chaucer*, pp. 202-03; Traversi, pp. 85-86.

[30]On the comic reversal of the two halves of the tale and the imagery of horses throughout, see esp. Kolve, *Imagery*, pp. 249-53, and Lancashire, "Innuendo," pp. 167-69. P. Brown analyzes the plot of RvT in terms of spaces controlled alternately by Symkyn and then by the clerks (pp. 229-34).

[31]As in the Reeve's phrase "whan I was bore," this phrase reduces all of life to the sexual act. In the primal thinking of the tale, where stealing and survival are all that matter, copulation is an act of paramount importance.

[32]In the territorial metaphor of the tale, the clerks encroach upon all of Symkyn's spaces, including, especially, the "privetee" of his women. Space operates, like time, as a literalized theme in the tale. On the importance of space as "functional element," see Frank, pp. 63-65, and P. Brown, pp. 225-36.

[33]Spearing and Spearing note that "the outcome [of the tale] is determined not by cunning, but by pure chance—a force that in the fabliaux tends to favor the young against the old" (p. 22). The young do win, but they win through superior vitality, a natural force, not by simple chance.

[34]In *The Parlement of the Thre Ages* time stops while dying Elde delivers a lengthy peroration upon the Nine Worthies (lines 265-654), a speech representative of the ages of man.

HE WIFE OF BATH: CHAUCER'S INCHOATE EXPERIMENT IN FEMINIST HERMENEUTICS

Susan K. Hagen

The Wife of Bath was never a living woman. She is a fiction, a creation of a fourteenth-century male poet of privilege. To few readers will these statements seem revelatory; to many they might seem naive or even superfluous. Nonetheless, they will become statements of increasing importance as Chaucerians become aware of what feminist critics are discovering about the ways male authors depict female experience.

Actually, it is Chaucer's success in creating in the Wife of Bath a character of such vivid personality that makes it all the more important that we remember her to be a fiction. Like others in that relatively small but eclectic troupe of literary characters who have taken on life beyond the confines of their fictions—Hamlet, Frankenstein, Scrooge, for example—she strides with her spurs, red stockings, and broad hips out of the pages of poetry and into our imaginations. By some she has been admired for her strident lustiness, by some condemned, by far more romanticized.[1] Recently, though, something in her actions has begun to ring untrue; she has been accused of being a traitor to self, of capitulating when she rewards the rapist-knight in her tale by fulfilling all his "worldly appetit" (III.1218).[2] It is in the context of such charges that we must remember that the Wife of Bath was never a living woman, that she is a fiction, a creation of a fourteenth-century male poet of privilege.

weak ✳

From this limitation comes the discrepancy of character that allows an apparently strong-willed female speaker to give a rude, aggressive, and insensitive male character his heart's desire. In creating the Wife of Bath, Chaucer faced the fundamental limitation of his own place in history. It may be that a related discrepancy perceived by Chaucer in human life first called into being a fiction such as the Wife of Bath. Chaucer criticism assumes that the poet recognized the inherent difference between what women are and what religious and secular authorities said they should be. If he perceived some sort of disparity between the experiences of actual women and the models provided by medieval texts (delineated by Hope Phyllis Weissman, pp. 94-95, as allowing only four paradigms: Eve, Mary, the fabliau virago, and the courtly lady),[3] his good Wife from beside Bath may be his experiment in portraying the feminine consciousness of that disparity.

In Chaucer's time women's experiences were never considered apart from their relationships either to God or to men.[4] Medieval women had two acceptable roles: religiously sanctified bride of Christ or socially validated wife. A woman's significance depended upon her relationship either to God or to his first created child, Adam.[5] It was assumed that a woman who did not choose chastity would marry.[6] From the time of Aristotle, who defined woman as a "misbegotten male," the result of a flawed sperm that formed her female, to the time of Aquinas, who saw woman as "naturally subject to man," in whom reason reigned (Erickson, p. 204), and on through Chaucer's time, the female was seen and judged in relation to the male, who provided the norm for human experience.[7]

Woman's experience thus could not fail to coincide with the

categories of religious and secular authorities. In the medieval world view, apart from those two patriarchal validators of female experience—God and man—there was no female experience. And these assumptions inevitably explain why the Wife of Bath is Chaucer's inchoate experiment in answering the imagined question "What happens when a woman's personal [in this case, secular] experience does not coincide with what the authorities say a woman's experience is to be?" The question is, in the final medieval analysis, nonsensical. Yet Chaucer, a poet of great human sensitivity, could imagine that marriage per se might not give all secular women what they desire most. The Wife of Bath is his attempt to push the limits of the humanly imaginable in the face of the doctrinally impossible, to push the question as far as he can before it renders itself nonsensical and catches him in a hermeneutical loop.[8]

The religious dimensions of that loop have only recently been uncovered by the work of feminist theologians. Rosemary Ruether posits human experience as the "starting point and the ending point of the hermeneutical circle." Ideally, models of interpretations should either be authenticated "through their ability to illuminate and interpret experience"[9] or (in their inability to do so) be discarded or "altered to provide a new meaning." Unfortunately, established systems of authority turn this relation upside down and attempt to dictate "what can be experienced as well as the interpretaton of that which is experienced" (pp. 12-13).[10] Hence the Wife of Bath's crisis with authority: faced with a model of interpretation that fails to illuminate her personal experience yet insists on prescribing the limits of her selfhood, the Wife voices her now famous preference for experience over the powers that be:

> "Experience, though noon auctoritee
> Were in this world, is right ynogh for me
> To speke of wo that is in mariage. . . ."

(Lines 1-3)

Although it might be argued that the Wife's separation of authority and experience is conditional upon the existence of authority (Gottfried, p. 207), it may as well be argued, as I do, that the experience of marriage is sufficient in itself for the Wife's conclusions about its woe. Indeed, the Wife's dispute with authorities has far less to do with whether there *is* woe in marriage than with whether she should ever have married in the first place, much less in the fifth. Consequently, instead of focusing on the conditionality of these lines we might more profitably focus on their context, "in this world," in gleaning Alisoun's attitudes toward authority.

As the Wife's ensuing commentary on scriptural interpretation (lines 4-162) makes clear, her problem with authority is confined to the authority of this world, not the next. Perfectly willing to follow commands direct from God or Jesus, at least as she interprets them, she refuses to accept as absolute what ordinary men have said.[11] In particular, she refuses to feel guilty for not being a virgin simply because Paul said it was best to be one. What God did not expressly command she concludes to be a matter of personal prerogative:

> "Wher can ye seye, in any manere age,
> That hye God defended mariage
> By expres word? I pray yow, telleth me.
> Or where comanded he virginitee?
> I woot as wel as ye, it is no drede,
> Th'apostel, whan he speketh of maydenhede,
> He seyde that precept therof hadde he noon.
> Men may conseille a womman to been oon,
> But conseillyng is no comandement.
> He putte it in oure owene juggement;
> For hadde God comanded maydenhede,
> Thanne hadde he dampned weddyng with the dede."
>
> (Lines 59-70)

"In this world" men may advise women to be virgins, but they cannot compel them to be. After all, "Poul dorste nat comanden, atte leeste, / A thyng of which his maister yaf noon heeste" (lines 73-74). Consequently, while allowing the higher value of chastity, for she freely admits that "The dart is set up for virginitee; / Cacche whoso may" (lines 75-76), the Wife of Bath simply will not rebuke herself for not being what she was not commanded to be.

The point here is not to defend the Wife of Bath's scriptural exegesis, for it is certainly not without indulgent self-interest, but to underscore her insistence on differentiating between what earthly authority and what heavenly authority have told her a woman must be and do. Refusing to allow male systems of inter-pretation to dictate her behavior, she challenges the authenticity of those systems:

> "*Men may devyne and glosen, up and doun,*
> *But wel I woot*, expres, withoute lye,
> God had us for to wexe and multiplye;
> That gentil text kan I wel understonde.
> . . . .
> *Glose whoso wole, and seye bothe up and doun*
> That they were maked for purgacioun
> Of uryne, and oure bothe thynges smale
> Were eek to knowe a femele from a male,
> And for noon oother cause—say ye no?
> *The experience woot wel it is noght so.*"
>
> (Lines 26-29, 119-24; italics mine)

That her use of the noun "men" is gender-specific cannot be doubted given her later allusion to Aesop's fable of the lion:

> "Who peyntede the leon, tel me who?
> By God, if wommen hadde writen stories,
> As clerkes han withinne hire oratories,
> They wolde han writen of men moore wikkednesse
> Than al the mark of Adam may redresse."
>
> (Lines 692-96)

Although the reasoning that brought her to this pronouncement is as sexually oriented as her scriptural exegesis—for she claims clerks write stories of adulterous wives when they themselves grow embittered and too old to perform sexually—the Wife's assertions regarding gender and judgment remain valid: First, clerks denigrate women as a function of their privileged, male, ecclesiastical status; and, second, were women's judgments to receive privileged, written status, they would cite equal or even greater condemnations of men. In fact, one of the tenets of modern gender awareness in literary interpretations is essentially a restatement of the Wife's conclusions; in the words of Annette Kolodny, interpretive reading and writing strategies "are learned, historically determined, and thereby necessarily gender-inflected" (p. 47).

The implication of the phrase "mark of Adam" also bears consideration. The Wife broadly means that men could never redress all the wrongs women would write of them were the tables turned, but the choice of the word "mark" draws attention to the physical image of a man over and against the image of a woman, Adam over Eve, maleness over femaleness.[12] For the medieval reader, such a visual image carries with it a tradition of male superiority over females. It reminds us that humanity has been seen normatively in the form of Adam, that the generic male has been the less-than-objective correlative by which all human experience has been judged.

Presenting a woman's experience from a female perspective, the Wife of Bath's entire performance stands in opposition to such androcentricity. She offers a new hermeneutics based on experience rather than the received authority of the exegete and glossator; she insists on interpreting any given text—even Scripture—in accordance with her experience rather than their dicta. Furthermore, she expresses herself in a fashion contrary to the linear and exclusive models of the patriarchal literary tradition (Ruether, pp. 89-90). By their criteria her narrative lacks focus: it turns back on itself, the Wife apparently losing her place at times; it contains asides and interjections that seem little more than chatty gossip or the results of a woman's inability to stick to the subject. Her story, like her horse, is an ambler. But her performance is flawed and her interjections superfluous only by the standards of a male hermeneutics that prejudges what is artful and what is meaningful.[13]

There is no need to deny that her narrative method is characteristically female, for it is deliberately so.[14] If we accept as good the androcentric hermeneutics the Wife of Bath rejects, we fall into the interpretive error that has long both plagued and protected traditional forms of literary scholarship (see Eagleton, pp. 79-80). In other words, to privilege as appropriately normative the rhetorical method from which she deviates is to predetermine the result of our investigation into what the text means.

I want to offer two examples of how the hermeneutical loop pervades criticism, because such an understanding allows us insight into the problem Chaucer faced in creating the Wife. Implicit acceptance of authority underlies John A. Alford's conclusions in an informative essay on the rhetorical and philosophical traditions behind The Wife of Bath's Tale and The Clerk's Tale, respectively. Beginning with the traditions of ancient Greece, Alford lays the foundation for his argument: "Dialectic is an art (*techne*), a system of philosophical inquiry that leads to knowledge; rhetoric is a knack (*empeiria*), based on experience, and leads merely to belief" (p. 110). Alford's choice of the word "merely" prefers the *knowledge* of philosophical inquiry to the *experience* of individual judgment, that is, it prefers the intellectual method the Wife of Bath eschews to the technique she employs. And while Alford may be far more descriptive of medieval attitudes than prescriptive of ultimate values, the bias toward androcentric authority is impossible to ignore in his word choice:

> Against this background [philosophy versus rhetoric] the
> conflict between the Clerk and Wife appears profoundly

111

> more significant. The Oxford logician is, in every respect,
> like the discipline he pursues (terse, moral, guided by knowl-
> edge, motivated by the desire for truth), while his rhetorical
> opponent from "biside Bathe" (garrulous, amoral, guided by
> "experience," motivated by the desire for bodily pleasure,
> personal wealth, and above all power) embodies all the faults
> typical of eloquence without wisdom. (P. 113)

Aside from the questionable validity of these characterizations,[15] the argument is circular because the values of the
prevailing authority are used to judge the Wife at fault for being
in opposition to those values. Alisoun herself becomes lost in a
loop of self-validating assumptions that men have presented as
aesthetic criteria.

Graham D. Caie's review of the glosses of The Wife of
Bath's Prologue in early Chaucer manuscripts provides an even
clearer instance of the critical acceptance of "auctoritee." Noting that most of the glosses are from St. Jerome's *Epistola
adversus Jovinianum*, Caie claims that "by means of them the
glossator could ensure that the reader was not deceived by the
Wife's false logic" (p. 351). But, surely, to use glosses—which
the Wife herself rejects ("Men may devyne and glosen, up and
doun" [line 26])—to prove the Wife's logic false is to beg the
question. Like Alford, Caie interprets the Wife of Bath by the
very androcentric hermeneutics she proclaims herself to oppose.
I am not here arguing that the Wife's feminist hermeneutics is
an ideal one, for, as Ruether points out, the replacement of
authoritarian androcentrism with reactionary gynocentrism continues to marginalize one gender, reducing males to something
less than fully human (p. 20). Nonetheless, to judge the Wife's
character by standards she rebels against is to ignore the
realities that gave birth to the fiction of her character.[16] We
should not limit what the Wife of Bath might represent as an alternative method of validating the self.

The opening section of The Wife of Bath's Prologue (lines
1-162) enacts an extended rebellion against prevailing inter-

pretations of Scripture,[17] especially in regard to marriage and coitus, in which she insists on the experiential reasonableness of her own readings. Nine times she counters the readings of "auctoritee" with phrases beginning "But . . ." (lines 21, 27, 32, 67, 77, 78, 80, 107, 135), each time stressing personal rationales. Indeed, her first use of the word "but" serves to introduce her series of refutations. Having just thanked God that she has been married five times to such worthy men, the Wife reports, *"But me was toold*, certeyn, nat longe agoon is / . . . [that Christ went to only one wedding, so] / That I ne sholde wedded be but ones" (lines 9, 13; italics mine). What follows, of course, is her rejoinder to that complaint. Significantly, when she has made her point and claimed the debt her husbands owe her, her words reject the exegesis of temporal authorities in favor of direct textual interpretation (regardless of the validity of her reading): "Right thus *the Apostel tolde it unto me*" (line 160; italics mine).

Throughout the remainder of the Prologue the Wife of Bath employs unabashedly antifeminist caricatures to justify her own actions in relation to her various husbands: a wise woman will set about getting herself a love when she has none (lines 209-10); no man can swear and lie half so boldly as a woman (lines 227-28); God gave women at birth the gifts of deceit, weeping, and lying (lines 400-02); intoxicated women have no defense from lechers (lines 464-68); women always desire what they cannot have and shun what is readily available to them (lines 515-20). Such appropriation of one's opponents' positions is hardly typical of scholarly disputation; indeed, the Owl loses the debate with the Nightingale over just such a technicality (*The Owl and the Nightingale*, lines 1635-52). The Wife, however, is not concerned with the rules of disputation; she simply reports candidly what personal experience has shown her to be true. Her frank references to "myn instrument" (line 149), "chambre of Venus" (line 618), *"bele chose"* (lines 447, 510), *"quoniam"* (line 608), and husbands "fressh abedde" (line 1259) stand in marked contrast to the verbal fastidiousness of some of her male pilgrim companions, such as the narrator's disclaimer of responsibility for anything crude in the tales (I.725-46, 3167-86), the Merchant's apology to ladies for his blunt description of Damyan's actions in the pear tree (IV.2350-51), and the Manciple's excuse for his use of the word "lemman" (IX.205-22).

The aspect of her narrative that is most obviously non-normative, though, remains her associative method of development. I use the word "associative" to avoid the negative connotations of the more frequently used adjectives "digressive" or "discursive"; nonetheless, the truth remains that the movement of her narrative is nonlinear. In the third line she introduces her topic, the woe that is in marriage, yet she does not even begin talking about marital tribulation until line 193 (where she describes how she manipulated her first three husbands), and she speaks of no woe that she herself suffered until line 481 (where she confesses that her fourth husband's delight in others caused her resentment). Nonetheless, while she delays her thesis (Patterson, "Wyves," pp. 657-58), she never loses sight of it, for in effect all the details that come between "wo that is in mariage" and the dalliances of her fourth husband develop the context by which we can know just how painful was the woe she eventually suffered.

Thus, as the text develops toward its promised statement, the context that will give that statement meaning deepens. Because we know how proud the Wife is and what control she had over her old spouses, we know how the wanderings of her young fourth husband could have disconcerted her. Because we know how she fought for her property and safeguarded her freedom, we know just how much she gave up to young Jankyn and how bitterly she suffered at his hand. Rather than relying on a traditional, single line of thematic development, the Wife of Bath turns to a development more akin to an epicycle: always moving essentially forward, but marking out an ever-widening background of experience that proves essential to her theme. Her method is certainly not linear, and it may not be efficient, but it is efficacious.

The Wife of Bath, then, embodies in personality, experience, and associative speech something deliberately different from the authoritative patterns for these traits. If in doing so she seems inordinately, even lasciviously, preoccupied with her own physical sexuality, we must remind ourselves that these are not the preoccupations of an actual woman but the projections of a male poet attempting to create a female consciousness to be juxtaposed to the "mark of Adam." It is therefore not surprising that her characterization takes on some of the negative tradition of Eve (Knapp, pp. 394-95) and that she becomes female sensuality set against male rationality. Chaucer did not have many other models to follow. Furthermore, as the product of an androcentric culture, Chaucer might easily see the character of women as defined by that difference that tempted even the reason of Adam to fall to the carnality of Eve. That the Wife of Bath sees herself more as a sexual being than anything else may result from the deep structures of medieval theology.

What is called for in understanding the Wife of Bath, then, is a reading of the tale that includes women's real experience rather than male projections of that experience.[18] We must critique Chaucer's would-be feminist hermeneutics with a genuine feminist hermeneutics that deconstructs both the androcentric authority and the projected gynocentric experience men would imagine in opposition to it. By doing so, we can learn what it is about the Wife of Bath that rings untrue.

As I stated earlier, the Wife of Bath is Chaucer's attempt to answer the question "What happens when a woman's personal experience does not coincide with what the authorities say a woman's experience is to be?" We see the disparity between reality and doctrine no more clearly than in her predicament with Jankyn. Regardless of her feelings for her first three husbands, she loved the next two, and with the fifth even violated her own rule that no one should be master of both her body and her goods (lines 313-14). As she relates, she wedded him

"with greet solempnytee,
And to hym yaf I al the lond and fee
That evere was me yeven therbifoore."

(Lines 629-31)

Essentially, she did what authority said women should do: she put both her possessions and herself under the charge of her husband. This action should have secured for her marital bliss and loving shelter, but it did not:[19] "But afterward repented me ful soore; / He nolde suffre nothyng of my list" (lines 632-33). For her, authority and experience did not complement each other. What should have brought her the love of her husband brought instead commands to stay at home, antifeminist tirades, and a box on the ear. Lee W. Patterson rightly calls this episode an analysis of "the suffering of an unloved spouse" ("Wyves," p. 679). Theirs is not a happy marriage.

And what does a woman do in a situation such as this? According to the Wife's words, she does anything she can to regain control, and she remains kind and true to her husband as long as he lives. Aside from the fact that the ruse the Wife uses to trick Jankyn into relinquishing his control is stereotypically antifeminist, and in spite of Alisoun's love for Jankyn, something about this scenario rings hollow. Perhaps it is too hard to believe that young Jankyn reformed so readily or that the strong-willed Wife of Bath forgave so completely. Moreover, if this ending of The Wife's Prologue leaves us a bit skeptical, the ending of her tale leaves us all the more unsatisfied.

After a dignified and moving speech in which she defends her lineage, poverty, unattractiveness, and age, the old woman of the tale becomes for her petulant rapist-husband precisely what he desires, a young, beautiful, and faithful courtly lady. Chaucer's experimental feminist hermeneutics is undercut by this transformation, as is the Wife's personality. The old woman justifies her alleged deficiencies by citing divine precepts and the example of Jesus, seen in opposition to material values. If Chaucer

116

had believed in the speech on "gentillesse" (lines 1109-1218), if he had believed that a woman's personal experience could directly follow the paradigm of Jesus' life and therein be free from the intervention of worldly authorities, and if he had dared to allow the Wife of Bath to believe it, there would have been no need for the old woman to change into anything at all.

Nevertheless, after the knight tells her to decide for herself whether to be foul and old but humble and true, or young and fair but dangerously untrustworthy, she becomes fair and young and "obeyed hym in every thyng / That myght doon hym plesance or likyng" (lines 1255-56). That she makes such an offer is at least perplexing, for immediately before proposing the choice, she had closed her self-vindicating speech with the offer of her body: "But nathelees, syn I knowe youre delit, / I shal fulfille youre worldly appetit" (lines 1217-18). That she then gives him all his delight unconditionally, especially after his less-than-gracious abdication of sovereignty over her (he ponders long and sighs sorely before answering [lines 1228-29]), is unsatisfying at best.

Several critics recently have offered explanations for why the Wife of Bath—or Chaucer—would have the old woman of the tale willfully transform herself into the male-defined being she defended herself against. Seeing the Wife of Bath as "imprisoned by the antifeminism of her culture, for in the tale's conclusion the image becomes her will" (p. 105), Weissman remains nonetheless generous to Chaucer as she claims that the Wife's self-indictment "represents Chaucer's profound and sympathetic insight into the effects of antifeminism on the feminine nature" (p. 107). Judith Ferster finds the Wife guilty of self-interested blindness because she ignores the implications of what she knows about the ability of antifeminist texts to define how she herself can be "read" as a woman; the Wife is "much more willing to see herself as the shaped text than as the shaping reader, and [uses] her sophisticated but partial hermeneutics to escape responsibility for exactly what she claims to want:

self-determination" (*Chaucer*, p. 122). In somewhat the same vein as Ferster, Stephen Knight regrets that the promise of female liberation from masculine and aristocratic oppression suggested in the old woman's speech is denied when she rejects sovereignty over the knight and becomes his property (pp. 98-104). Arlyn Diamond finds the old woman "with all her powers of *faery*, willingly [reducing] herself to the status of a creature lacking any will of her own" (p. 72), a reassuring message to the tale's male audience that

> the most aggressively virile males need not be afraid—even witches will capitulate to their need of masculinity, if they are given some token respect. The knight and his bride, like Jankyn and Alisoun, achieve absolute happiness because the woman, assured of sovereignty, really only wants to make her man happy. (P. 73)

Following the feminist hermeneutical method that has informed this essay, though, another explanation takes form, one which need not exclude those above. As a fourteenth-century male poet of privilege Chaucer simply could not entertain any other consequence of the hermeneutics he was creating. He could imagine no other result for his experiment than for woman's will to be man's will for woman, for apart from—and in relation to—man, there was no will for a secular woman capable of authentication in the Middle Ages. Ultimately, the gynocentric hermeneutics Chaucer created for the Wife of Bath had to give way to the androcentric world view of his own historical circumstance. Chaucer might reverse standard patriarchal hierarchies for a time, but in the final analysis neither he nor anyone else in the fourteenth century could transcend them. Gender meant man or woman, master or servant, one or the other. Consequently, women could be pictured by Chaucer only as something other than men, defined not by *what* they are in and of themselves but by *how* they are different from men. In a time when men reigned as the normative models for human experience, a gynocentric hermeneutic carried to its logical conclusion would have been akin to imagining the advent of the apocalypse without assurance of the heavenly hierarchy.

An alternative to a dichotomous world view, such as a truly humanocentric—or even an ecocentric (Ruether, pp. 72-92)—world view, was essentially unthinkable in the fourteenth century. Consequently, no matter how sympathetic Chaucer was to the perceived incongruities of women's lives, he could define women's problems, desires, and wills only in relation to men.[20] For Chaucer to have done otherwise would have rendered the prevailing interpretive systems inauthentic, thereby denying the religious and secular patriarchy that gave his culture—and much of his writing—stability and meaning. The ramifications of such an action would be not mere challenging of the prevailing institutions but a full scale battering of the underlying hermeneutical structure that gave those institutions meaning and validated their spiritual and temporal authority.[21] It would be no less than to question the privileging of Adam over Eve, rationality over physicality, recorded wisdom over personal judgment. Chaucer was neither culturally nor historically of a time that would allow such heterodoxy. As epistemologically limited as his own noble knight Theseus, Chaucer makes what he surely saw as virtue out of what was for him necessity. And while one might hold Chaucer responsible within his limitations, one ought not blame him for them. Even if his experiment in feminist hermeneutics is inchoate, he was thwarted by limitations that his critics are beginning to grow beyond only now, six hundred years later.[22]

NOTES

[1]See Malvern for an appreciative reading of how the Wife puts her energy to the use of satire; for examples of other sympathetic readings, see Pearsall (*CT*, pp. 71-91) and David (*Strumpet*, pp. 135-58). Robertson presents probably the most familiar condemnation of the Wife of Bath as a representation of "car-

nality, with reference both to the Scriptures and to life generally" (*Preface*, p. 331). Others deem her a possibly murderous nymphomaniac (Rowland, "Dame Alys" and "Death") or a dangerous sociopath (Sands). Still others see her as part of "God's plenty" (Dryden, p. 174) or as "the most memorable of [Chaucer's] characters . . . represent[ing] practical experience as against received authority, female freedom as against male domination, and unblushing sensuality as against emotional austerity" (Muscatine, *Chaucer*, p. 204).

[2]See especially Diamond; Ferster, *Chaucer*, pp. 122-38; Patterson, "Wyves," pp. 682-83.

[3]In discussing images of women in medieval literature, Ferrante concludes, "When they [men in the late thirteenth century] think of women as real beings, they tend to see them only as child-bearers, or as temptresses, and the literary possibilities are slight or negative" (p. 13); see also her chs. 1 and 3. For a catalog of antifeminist texts, see Utley.

[4]Noting that in the GP the Wife of Bath is "defined by her marital status" rather than by her excellence in cloth-making, Gottfried concludes, "At the same time we remember that it is the custom of patriarchal society to classify women according to their marital status, we should bear in mind that, as we shall see, the *Wife of Bath's Prologue* in no way challenges the assumption that the worth of women can only be measured by their relationship to men. The Wife herself not only concurs, but encourages her audience to judge her on the basis of her wifely success, the measure of her matrimonial experience" (pp. 204-05). Cf. Carruthers, "Wife," who attributes far greater thematic importance to the Wife's economic enterprises and "maistrye" of her husbands. It should be noted that Chaucer's perception of women is also bounded by class, and although I do not address this directly, it remains a contextual premise for the essay. Delany makes the point explicit: "It is easy enough to say, then, that the remarkable *Book of Margery Kempe* gives us a social reality that Chaucer could neither observe firsthand nor sympathize with if he saw it. As a man, as a devout Catholic, as a highly placed civil servant and courtier, as a poet in the continental courtly tradition, he could scarcely be expected to see the bourgeois woman in other than the conventional doctrinal and literary terms" (*Writing*, pp. 83-84).

[5]Finding the Wife's "Venerian" femaleness (line 609) due more to her estate than to her horoscope, Crane makes the following points about women's

estate: "Estates literature distinguishes not only among ways of life (workers, nobles, clergy) but also between women and men. Secular women are assigned to a separate female estate. This fourth estate is subdivided according to women's social status in their relations to men rather than according to professions or work in the world: women are maidens or spouses or widows; they tempt, bear children, and so on. This social formulation of social identity obviously makes women's significance dependent on their relations to men, providing little justification for Alison's claims to supremacy" (p. 22).

[6]In her discussion of patristic attitudes toward women, Erickson notes: "Here it must be remembered that while men had at least three sexual alternatives, in the thinking of churchmen, women had only two. Men could either marry, become ascetics, or live as bachelors. Women could choose only between marriage and the semi-cloistered life of a consecrated virgin. The idea of spinsterhood was foreign to the thinking of patristic theologians; they assumed that any woman who did not choose virginity would marry" (p. 191).

[7]Never losing sight of the fact that many primary texts were written by men and concern limited social strata of women, Lucas provides a responsibly researched study of medieval attitudes toward women.

[8]See Crane for a related discussion of Alisoun's inability to define the sovereignty she desires because of her historical lack of a rhetorical language in which to express that desire. See Ferster, "Interpretation," for a summary of the principles of modern hermeneutics (pp. 150-51).

[9]For Ruether, experience "includes experience of the divine, experience of oneself, and experience of the community and the world, in an interacting dialectic" (p. 12).

[10]Although not writing in hermeneutical terms, Patterson draws a related conclusion concerning "Chaucerian ambivalence towards 'auctoritee'—both as received authority and achieved authorship" ("Wyves," p. 691).

[11]Fiorenza provides a carefully argued discussion of the political and social issues that may have mediated the original revolutionary character of the Jesus movement into a stance more in keeping with the prevailing authorities in the Pauline epistles.

[12]Fisher glosses "mark of Adam" as meaning "image, i.e., men" (p. 118); *The Riverside Chaucer* as "male sex" (p. 114); Baugh as "all in the image of Adam, all men" (p. 393).

[13]See Patterson, "Wyves," for an appreciative reading of the Wife of Bath's characteristically feminine style and her use of the rhetorical technique *dilatatio*.

[14]The Wife of Bath's narrative style may be tellingly compared with the Clerk's, which is characteristically androcentric. His rhetoric is formal and his plot linear, he deals in absolutes and superlatives, he professes to be discussing relationships between abstract concepts rather than between real people, and he resolves the tension in his tale arising from Walter's unjustified treatment of Griselda by recourse to authority. Alford investigates the differences in style between the two pilgrims in specifically medieval terms.

[15]Certainly not all critics accept that the Wife of Bath covets power. The sovereignty she desires has been interpreted as having a range of meanings, from personal prerogative to economic independence to the romance genre (Hagen; Delany, *Writing*; Fradenburg).

[16]Schibanoff offers a critical approach that breaks this loop by showing the Wife of Bath as Chaucer's vision of the new reader of the late fourteenth century who had within her hands both the newly available written text and the power to interpret it apart from the scholarly and ecclesiastical authorities.

[17]The Wife of Bath also openly rebels against secular or oral texts. As she harangued each of her first three husbands, she challenged them: "After thy text, ne after thy rubriche, / I wol nat wirche as muchel as a gnat" (lines 346-47), and

> "Been ther none othere maner resemblances
> That ye may likne youre parables to,
> But if a sely wyf be oon of tho?"
>
> (Lines 368-70)

[18]Diamond implies an answer: "'Experience' is female, 'auctoritee' male. 'Auctoritee' tells us that Chaucer's portrait of the Wife of Bath is a master-

piece of insight into the female character. Yet the general critical consensus at this point, which is familiar to anyone who has read Chaucerian scholarship, does not convince me. My disbelief is based on my inability to recognize myself, or the women I know, or have known in history, in this figure compounded of masculine insecurities and female vices as seen by misogynists" (p. 68).

Greene and Kahn offer a definition of feminist scholarship relevant here: "Feminist scholarship undertakes the dual task of deconstructing predominantly male cultural paradigms and reconstructing a female perspective and experience in an effort to change the tradition that has silenced and marginalized us. . . . Feminist scholarship, then, has two concerns: it revises concepts previously thought universal but now seen as originating in particular cultures and serving particular purposes; and it restores female perspective by extending knowledge about women's experience and contributions to culture" (pp. 1-2).

[19]The same can be said for patient Griselda. Her actions were in every way superlative, yet we can hardly say that the first twelve years of her marriage were happy ones. This is especially disturbing when we are forced to admit, as Morse has convincingly argued, that, like it or not, many medieval readers of the Griselda story accepted her as a real-life example of how women should behave in marriage. Even the Clerk expresses some discomfort at Walter's needless testing of his wife and at her submission to his most brutal demands (IV.456-62, 561-63, 694-707). Nevertheless, the Clerk refuses to address this tension at the end of his tale, opting instead to obfuscate the matter by an interpretive reading of his own tale based on scriptural authority.

[20]Delany makes many similar points as she compares Chaucer's LGW with Christine de Pisan's *Livre de la cité des dames* as each poet's "anxious confrontation with the western misogynistic tradition in literature" ("Rewriting," p. 75). In particular, she cites Chaucer's inability to see his own antifeminism, discovering resemblances between Chaucer's Alceste and Homer's Penelope: "I believe that Homer intends to say two things about women: one, that women are capable of moral choice and action; two, that from a comic viewpoint woman's 'natural' role is that of subordination to men. I suggest that Chaucer would support both statements. Neither poet considers the second notion misogynistic, but rather a fact of life, a more or less self-evident verity, a socially necessary and valuable arrangement which is for Chaucer, moreover, a consequence of the Fall" (pp. 81-82).

[21]Note the difference between recent campaigns for equal pay for women for equal work and the call for job parity. The first challenges the prevailing system; the second challenges Western culture's evaluation of the relative worth of tasks traditionally performed by men and those traditionally performed by women. It does not challenge our economic institution; it challenges the value structure upon which our economic institution is based.

[22]Showalter ventures the following: "Perhaps modern criticism, instead of graciously taking [feminist critics] into its historical embrace, will learn some lessons about itself from our anomalous movement, and will begin to question the myths of its own immaculate conception in the realms of pure and universal thought. At that point too, the power of gender will cease to be the special intellectual property of feminist criticism, and will be seen as a crucial determinant in the history of all forms of reading and writing" (p. 42).

Y SPIRIT HATH HIS
FOSTRYNG IN THE BIBLE":
THE SUMMONER'S TALE
AND THE HOLY SPIRIT

Jay Ruud

The scatological aspects of Chaucer's Summoner's Tale have offended the tastes and sensibilities of many readers and critics.[1] Over the past twenty years, however, appreciation of the tale's artistry has grown tremendously, to such an extent that John V. Fleming, for example, is able to say that the tale is "a creditable entry for the Harry Bailly Prize" ("Satire," p. 19).

Much of the criticism has looked at the tale either as it relates to the violent Friar-Summoner quarrel (an approach Chaucer encourages by having the Friar interrupt the Summoner's discourse) or as it reveals the psychology of the Summoner-narrator.[2] But there are particular problems with a dramatic reading of The Summoner's Tale: if we are to see the tale as the product of an enraged narrator, how are we to explain the plethora of learned allusions and the brilliantly ironic tone, particularly in the depiction of the friar?[3] It seems more fruitful to consider the tale in and of itself, what it does and how it works, independent of any pilgrim narrator. When our attention is shifted from the roadside drama, it becomes clear that the depiction of Friar John

in the scene with Thomas and his wife is as brilliant as anything
Chaucer ever wrote, comparing in technique with some of the
portraits in the General Prologue.[4] The friar's character embodies every known complaint about his estate but seems life-
like because he himself does all of the talking (Mann). The difference is that while in the General Prologue or Wife of Bath's
Prologue our sympathies are often raised as we see things from
the character's point of view, here the friar condemns himself
out of his own mouth: he speaks continually of the Franciscan
ideal, but his actions show him to be the precise opposite of that
ideal.[5]

The Franciscan ideal challenged friars to live lives emu-
lating the first apostles after they had received the Holy Spirit at
Pentecost, and the association of friars with the Holy Spirit was
widely recognized in the Middle Ages. The Summoner's Tale, in
fact, plays not only on this association but on various connotations, literal and figurative, of the term *spirit*. Recognizing the
corpus of scholarship that has dealt with this theme, I wish here
first to explore the ways in which those varying connotations affect The Summoner's Tale. More specifically, I then want to
consider important, hitherto unnoticed allusions to Abraham and
how they relate to the gift of the Holy Spirit. Finally, I intend to
examine the theme of wrath in the tale, to show that in fact it is
clearly subordinate to and encompassed by the greater theme of
the spirit.

CONNOTATIONS OF THE SPIRIT

Friar John has apparently presented himself so consistently
as heir to the Apostolic Spirit that his acquaintances think of him
in those terms. The lord of the village, into whose house Friar
John flees after his altercation with Thomas, tells him, "Ye been
the salt of the erthe and the savour" (III.2196), echoing Scripture
(Szittya, "Friar," p. 33). But Christ's words to the apostles were a

warning, for if the salt loses its "saltness" it is good for nothing but disposal. The allusion may imply that Friar John's apostolic pose ought to be genuine or else he is good for nothing but to be thrown out and "trodden under foot" (Matthew 5.13).

That Friar John thinks of himself in terms of inheriting the Apostolic Spirit is clear throughout his discourse. In order to paint himself as intensely spiritual, he uses the rhetoric of the Spiritual Franciscans—those who, in the face of widespread opposition from revisionist Conventuals and of papal decrees, maintained their insistence upon adherence to St. Francis's strict First Rule (P. Olson, *CT*, p. 215; J. Fleming, "Satire," p. 6). He claims for himself a life of ascetic abstinence, declaring,

> "My spirit hath his fostryng in the Bible.
> The body is ay so redy and penyble
> To wake, that my stomak is destroyed."

(Lines 1845-47)

In practice, of course, the friar's actions are far removed from his speech, as he shows when he orders his gourmet meal. By nourishing his spirit through asceticism, poor Friar John has so destroyed his stomach that it can manage to hold down only the most delicate of dishes:

> ". . . of a capon but the lyvere,
> And of youre softe breed nat but a shyvere,
> And after that a rosted pigges heed. . . ."

(Lines 1839-41)

Ascetic fare indeed! The friar consciously and deliberately implies for himself apostolic status when he tells Thomas that his manner of confessing is superior to that of Thomas's parish priest, because

> "I walke and fisshe Cristen mennes soules
> To yelden Jhesu Crist his propre rente;

127

To sprede his word is set al myn entente."

(Lines 1820-22)

Not only do the words echo Christ's promise to his first disciples to make them "fishers of men" (Szittya, "Friar," p. 31; Levy, p. 52), but they also suggest that he has inherited the privilege of hearing confession and imposing penance as granted to the apostles when Jesus breathed into them the Holy Spirit: "he breathed on them, and said to them, 'Receive the Holy Spirit. If you forgive the sins of any, they are forgiven; if you retain the sins of any, they are retained'" (John 20.22-23). And they suggest that he has received, as well, the apostolic gift of tongues that gave those disciples the power and ability to spread the gospel through the Word, through preaching (R. Clark, "Thomas," p. 174).

Friar John further utilizes Spiritualist rhetoric to claim that he and those of his order have received special spiritual gifts because of the cleanness of their lives, which are patterned after those of the apostles. He claims to have had a divinely inspired vision of Thomas's son borne to bliss a half hour after his death—and adds that "oure sexteyn and oure fermerer" had the same vision (line 1859). The friars can be granted such a vision, he insists, because

> "We lyve in poverte and in abstinence,
> . . . .
> Whoso wol preye, he moot faste and be clene,
> And fatte his soule, and make his body lene.
> We fare as seith th'apostle; clooth and foode
> Suffisen us, though they be nat ful goode.
> The clennesse and the fastynge of us freres
> Maketh that Crist accepteth oure preyeres."

(Lines 1873, 1879-84)

Thus, of course, friars are the ones whose prayers can restore Thomas to health. The efficacy of those prayers is highly questionable, however; Thomas, long bedridden, complains that although

128

he has given "ful many a pound" to various friars, he is "never the bet" (line 1951).

While Friar John's answer about the mistake of spreading his resources too thin—"What is a ferthyng worth parted in twelve?" (line 1967)—foreshadows the climax of the tale with an outrageous pun, it also provides the context of his next deliberate equation of the friars with the apostles. In justifying the friars' exacting of the contributions for their spiritual "labour" or prayer, Friar John quotes "the hye God" as saying that "the werkman worthy is his hyre" (lines 1971-73), echoing Luke 10.7, where the apostles are instructed to live by humbly accepting the gifts and hospitality of the people to whom they minister. The saying, however, is twisted from its original context (and St. Francis's understanding of it) to mean that people like Thomas had an *obligation* to pay the friar what he had "earned" (Szittya, "Friar," pp. 31, 40).

The friar's failure to live up to the apostolic ideal he hypocritically espouses is clear from his words and actions. More subtle are his failures to live up to the precepts of Luke 9-10 and of Matthew 10, those gospel passages wherein Christ instructs his apostles as to how they are to go into the world—passages that St. Francis had forged into principles for his order in his First Rule of 1221 (Szittya, "Friar," pp. 39-40; P. Olson, *CT*, p. 214; J. Fleming, "Satire," p. 13). Friar John has a "scrippe and tipped staf" (line 1737), though Christ had commanded his apostles to carry neither bags nor staffs (Matthew 10.9-10; Luke 9.3, 10.4). The apostles were instructed to go in pairs (Luke 10.1), but this friar has two other companions, his "felawe" and a certain "sturdy harlot" who carries a sack for all that they collect by begging (lines 1740, 1754-56). Christ told the apostles to visit only one house in a village (Luke 10.8), but this friar "gan to poure and prye" into "every hous" (line 1738). The apostles were to eat the food provided for them (Luke 10.8); Friar John orders a gourmet meal. The apostles were given the charge of healing the sick (Luke 10.9); Friar John makes the sick Thomas

129

more choleric.[6] The apostles' first words upon entering a house were to be *"Pax huic domui"* ("Peace to this house"). If a man of peace were in the house, then that peace would rest upon him; if not, it would come back to rest upon the apostle himself (Luke 10.6). In The Summoner's Tale no peace rests upon the sullen Thomas, but no peace comes to rest upon the wrathful friar either. His first words are the rather ambiguous *"Deus hic!"* (line 1770). Is Friar John presumptuous enough to imply that God is in the house—at least in the spirit—now that he has arrived?

Chaucer intends the friar's pretensions to apostolic gifts of the Holy Spirit to be exposed by the realities of the tale: he is a false apostle.[7] Moreover, if we look further at the implications of the term *spirit*, a deepening pattern of images emerges. St. Paul, for example, described a number of "gifts of the spirit": uttering wisdom, uttering knowledge, having faith, healing, working miracles, prophesying, distinguishing spirits, speaking in various kinds of tongues, and interpreting tongues (I Corinthians 12.4-11). Friar John perverts the gift of "uttering wisdom and knowledge," which might be manifested by good preaching, into greedy preaching to obtain contributions for trentals (lines 1713-32) and ineffectual preaching on wrath at the bedside of the captive Thomas (lines 1981-2093). The sermon on wrath contains three exempla, none of which shows the evil effects of wrath upon the one who sins; each instead shows the evil effects of the sinner upon others, so that the theme of the sermon is, in fact, that Thomas had better not arouse the wrath of his wife (M. Fleming, pp. 90-91; J. Fleming, "Satire," p. 15; P. Olson, *CT*, p. 217):

> "Be war, my sone, and herkne paciently
> That twenty thousand men han lost hir lyves
> For stryvyng with hir lemmans and hir wyves."
>
> (Lines 1996-98)

The sermon, as it turns out, is a disaster, since this sermon against the sin of ire serves only to arouse the anger of the person who hears it, which results ultimately in the preacher's own display of the very sin against which he has preached.

As for the gift of prophecy, Friar John certainly pretends to this gift when he describes the vision he supposedly had the night Thomas's child died. But this vision obviously is a fabrication made up on the spot that serves the friar's purposes and nothing more. He has no real gift of prophecy (Levitan, p. 237). The gift of tongues ("And they were all filled with the Holy Spirit and began to speak in other tongues, as the Spirit gave them utterance" [Acts 2.4]) is in Friar John reduced to the French phrase *"je vous dy sanz doute"* (line 1838), by which John seems to display his "social or educational superiority" (J. Richardson, "Notes," p. 877; see also Levitan, p. 239). The friar also uses a few Latin tags (e.g., the *"Deus hic!"* and *"cor meum eructavit!"* [line 1934]), the first of which implies a hiccup, the second a belch. If there is a gift of the spirit here, it is more like the wind of a fart than an ineffable holy presence. Furthermore, the friar's enraged silence upon entering the great lord's house is, as Penn R. Szittya suggests, a direct reversal of the gift of tongues and the power of language conferred at Pentecost ("Friar," p. 27). As Chaucer systematically undercuts the friar's pretension to Apostolic Spirit, so too he clearly eliminates the claim that the friar possesses any of St. Paul's spiritual gifts.

For a more popular enumeration of the "gifts of the spirit" the medieval Church also looked back to the promises of Isaiah, which spoke of the Messiah, the branch of Jesse: "the Spirit of the Lord shall rest upon him, the spirit of wisdom and understanding, the spirit of counsel and might, the spirit of knowledge and the fear of the Lord" (11.2). Following this popular tradition, the English hermit Richard Rolle of Hampole lists the "Seven gyftes of þe Hali Gaste" in his *Form of Living* as "wysdome, understandyng, cownsayle, strengh, connyng [that is, knowledge], pyte, and þe drede of God" (Rolle, pp. 116-17; see R. Clark, "Wit," p. 50). Most appropriate for Friar John is Rolle's definition of "cownsayle" as "doyng away of worldes rytches and

131

of delytes"; the gluttonous friar who begs for worldly goods is clearly not in possession of this particular gift. Similarly, "wysdome" is the "forgetyng of ertly thynges, and thynkyng of heven"; the only time Friar John seems to think of heaven is when he makes up the story of the dead child's resurrection, and that is only to excuse his own neglect of Thomas and his wife in their sorrow. Most interesting is Rolle's definition of "connyng," which is what "makes a man in gude hope, noght rusand hym of his rightwisnes, but sorowand of his syn; and þat man geder erthly godes anely to þe honoure of God, and prow [profit] til other men mare þan til his self." Friar John spends most of the tale boasting ("rusand") of his righteousness and the spiritual benefits it brings, and his chief purpose is to gather goods not to honor God but to honor himself and his own order.[8]

The term *spirit* also connotes essence as opposed to outward form. This biblical sense underlies line 1794—"lettre sleeth, so as we clerkes seyn"—playing as it does upon II Corinthians 3.6, "The written code kills, but the Spirit gives life." The friar fails to complete the quotation, in effect replacing the real spirit by glossing. As D. W. Robertson, Jr., has pointed out, Chaucer is here satirizing not spiritual interpretation of the Bible per se but its abuse (*Preface*, p. 332). "Glosynge is a glorious thyng, certeyn" (line 1793), says Friar John when he explains that his preaching is "Nat al after the text of hooly writ, / For it is hard to yow" (lines 1790-91). Later, in explaining the scriptural basis for the high status of friars, he smoothly states, "I ne have no text of it, as I suppose, / But I shal fynde it in a maner glose" (lines 1919-20). Robertson explains that the friar here neglects the literal sense of Scripture altogether, substituting instead his own beliefs. This method, of course, abuses the idea of spiritual interpretation (p. 332).

This glossing is related both to the traditional gifts of the spirit and to the nature of the Holy Spirit. Roy Peter Clark notes that of St. Paul's list of spiritual gifts, four relate directly to the use of language. Glossing was the ability to interpret, that is, the manifestation of the spiritual gift of "wit" (defined as the "capacity of the intellect which made one skillful in the use of language"); the friar's intentional distortion of Scripture "bastardizes the faculty of wit granted by the Holy Spirit" ("Wit," pp. 52, 55).

The nature of the Holy Spirit is further defined in John 6.13, where Jesus speaks of the coming "Spirit of truth," to which Chaucer clearly contrasts the mendacity of the friar. Truth is universally recognized to be the nature of the Holy Spirit—note how the Holy Spirit is called "Saint Truth" throughout *Piers Plowman* (see B V.58-59). Bernard S. Levy describes how the friars justified "their glossing of the Bible on the basis of this pretension to direct inspiration [by the Holy Spirit], since for the Church, the Holy Ghost is considered to be the source of Truth" (p. 48). The friar's false glossing is a direct violation of the truth of the Holy Spirit.

The letter/spirit dichotomy of Corinthians is related to the larger flesh/spirit distinction that Paul emphasizes in many epistles (Romans 7.6, 8.4; Galatians 5.16-17). It need hardly be asked whether Friar John is guided by the spirit or by the flesh. Paul A. Olson calls him "an Epicurean materialist, more obviously materialistic than Epicurean" (*CT*, p. 214). His gluttony, his avarice, his hypocrisy, and most of all his wrath mark him as a creature of the flesh. Recent critics see as blind materialism his obsession with the problem of carrying out to the letter the terms of the oath he has sworn—that is, the problem of "arsmetrik" involved in dividing Thomas's "ferthyng" into twelve equal portions (Carruthers, "Letter," p. 212; J. Fleming, "Satire," p. 17). Particularly instructive is the friar's concern that dividing money dilutes its value: "What is a ferthyng worth parted in twelve?" (line 1967). Alan Levitan sees this as a "materialistic reversal of the Holy Spirit's nature," since "the Holy Ghost, like *caritas*, is not diminished in strength when it is shared" (p. 240).

In the biblical sense, moreover, *spirit* is also "wind" or "air." The Hebrew *ruah* ("spirit") is the word used, for instance, in

Genesis 8.1 when God makes "a wind blow over the earth." Christ plays on both meanings when he says that the spirit "blows where it wills" (John 3.8). Since the friar's glossing replaces the spirit, his "spirit" is simply air that he breaks with his words. As Chaucer's wonderfully windy eagle in *The House of Fame* tells Geoffrey:

> "Soun ys noght but eyr ybroken;
> And every speche that ys spoken,
> Lowd or pryvee, foul or fair,
> In his substaunce ys but air. . . ."

> (Lines 765-68)

The Summoner's Tale's implied image of speech as broken air, which is also flatulence, is suggested in these lines as well (Leyerle, "Eagle," pp. 254-55).

Spirit also implies "life," because the breath of the body was the sign of the body's life. The spirit of God, however, brings new life, like the restoring spirit of Zephyrus in the General Prologue. The friar's glosses, designed only to bring him money, bring no life. By contrast, Christ speaks of the spirit giving life and of his words being both "spirit and life" (John 6.63), punning on both meanings of *spirit*. The friar's words are spirit only in the sense of air, without the life that they should give. Spirit as mere airy wind occurs in the Bible, denoting something worthless, insubstantial, and impossible to hold. The preacher of Ecclesiastes gives up his struggle to gain wisdom because it is foolish and "striving after wind" (1.14, 17). In the same vein, the writer of Proverbs admonishes that he who troubles his own house "will inherit the wind" (11.29). The air that is broken by Thomas in his priceless gift to Friar John is the sublimely appropriate spiritual inheritance for this particular "Spiritual" Franciscan (Levy, p. 50; R. Clark, "Wit," p. 50; Birney, p. 115; Levitan, p. 240).

IMAGERY OF ABRAHAM

The flesh/spirit distinction is taken up by St. Paul in several letters wherein he discusses the fleshly and the spiritual heirs of Abraham.[9] According to Church doctrine, God's promise to Abraham that his descendants would be as numerous as the stars and that through him all nations on earth would be blessed (Genesis 12.2-3, 15.4-5) was fulfilled with the coming of the Holy Spirit. Christians are seen in Paul's letters as the spiritual heirs of Abraham:

> So you see that it is men of faith who are the sons of Abraham. . . . Christ redeemed us from the curse of the law . . . that in Jesus Christ the blessing of Abraham might come upon the Gentiles, that we might receive the promise of the Spirit through faith. . . . And if you are Christ's, then you are Abraham's offspring, heirs according to promise. (Galatians 3.7-29)

Related to this doctrine is Paul's description of true circumcision (Romans 2.25-29). Abraham initiated the ritual of circumcision as a sign of his covenant with God (Genesis 17), but Paul says, "he is a Jew who is one inwardly, and real circumcision is a matter of the heart, spiritual and not literal" (Romans 2.29). The distinction is between physical inheritance and spiritual inheritance: those who follow Christ, who are "of the Spirit" in the Christian sense, are the spiritual heirs of Abraham. Elsewhere Paul allegorizes Abraham's sons, indicating that Ishmael, the child born of the flesh, was disinherited in favor of Isaac, "him who was born according to the Spirit" (Galatians 4.29). In Romans, Paul repeats the same formula, though here the spiritual heirs are God's children: "all who are led by the Spirit of God are sons of God. . . . We are children of God, and if children, then heirs, heirs of God and fellow heirs with Christ" (8.14-17). Paul fur ther distinguishes the two kinds of descendants:

> not all are children of Abraham because they are his
> descendants; but "Through Isaac shall your descendants be
> named." This means that it is not the children of the flesh
> who are the children of God, but the children of the prom-
> ise are reckoned as descendants. (Romans 9.7)

Thus the spiritual children of Abraham are the children of God, and the heirs of the Holy Spirit are heirs to the promise made to Abraham.

Two vivid images within The Summoner's Tale contain strong echoes of Paul's equation of the inheritance of Abraham with that of the Holy Spirit. The first is the graphically memorable image of the natural "heritage" of friars in the Summoner's Prologue: a friar, borne to hell in a vision, sees no friars there and wonders if friars have "swich a grace" (line 1683) that none ever come to this place. His angelic guide disillusions him; he tells Satan to lift his great tail, at which thousands of friars fly out like so many bees around a hive. Eternal damnation in the "develes ers" is, says the Summoner, the friars' "heritage of ver-ray kynde" (lines 1705-06). The assertion that the friars have as their eternal inheritance not Abraham's promise of salvation but rather the devil's arse shows that the friars are not St. Paul's spiritual heirs but children of the flesh. That the allusion in the Prologue is in fact to Abraham is suggested by the iconography of the passage.[10] A popular depiction of Abraham in the art of the late Middle Ages relied on the biblical description of the Bosom of Abraham: the beggar Lazarus, having had nothing in life, is portrayed as "carried away by the angels to Abraham's bosom," while the rich man Dives is sent to hell, from which he pleads in vain to Father Abraham for some relief (Luke 16.22). Chaucer certainly had this story in mind when he wrote The Summoner's Tale, for he has Friar John allude to this very passage in his long digression on the efficacy of friars' prayers:

> "We han this worldes lust al in despit.
> Lazar and Dives lyveden diversly,

And divers gerdon hadden they therby.
Whoso wol preye, he moot faste and be clene,
And fatte his soule, and make his body lene."

(Lines 1876-80)

Luke's story of Dives and Lazarus influenced artistic representation of heavenly bliss throughout the Middle Ages. In portrayals of the Last Judgment, for instance, it was traditional to
depict Abraham holding the little souls of many elect in his
bosom; the Last Judgment of the tympanum at Saint-Etienne
Cathedral in Bourges (ca. 1270-80) is perhaps the best-known
example. Moreover, the iconography of Abraham's Bosom was
well known to literary artists of fourteenth-century England. In
Piers Plowman, for example, Abraham is the personification of
faith. When he meets the dreamer, the dreamer says:

Thenne hadde y wonder of his wordes and of his wyde clothes,
For in his bosome a baer thyng and þat blessede ofte.
And y lokede in his lappe; a lazar lay þerynne,
With patriarkes and profetes pleynge togyderes.
"What waytest thow?" quod Fayth, "and what woot thow haue?"
"I wolde ywyte," quod y tho, "what is in thy lappe?"
"Loo!" quod he, and lette me see. "Lord, mercy!" y saide,
"This is a present of moche pris, what prince shal hit haue?"

(C XVIII.270-77)

This gift of Abraham—his inheritance—is for the poor rather
than for princes. As Friar John says, it is for Lazarus rather than
for Dives. The friar, although he verbally puts himself with
Lazarus, by his actions belongs with Dives. As Abraham lifts his
"wyde clothes" to reveal the souls of the elect clinging to his
bosom, from which they receive their spiritual inheritance, so
Satan lifts his tail to reveal the souls of the friars swarming like
bees around "the develes ers," where they have their "heritage
of verray kynde."

The juxtaposition of the fleshly inheritance of the friars and

137

the spiritual inheritance of the saved may be reinforced by the simile of the bees. In Chaucer's text, we are told,

> "Right so as bees out swarmen from an hyve,
> Out of the develes ers ther gonne dryve
> Twenty thousand freres on a route,
> And thurghout helle swarmed al aboute,
> And comen agayn as faste as they may gon,
> And in his ers they crepten everychon."
>
> (Lines 1693-98)

Any description of a man in a vision being shown the pains of hell might have suggested Dante to the audience.[11] One may then remember the description in *Paradiso* XXXI of the souls in bliss traveling like bees from God to the mystic rose:

> But the other host—who, as it flies, sees and sings His glory who enamors it and the goodness which made it so great— like a swarm of bees which one moment enflower them- selves, and the next return to where their work acquires savor—was descending into the great flower which is adorned with so many petals, and thence reascending to where its love abides forever.[12]

If one may recognize such an allusion, then the contrast between the heirs of the flesh and the heirs of the spirit is quite striking. Dante's bees bring the light of God's love to the souls of heaven, to whom they "porgevan de la pace e de l'ardore / ch'elli acquistavan" (XXXI.17-18); that is, they give those souls the peace and the ardor which they obtain from God's light and then repeatedly return to the source of that light. Similarly, Chaucer's bees bring the nectar of Satan's nether parts "thurgh- out helle . . . al aboute" and then return to their source. The savor of the mystic rose graphically contrasts to that of the devil's ass.

That Friar John represents the fleshly heir, not the spiritual heir, is suggested by another of the tale's memorable images: the picture of the friar eagerly groping down the back of the bedridden Thomas. It is a picture that some recent critics have convincingly associated with doubting Thomas and his groping of the wounds of Christ, and, by extension, with the groping of the stigmatic wounds of St. Francis on his deathbed (R. Clark, "Thomas"; P. Olson, *CT*, p. 231). I would add to these another possible allusion, which would extend the pattern of patriarchal imagery begun in the Prologue. When bedridden Thomas invites Friar John to put his hand down his back "and grope wel bihynde" in order to find "A thyng that [he had hidden] in pryvetee," he first requires him to "swere on [his] professioun" to divide the gift equally among the others of his convent (lines 2135-43). The scene is reminiscent of the biblical tale of Abraham, old and presumably bedridden himself, saying to his servant,

> "Put your hand under my thigh, and I will make you swear
> by the Lord, the God of heaven and of earth, that you will
> not take a wife for my son from the daughters of the
> Canaanites, among whom I dwell." (Genesis 24.2-3)

The elements of the old man in ill health, the request that the visitor put his hand under the old man's thigh, and the demand to swear an oath are present in both stories.

Why might Chaucer allude to this scene in Genesis? Abraham is concerned that his son Isaac, the heir of the promise, not be contaminated by the ways of the flesh represented by the Canaanite women. It is a concern that his descendants be true and pure, that is, in Paul's terms, be spiritual descendants. There is, in fact, a pattern in Genesis of this sort of bedside scene. When, blind and bedridden, old Isaac is tricked into blessing Jacob rather than his first-born brother Esau, Jacob becomes the preferred son, the heir of the promise (Genesis 27). Similarly, in Jacob's old age he calls his son Joseph to him. Requiring Joseph to "put thy hand under my thigh" (Genesis 47.29), he obtains an oath from Joseph to bury him in Canaan rather than in Egypt. Joseph then presents his two sons to be blessed, putting the younger son Ephraim on Jacob's left and the elder Manassah on

Jacob's right. But Jacob, crossing his hands, gives the greater blessing to the younger child (Genesis 48). What all of these scenes have in common is the passing on of the blessing, the spiritual inheritance, from the old man to his descendants. In each case—Isaac, Jacob, and Ephraim—it is the younger son rather than the older son or the legitimate heir of the flesh who is the spiritual heir of the blessing passed from God through Abraham. This inheritance is, to judge by the friar's rhetoric of Lazarus, the special gift to which he believes he is entitled. But, in fact, that is not the gift that Friar John is eager to receive. He is a creature of the flesh who thinks he will receive gold or some precious jewel and, as it turns out, his inheritance is spirit of a particularly fleshly sort: "Amydde his hand [Thomas] leet the frere a fart" (line 2149). The friar literally "inherits the wind" (Proverbs 11.29).

THE FRIAR'S SIN

The friar's immediate reaction to Thomas's gift is to fly into a rage. Indeed, critics have argued that The Summoner's Tale is principally a story about wrath, and that the elements of anti-fraternal satire and biblical parody (which expound the letter/spirit dichotomy) are merely among the tale's interesting trappings (M. Fleming; J. Fleming, "Satire," p. 10). The theme of wrath does loom large, but the story is, I believe, chiefly about the spirit of God in all of its meanings contrasted to the flesh (man's lower nature) as demonstrated by the friar. Of all the deadly sins, ire seems most associated with the flesh and directly opposed to the spirit and so is the appropriate sin for this particular friar.[13]

Friar John's sermon is about wrath: it arouses wrath in Thomas, and, as it turns out, the hypocritical friar is preaching against the sin he ends up committing himself. Wrath was, in fact, considered a particular enemy of the Holy Spirit. In Middle

English the word *spirit* could mean "the emotional part of man as the seat of hostile or angry feeling."[14] In *Piers Plowman*, for example, St. Truth, identified with the Holy Spirit, dwells in the human heart, and wrath is his foe (C VII.255, 261-63); in the B-text, moreover, Ire is personified as a friar (V.135). If Friar John could be called a child of the spirit, perhaps it is because he embodies this kind of wrathful spirit.

The traditional opposition of wrath and the Holy Spirit appears in the complementary imagery conventionally associated with each. The Holy Spirit was usually pictured as a dove, but often it was imaged as fire, like the tongues of fire that descended upon the apostles (Acts 2). Fire, the burning of rage, is of course an appropriate image of anger.[15] When Thomas finally can take no more of Friar John's "false dissymulacioun," he "wax wel ny wood for ire; / He wolde that the frere had been on-fire" (lines 2121-23). As Szittya notes, this image clearly reverses the "alighting of spiritual fire" in Acts, driving home the picture of the friar as a false apostle ("Friar," p. 26).

Also pertinent is St. Paul's catalog of the "fruits of the Spirit": love, joy, peace, patience, kindness, goodness, faithfulness, gentleness, self-control (Galatians 5.22). Anger is the polar opposite of these qualities. It engenders in Friar John hate rather than love, discord rather than joy and peace; it puts him out of patience, causing "backbiting" and broken relationships rather than fidelity; and it surely makes him lose his self-control, as he starts up "as dooth a wood leoun" or "wilde boor" grinding his teeth (lines 2152, 2160-61). In the words of Chaucer's Parson, "This Ire is so displesant to God that it troubleth his hous and chaceth the Hooly Goost out of mannes soule, and wasteth and destroyeth the liknesse of God" (X.544).[16] Surely the bestial similes that describe the friar in his state of rage—"wood leoun," "wilde boor"—betoken the destruction of God's likeness and the flight of the Holy Ghost from his soul (see J. Fleming, "Satire," p. 17).[17]

Measuring Friar John's behavior by the Parson's statements

about ire, one sees that this sin dominates his character. When, for example, Friar John "chideth" Thomas well, as the wife asks him to (line 1824), the action demonstrates ire; according to the Parson, chiding is when an angry man reproves his neighbor, "if he repreve hym uncharitably of synne" (X.626; see J. Fleming, "Satire," p. 12). Since the friar's goal in chastising Thomas is clearly not charitable, except in the sense that he hopes Thomas will give him a contribution "for seinte charitee" (line 2119), his quick condemnation of the sin (for which he has only the frustrated wife's word) surely fits the definition of chiding. Lying, another aspect of ire, is "fals signyficaunce of word, in entente to deceyven his evene-Cristene" (X.608). Certainly most of what the hypocritical friar says to Thomas and his wife is a lie, as is, for example, the spur-of-the-moment vision that he "recalls" in response to hearing that their child has died since his last visit (lines 1854-68). The Parson also associates flattery with ire (X.612-17). The friar's words to the wife demonstrate flattery ("Yet saugh I nat this day so fair a wyf / In al the chirche" [lines 1808-09]), and he flatters her again a little later, when he feigns taking her into his confidence:

> "I prey yow, dame, ye be nat anoyed,
> Though I so freendly yow my conseil shewe.
> By God! I wolde nat telle it but a fewe."
>
> (Lines 1848-50)

The oath "By God!" displays another sign of anger, swearing, which according to the Parson "is expres agayn the comandement of God" (X.587). Moreover, when the friar rises in rage from Thomas's bedside he cries out "A, false cherl . . . for Goddes bones!" (line 2153), displaying the most wrathful kind of swearing, the sinful "dismembrynge of Crist" (X.591).

Chaucer's Parson also lists vengeance among the attributes of ire, which he defines as the "wikked wil to been avenged by word or by dede" (X.534). Friar John displays this desire in his last words to Thomas ("Thou shalt abye this fart, if that I may!"

[line 2155]), as well as in his words with the lady of the village ("But I on oother wyse may be wreke, / I shal disclaundre hym" [lines 2211-12]). Ire also involves "spiritueel manslaughtre," which includes backbiting, for it "as wikke is to bynyme his good name as his lyf" (X.565-66). Early in the tale Friar John defames the parish priests' manner of hearing confession:

> "Thise curatz been ful necligent and slowe
> To grope tendrely a conscience
> In shrift. . . ."

(Lines 1816-18)

The word "grope" is, of course, carefully chosen, as we discover later what a "tender groper" Friar John really is. Backbiting occurs again when Friar John compares the holy lives of friars to those of the secular clergy "that swymmen in possessioun" (line 1926) and then applies to them Jerome's insulting description of Jovinian. Finally, the friar's blind rage exposes fully his backbiting character when he declares to the lady of the village, "I shal disclaundre hym over al ther I speke, / . . . / To every man yliche, with meschaunce!" (lines 2212, 2215).

Chaucer has been at pains to paint a picture of a man inclined to ire in its various forms. The friar, in outward show the heir of the Apostolic Spirit, in fact possesses none of the fruits that that spirit was supposed to yield. In what may well be an allusion to the image of the Bosom of Abraham, the bliss which is the inheritance of the true spiritual heir of the promise, Friar John ironically warns Thomas against "Ire that in thy bosom slepeth" (line 1993). While Abraham's spiritual heirs sleep in his bosom, ire sleeps in the bosoms of its own fleshly heirs, who include the friar himself.

The Summoner's Tale is not simply the scurrilous bit of offensive scatology that readers have for years thought it to be. Recent critics who have explored the nature of its satire and biblical parody have shown how rich a tale it is. But that satire and parody contribute to the larger theme of spiritual heritage.

JAY RUUD

Thus, ultimately, the squire Jankyn's climactic insult is not simply Chaucer's most indelicate joke; it is sublimely appropriate to the friar, who has perverted the Holy Spirit. The breaking of a fleshly kind of wind images the friar's befouling of the Holy Spirit he is supposed to embody. It is no accident that the closing image of the cartwheel parallels iconographic depictions of the Holy Spirit descending upon the disciples at Pentecost.[18] In his purely materialistic life of the flesh and his overriding sin of ire (which directly opposes the Holy Spirit), Friar John displays by contrast what it means to be a true spiritual heir of the blessing of Abraham and the Holy Spirit of the apostles.

NOTES

[1]For a summary of negative criticism of the tale, see Birney, p. 109.

[2]Zietlow, for example, claims that the tale illustrates the Summoner's triumph over the Friar, since in his depiction of Friar John he has destroyed Huberd's "ability to maintain a social front" (p. 17). Howard sees the Friar-Summoner quarrel breaking out because their "male defenses are up" as a result of the Wife of Bath's performance, making them "have at each other" rather than at Alisoun: the SumT shows him to be "gross and infantile," with a childish love of puns (pp. 256-57). Pearsall sees the puns on "ferthyng" (line 1967), "fundement" (line 2103), and "ars-metrike" (line 2222) as demonstrating and "wittily prolong[ing]" the Summoner's anality ("Comedy," p. 140). Owen makes a similar observation, stressing an unwitting self-exposure of the Summoner's anal fixation (*Pilgrimage*, p. 167). M. Fleming pushes the dramatic interpretation furthest, declaring that "Chaucer is defining the character of the Summoner by his tale" (p. 94) and that the tale's emphasis on wrath reveals the sort of person the Summoner is (p. 96). J. Richardson also believes that the Summoner's portrayal of a vindictive, angry friar is a projection of himself ("Friar," p. 232). For Carruthers the tale reveals the narrator as one who "reduces all things to the literal level, refusing to see any higher truth" ("Letter," p. 209).

[3]C. David Benson insists that "the cleverness and learning" of the SumT is clearly *not* suggested by the way the narrator is depicted outside of the tale; in

144

fact, what is suggested is "rather the reverse" (*Drama*, p. 12). Burlin, who takes a largely dramatic view of the tale, still says that the friar's final humiliation is "beyond the genius of the Summoner" (p. 165). Even Howard admits that "the gross Summoner isn't capable of such satiric deftness" (p. 257).

[4]Szittya compares the tale to the WBPro in terms of its use of "allusive irony," whereby Friar John, like the Wife, quotes for support precisely those scriptural or patristic passages that were most often used against them by critics of friars and women ("Friar," p. 45).

[5]The Franciscan ideal has been explained a number of times in relation to this tale. Important for the SumT is that some friars claimed to have obtained special gifts and inspiration through the Holy Spirit. Like the original apostles at Pentecost, friars were to have received this special inspiration by living according to Christ's instructions when he sent the apostles upon their mission (P. Olson, *CT*, p. 227; Szittya, "Friar," p. 34; Williams, "Chaucer," p. 501; J. Fleming, "Satire"). Followers of the Franciscan Joachim de Fiore went so far as to claim that a new age of the Eternal Gospel was to begin ca. 1260—an age of the Holy Spirit that would supersede the age of the New Law, as that age had superseded the age of the Old Law. Specially endowed with the Holy Spirit, the friars were to be the forerunners of this age, much as John the Baptist was the forerunner of the Christian age (Levy, p. 48; Levitan, pp. 236-37). Less radical but in the same vein was Grossi, the Carmelite General, a contemporary of Chaucer's. J. Fleming notes that Grossi "maintained as an historical fact that friars of his order received the Holy Ghost with the Apostles on Pentecost and were baptized by them in the presence of the Virgin Mary" ("Satire," p. 19). Szittya, who sees the allusion to Joachim de Fiore as too obscure, notes instead the much more natural reason for associating the Franciscans with Pentecost, the day of the descent of the Holy Spirit on the disciples: the General Chapter of the Franciscans met approximately every third year at Pentecost. Szittya speculates that St. Francis chose the Feast of Pentecost surely "because of its symbolic connection with the apostles, whose life he strove devoutly to imitate" (pp. 28-29).

[6]His ministrations to Thomas are, in fact, the precise opposite of what sound medical advice of the time would have prescribed; where doctors would have encouraged a careful diet and warned against serious meditation and sorrow, Friar John tells Thomas how important it is to fast and forces him to reflect at length about the importance of sorrow for sin (Gallacher, p. 200).

Furthermore, and most ironically, doctors warned that the "patient should under no circumstances be made angry" (p. 205).

[7]Haskell ("St. Simon") argues that the saint evoked by Thomas (line 2094) is in fact intended to allude to Simon Magus, the arch-false apostle of Acts and of Christian legend, and she describes a number of parallels between the legend of Simon Magus and the SumT. Obviously such allusions to Simon would suggest Friar John's pretended apostlehood as well. Haskell's parallels, however, are not entirely convincing.

[8]Friar John's insistence that he wants money from Thomas to help build a convent *is* sincere. In the internal Franciscan controversy, the building of such edifices was, "in Spiritual propaganda . . . the very type of mendicant dissoluteness" (J. Fleming, "Satire," p. 6).

[9]Lancashire explores a number of Old Testament events involving Moses and Elijah that the medieval Church saw as prefiguring Pentecost. The friars "parody Elijah and the new Moses, those from whom their order is traced, but imitate the old Moses in practicing the superseded Law" ("Moses," p. 28). While these parallels are useful to see, the allusion to the Bosom of Abraham in the story of Lazarus and Dives (line 1877; and perhaps line 1993) is more fruitful in its relation to the theme of the spirit. Nonetheless, the Mosaic imagery complements the Abraham allusions: those who follow the Old Law remain Abraham's heirs in flesh, not in spirit.

[10]Christian art generally pictured three major scenes from the life of Abraham: Abraham and Melchizadek, Abraham and the three heavenly visitors, and Abraham and Isaac, prefiguring respectively the Eucharist, the Trinity, and the Crucifixion. J. Fleming has argued convincingly that the anecdote of the SumPro parodies the image of the Maria Misericordia, another popular theme in art and in fraternal anecdotes, and one used by a number of lay confraternities. Fleming relates this to the SumT by noting the traditional Pauline contrast of wrath with mercy (Eph 2.3-5) and of vessels of wrath with vessels of mercy (Rom 9.22). (The latter part of the argument is weak because the scriptural "vessels of wrath" are those who are to receive the wrath of God, not those who, like the friar, are wrathful themselves; admittedly, Fleming calls his argument "technical in nature and somewhat removed from Chaucer's immediate text" ["SumPro," line 105].) While the Maria Misericordia image undoubtedly influenced the SumPro, I suggest that

Chaucer's use of words like "heritage" suggests an allusion, as well, to Abraham.

[11]It is likely that Chaucer's description of Satan's tail ("Brodder than of a carryk is the sayl" [line 1688]) alludes to Satan's wings in *Inferno* XXXIV.48; see J. Richardson ("Notes," p. 877).

[12]Trans. Singleton (Dante, *Paradiso*, p. 347). The Italian text reads:

> ma l'altra, che volando vede e canta
> la gloria di colui che la 'nnamora
> e la bontà che la fece cotanta,
> sì come schiera d'ape che s'infiora
> una fïata e una si ritorna
> là dove suo laboro s'insapora,
> nel gran fior discendeva che s'addorna
> di tante foglie, e quindi risaliva
> là dove 'l süo amor sempre soggiorna.
>
> (XXXI.4-12)

[13]Many critics believe that the main concern of the tale is not ire but hypocrisy. The hypocritical friar was a popular literary convention: Faus Semblant is, for example, portrayed as a friar in illustrations of the *Roman de la Rose* (Levitan, p. 236). Adams notes that while a number of abuses are attacked in the tale, "hypocrisy is the abuse which dramatically underlies the entire structure" (p. 127); see also Williams, "Chaucer," p. 507; M. Fleming, p. 53. Clearly Chaucer is concerned with painting a vivid (if obviously conventional) portrait of a religious hypocrite. Even in his great rage Friar John remembers his facade of humility when he corrects the lord's addressing him by the title *maister* (lines 2185-88). The denial is ludicrous, since in the same breath Friar John boasts "I have had in scole that honour," and since he has just been called "maister" by both Thomas and his wife (lines 1781, 1800, 1836) without raising any protestation (Lancashire, "Moses," p. 28). Szittya explains that one of the major charges leveled against the friars was that they wanted the title *maister* ("Friar," p. 42).

[14]*OED*, s.v. *spirit* sb., which quotes the Lollard Bible (1382): "Thanne the Lord rered ageins Joram the spirite of the Philisteis, and of Arabes" (2 Chr 21.16).

[15]Citing St. Gregory's homily on Pentecost, Levy sees the theme of wrath in the tale as "a clear reflection of the parody of Pentecost" since "the hearts of friars are kindled with wrath" in direct contrast to the Holy Ghost's kindling of the apostles' hearts with holy fervor (p. 56).

[16]Merrill also uses the ParsT to examine Friar John's sermon, applying most of the Parson's comments to the Friar-narrator. Noting that flattery is an aspect of ire, he also cites the irony of Friar John's second exemplum, which suggests that "the best way to deal with a man of high degree is to flatter him," and the friar's immersion in the sin of anger when he "toadies to the lord of the village" (pp. 348-49).

[17]Wrath is not only a sin of the spirit but, according to St. Augustine, "leads to despair and the abandonment of hope for salvation and thus leads back to the world of material sins" (qtd. M. Fleming, p. 97). In medieval theology, despair was the unforgivable sin, repudiating the workings of grace and blaspheming the Holy Spirit (Mt 12.31-32, Lk 12.10, Mk 3.28-30).

[18]Levitan reviews the iconography of Pentecost, pointing especially to the twelfth-century Pentecost Dome of St. Mark's Cathedral, Venice, which shows the twelve apostles receiving the Holy Ghost as if at the spokes of a large wheel (p. 243). Also of interest is Dante's *Paradiso* X, where friars are depicted as revolving on great wheels, and *Paradiso* XIII, where the image actually becomes a chariot wheel (Levitan, pp. 241-42). On the parody of Pentecost, see also Levy and P. Olson, *CT*.

ORDS, CHURLS, AND FRIARS: THE RETURN TO SOCIAL ORDER IN THE SUMMONER'S TALE

Linda Georgianna

One of the great pleasures of reading and teaching *The Canterbury Tales* is the common experience of stumbling unexpectedly over a passage that one had formerly, for whatever reason, mentally deleted from one's account of the tale. At the NEH Chaucer Institute we were frequently forced to adjust our understanding of a tale in order to incorporate one of these forgotten passages into our reading. The passage that concerns me here comes near the end of The Summoner's Tale, when the friar turns to the lord of the local manor for satisfaction after having been humiliated by his former patron, the churl Thomas. While the tale's epilogue, which consists of the squire's clever if irreverent solution to the friar's "probleme," has received some attention (Levy; Levitan; Szittya, *Tradition*; R. Clark, "Wit"; Hanning, "Roasting"), the preceding interactions between Friar John and the lord have been largely ignored by Chaucer critics. In fact, the tale as a whole is less frequently highlighted by literary critics than by historians, who often cite it as evidence of widespread contempt for friars in late fourteenth-century England (e.g., Trevelyan, pp. 114-17, Du Boulay, p. 44). Literary critics usually treat the story of Friar John and the latter-day doubting Thomas as a fabliau of sorts and discuss it primarily as an extension of the Summoner's vicious and coarse personality. What has been called the dramatic theory of the tales, that is, the tendency to view the tales primarily as reflections of the personalities of their tellers, may not govern all tales, but it has served, in the work of Janette Richardson ("Friar") and Charles A. Owen, Jr. (*Pilgrimage*, pp. 158-68), for example, to illuminate the Friar's smooth tale of a greedy, malicious, and stupid summoner and the Summoner's revenge in the form of a story about a hypocritical, arrogant, and smooth-talking friar.

Helpful though it is to recognize the dramatic interplay between these characters and their tales, important aspects of The Summoner's Tale are lost when it is viewed exclusively in terms of its teller's personality (Pearsall, *CT*, pp. 223-24). The scatological humor of the Summoner's story, introduced in his unforgettable image of a nest of friars living under the devil's tail and culminating in Thomas's gift to Friar John of a monumental fart, certainly corresponds well enough to the crude vulgarity suggested by Chaucer's portrait (I.623-68) of the grotesque "gentil harlot" (line 647) of the General Prologue. But other parts of the tale, especially the passage depicting the friar's interchange with the lord of the manor, are not particularly illuminated by this approach, which may be why the passage is often omitted from critical accounts. The passage focuses our attention on the reactions of the aristocracy to the friar's humiliation and thereby suggests both a sensibility and a set of concerns quite alien to Chaucer's Summoner, whose bullying and blackmailing techniques, successful enough when used against powerless villagers, were unlikely to be employed against the upper classes. The summoners Chaucer describes—corrupt minor officials in the rural archdeacons' courts who systematically fleeced widows and "lewed" men with the help of an elaborate spy network of local pimps and prostitutes[1]—would hardly gain easy admittance to the dining halls of lords and ladies. In the passage in question it is not the Summoner who speaks but the poet: Chaucer invites his courtly audience to move beyond the Summoner's churlish, scatological humor and share in a more private joke, a genteel and more pertinent attack on the friars' pretensions to social positions of power in the halls of the rich.

In addition to highlighting an aristocratic response to fabliau material, the passage is unusual in other respects. The genre of the fabliau leads us to expect a quick, even abrupt, conclusion immediately following the tale's climax. In both The Miller's Tale and The Reeve's Tale, for example, the primary targets of ridicule get their come-uppance and promptly "doun gooth al" (I.3821) as the tales summarily end. The closest known analogue to The Summoner's Tale, Jacques de Baisieux's *Li Dis de le vescie a prestre*, follows this pattern: the sick priest delivers his gift, in this case a testamentary gift of a bladder, and the tale ends after a few lines of sharp moralizing commentary. But in Chaucer's version of the tale of the rude gift, it is as though Friar John's love of glossing the text has proven contagious: one new character after another—lord, lady, squire, and "ech man" of the lord's household (III.2287)—is introduced specifically to provide or respond to increasingly elaborate glosses on the making, meaning, and consequences of Thomas's rude fart. Not content to limit the friar's humiliation to the ill-bred acts of churls, Chaucer allows Thomas's contempt for the friar to be shared by the upper classes as well, including his own courtly audience, whose values and outlook might well correspond to those of the noble household depicted in the passage.[2]

The friar himself offers the first angry gloss as he leaps away from Thomas's bedside:

> "A, false cherl," quod he, "for Goddes bones!
> This hastow for despit doon for the nones.
> Thou shalt abye this fart, if that I may!"
>
> (Lines 2153-55)

By denouncing Thomas as a "cherl" the friar makes a belated attempt to put the villager in his feudal place as a social inferior. The term "cherl" refers in part, of course, to the crudity or bad manners of Thomas's gift. But "cherl" is primarily meant, especially in the context of the friar's visit to the lord's court, as a stinging reference to Thomas's social class as commoner rather than as of noble birth (Havely, p. 147, Burnley, pp. 150-51). This passage marks its first use in the tale, but from now on the term "cherl" will be repeated insistently by each new character, appearing ten times within 137 lines, an extraordinary density far greater than anywhere else in Chaucer. "Cherl" is, in fact, the dominant term of the passage, and the key to its concern with social status and social transgression.

Having been insulted by a mere churl, the friar turns for redress to the traditional feudal hierarchy embodied in the local lord. In drawing our attention to the noble's response to the meaning of an act whereby a lowly churl reduces to a helpless object of ridicule an ambitious, socially pretentious friar, Chaucer invites us to consider the uneasy social relations among lords, churls, and friars as represented in the tale. In calling Thomas a "cherl" and his act one of "despit" (disdain), the friar indicates that he reads Thomas's gift as an insult to his status: he thus unwittingly raises the question of just what his position is in relation to the other social groups represented in the tale—wealthy villagers like Thomas, other religious groups in the spiritual hierarchy, and the upper classes. Before I examine the relationship between the friar and the lord's household, I will briefly define the social connections that bind the friar to the two other groups, as represented by Thomas's household and other clergy.

Up to the delivery of Thomas's gift the relative social status of the friar and Thomas has not been a prominent issue, although signs of a rather confused social relationship are evident. At the beginning of Friar John's visit both Thomas and his wife are deferential to the visiting "maister" (lines 1781, 1800, 1836), respectful of his status as a learned member of the religious hierarchy. The friar hardly discourages such deference with his pretentious blend of courtly, academic, and spiritual language punctuated by fashionable French tags. But at the same time the friar cultivates a seeming social equality between himself and Thomas, and he is himself deferential toward Thomas's wife. The friar "curteisly" greets Thomas by his first name as a "freend" (lines 1770-71) and Thomas's wife as "oure dame" (lines 1797, 2128). He goes even further in addressing Thomas as his "brother" (lines 1944, 2089), suggesting that close familial ties bind the two. Of course, the term refers specifically to a formal religious confraternity (J. Fleming, "SumPro," pp. 101-05). Thomas and his wife have become lay brothers or special bene- factors for whom the friar's convent has promised to pray (lines 2126-28). Yet another relation is suggested in the elaborate courtly attention the friar pays to Thomas's wife, calling himself the lady's "servant" (line 1806) in the typical reversal of male/ female dominance in the courtly love relationship.

But in spite of this confusion of implied personal relation- ships—master, friend, brother, servant—only one relation actually binds the friar to Thomas: the cash nexus, a mutual understanding of the impersonal and strictly mercantile basis of this particular brotherhood. Both men appear to operate as free agents, inde- pendent of the older feudal hierarchy.[3] Thomas is presented in the tale's opening not as a churl or commoner but as a "goode man" (line 1768), an independent householder who maintains a "mey- nee" (line 2156) and has accumulated some wealth, as is shown by the allusions to the considerable amount of gold and the many fine meals Thomas has given the friar in the past.[4] Although his illness is of long standing, Thomas seems to have no trouble meet- ing his expenses, which suggests that his financial well-being does not currently depend on work wages or the pursuit of a craft.

The friar's independent status is insistently expressed in two related ways. First, Chaucer emphasizes both literally and meta- phorically the friar's eagerness to "walke allone" (line 1862). For all of his talk—especially at the end of his plea for an offering—of "oure foode," "oure cloystre," "our pavement," "oure wones," and "oure bookes" (lines 2099-2108), the friar (who was nowhere in sight when Thomas's child died, who is fully prepared to eat a roasted pig's head, capon liver, and soft bread with no thought of sharing with his poor, oyster-eating brothers, and who could ask with so much feeling, "What is a ferthyng worth parted in twelve?" [line 1967]) is motivated not by brotherly charity but by self-interest of the coarsest variety. Indeed, after all of the "we"s and "oure"s the friar's last words as he gropes about Thomas's buttocks for the promised gift concern himself alone: "'A!' thoghte this frere, 'That shal go with *me!*'" (line 2144; italics mine). That the reference is singular is reinforced by the departure of Friar John's companion for town (line 1778), a fact about which we are informed just as the friar sits down to enjoy the delights of Thomas's hospitality *without* his brother. It is no wonder that Friar John speaks with awe of those "trewe freres" (line 1860) who have attained such venerable age in the convent that they may "walke allone" (Hanning, "Roasting," p. 13; Havely, pp. 139-40). Friar John is by disposition one who walks alone and takes for himself.

This independent disposition is reinforced by the friar's attitude toward other religious groups. Although the friar is occasionally willing to associate himself with the whole order of mendicant friars (as when he degrades the prayers of "burel folk" [lines 1869-1914]), for the most part the largest social group with which he is willing to be identified is his own convent of thirteen friars, which he represents repeatedly as an independent unit operating in competition with rival religious companies (Williams, "Limitour," p. 469; Havely, p. 136). When in his fateful pronouncement the friar asks Thomas, "What is a ferthyng worth parted in twelve?" he goes to the heart of this ethos. Religious orders, as represented by the friar, are not one of the three estates occupying a set place in a mutually dependent religious and social hierarchy but are, rather, a multiple set of rival units competing for a limited quantity of farthings.

When the friar tells Thomas that he has been preaching to the townspeople and has "taught hem to be charitable, / And spende hir good ther it is *resonable*" (lines 1795-96; italics mine), he suggests that the charity he has in mind is strictly limited to results that can be measured and compared. Charity thus implies neither a personal bond nor a free gift but a reasonable calculation of value. In fact, the whole thrust of the friar's pitch, both to the townspeople and to the bedridden Thomas, is that his convent's prayers represent a better because more effective product than those of competing curates, monks, and rival houses of friars; indeed, the friar takes every opportunity to undermine the motives, methods, or results of those who also claim to provide prayers for the faithful. The friar's favorite epithet for his fellow friars is "werkeris" (line 1937; and see lines 1973, "werkman"; 2114, "werchen"); he presents his convent throughout as a small but efficient and highly specialized work force, whose "labour" (line 1971) ensures a better product than that of rival companies.[5] "Oure orisons been moore effectueel" (line 1870) than those of others, the friar explains to Thomas's wife: "The clennesse and the fastynge of us freres / Maketh that Crist accepteth oure preyeres" (lines 1883-84). The friar speaks not of the friars' spiritual condition but of the state of their bodies, the "clene, . . . lene" bodies (lines 1879-80) of himself and his fellows. Prayers are thus represented as commodities, an almost physical product of the body, which friars specialize in producing in exchange for equivalent, tangible rewards of wheat, cheese, and money. Whether the competition is mere "burel folk," whose ordinary prayers cannot produce the divine revelation enjoyed by the friars (lines 1854-72), or the more specialized prayers and masses of parish priests, monks, or rival houses of friars, the friar presents his convent as more worthy of the people's farthings because these "werkeris of Goddes word" (line 1937) are more productive of more or better prayers than all others:[6]

> "And therfore may ye se that oure preyeres—
> I speke of us, we mendynantz, we freres—

Been to the hye God moore acceptable
Than youres. . . ."

(Lines 1911-14)

From the very beginning of the tale the friar establishes his mode of free enterprise, with its strong emphasis on accounting procedures and competitive market forces. Because trentals, for example, appeal by their very terms to a desire to translate the process of salvation into a form of reasonable accounting (*DTC* 15:1408-14; Havely, p. 136; Le Goff, pp. 227-28), they allow the friar to mercantilize even further the business of seeking mercy by touting the speed and efficiency of his house's ability to produce thirty masses "hastily ysonge," as opposed to the "waste" of the operations of parish priests, who "syngeth nat but o masse in a day" and can thus deliver far fewer souls to heaven than can the friars (lines 1720-29). Indeed, the friar's hawking of his order's version of trentals lends a whole new meaning to the term "mass production."[7]

The friar's business with Thomas, then, is a form of private enterprise that depends on his ability to persuade the wealthy villager to pay the friar for his "werk" so that the friars, in return, can continue to produce "effectueel" prayers on Thomas's behalf. "The werkman worthy is his hyre," the friar explains (line 1973), transforming what was originally a biblical message about the unimportance of the things of this world into a commercial message that reminds Thomas the employer of his obligation to pay his workers, the friars. The friar even refers to the bedridden Thomas as learning "to wirche" (line 1978) in a new way by giving donations to the friars' building fund. Thus the confraternity that the friar frequently refers to has in the context of so much mercantile vocabulary more in common with market guilds and merchant societies than with any apostolic mission to preach and save souls. It is a brotherhood of independent operators interested in fair market practices and profitable business relations (P. Olson, *CT*, p. 233).[8]

156

Thomas understands the friar's motives as a free agent perfectly well and has, in fact, so far fully accepted the terms of the arrangement, freely giving gold and expensive hospitality to his business partner and "brother" in exchange for prayers that will make him well. When Thomas finally complains to the long-winded friar, his decision to break off the partnership is based precisely on the same market values that have governed the friar's sermon (Aers, p. 42). He complains that he has not received equal value for money spent: having paid his brother "ful many a pound" (line 1951), Thomas remains ill and bedridden. The friar, reminding Thomas of their implied contract of prayers for alms, warns:

> "Thomas, Thomas! So moote I ryde or go,
> And by that lord that clepid is Seint Yve,
> Nere thou oure brother, sholdestou nat thryve.
> In our chapitre praye we day and nyght
> To Crist, that he thee sende heele and myght
> Thy body for to weelden hastily."
>
> (Lines 1942-47)

Surely the St. Ive here referred to is not Ivo of Chartres (as Cline, p. 482, proposes) but Ivo Helory of Brittany (1253-1303; see Robinson, p. 708, and Havely, p. 142). This St. Ive is characterized by Lester K. Little (p. 216) as one of the new twelfth-century urban saints, the patron saint of lawyers, known both for his professional legal skill and for his zeal in establishing numerous lay societies of confraternity. The legal reference highlights the fact that the confraternity here referred to represents less a spiritual transaction than a quasi-legal business arrangement. The friar warns Thomas that his ability to "thryve"—in this case by means of a return to physical health—depends upon his remaining the friar's brother by continuing to pay for the prayers that the convent produces by working overtime ("day and nyght") on Thomas's behalf.

Thomas, however, immediately and sardonically replies that

his money has not been well invested, for he has received in exchange only ineffectual prayers that have not made him feel one whit the better:

> "God woot," quod he, "no thyng therof feele I!
> As help me Crist, as I in fewe yeres,
> Have spent upon diverse manere freres
> Ful many a pound; yet fare I never the bet.
> Certeyn, my good have I almoost biset.
> Farwel, my gold, for it is al ago!"
>
> (Lines 1948-53)

The pun here on "good," meaning both "goods" and "good," is telling. For Thomas, to "fare" better has less to do with any spiritual or metaphysical good than with an even and reasonable exchange of goods for physical health.

But when Thomas pays the friar with a fart, he abruptly abandons the cash-based profit economy just described and turns to the much older gift economy on which feudalism was based.[9] In fact, Thomas's gift is not unlike the gown given by the lord to his squire in return for the squire's solution to the "probleme" of calculating precisely the division of a fart.[10] Rather than being an impersonal medium of exchange, as is money, the gown is a token of the giver's regard for the recipient. The gift itself cannot be easily exchanged, nor can its value be precisely calculated. Rather, it is the act of giving that is all-important: in the case of the gown, the gift shows the squire to have moved higher in his lord's esteem; in the case of the fart, the friar quite rightly perceives the gift as an insult to his status, a case of "despit." Friar John's denouncement of Thomas as a churl takes us back into the world of feudal relations, which the groping friar has set aside in the interest of cultivating his business with Thomas.

The shift from Thomas's house to the lord's court completes the move from the horizontal relations of independent agents in a mercantile brotherhood to the vertical relations of older feudal practices associated with the manor. At first the differences may not appear great, mainly because the friar himself seems equally at home in both worlds. Just as the friar has penetrated both the village generally and Thomas's home in particular, effortlessly displacing first the cat and then Thomas's wife at the sick man's bedside, so too he has managed to become a regular guest in the dining hall of the lord of the manor.[11] Immediately following his angry characterization of Thomas as a churl, the friar wastes no time in seeking redress at the court of the lord in whose demesne Thomas's village lies:

> He grynte with his teeth, so was he wrooth.
> A sturdy paas doun to the court he gooth,
> Wher as ther woned a man of greet honour,
> To whom that he was alwey confessour.
>
> (Lines 2161-64)

The friar's position in relation to both the lord and Thomas will deteriorate steadily during the course of the passage. In his entrance to the court, however, he is confident enough of his status, both as a friar and especially as the nobleman's longtime confessor, to interrupt the lord and his lady at table and to appear before the noble household so discomposed that he can barely speak for "rage" (lines 2166-68). A further indication of the friar's privileged status is that the lord, like Thomas earlier, registers no objection to the intrusion. On the contrary, he greets the friar warmly and by name (the name's first and only appearance in the tale). Immediately apprehending Friar John's angry mood, the lord invites him to "Sit doun anon, and tel me what youre grief is, / And it shal been amended, if I may" (lines 2174-75). But, as it turns out, the lord is not inclined to "amend" the friar's insult; instead the nobles, as represented by the lord, his lady, his squire, and each man of his household, ultimately add to the friar's humiliation, mocking him and divesting him of his roles as teacher and confessor in a "Rabelaisian" (P. Olson, *CT*, p. 233) flight of fancy concerning how,

159

properly, to divide a fart thirteen ways. Rather than avenge the
friar by fining or disciplining the villager, the lord ultimately
sides with Thomas. Playfully, he transforms the churl into a
shrewd master (line 2238, "shrewedly"), someone who is "no
fool" (line 2292) but a man of "ymaginacioun," "subtiltee," and
"heigh wit" (lines 2218, 2290-91). What is most striking about
the passage, and what has gone almost unnoticed, is its emphasis
on hierarchy and feudal order, from which the mercantile friar is
finally all but excluded.[12]

In many ways the scene at the lord's court repeats in small
the earlier episode at Thomas's house. Not only does the friar
gain the same easy entrance to the manor as in the village, but
also, as was the case earlier with Thomas, the friar prepares the
path to his own humiliation by the way in which he frames his
appeal. This time, however, the friar represents himself not as
the friend, fellow worker, and brother of wealthy villagers, an
independent operator intent on beating out the competition, but
as a member of the social and religious hierarchy who has been
insulted by a mere churl.

In his first speech to the lord Friar John appeals directly to
feudal status: the lord's, the churl's, and, by implication at least,
his own. Having just been given his name by the lord, the friar
now seeks his rightful place:

> "I have," quod he, "had a despit this day,
> God yelde yow, adoun in youre village,
> That in this world is noon so povre a page
> That he nolde have abhomynacioun
> Of that I have receyved in youre toun."
>
> (Lines 2176-80)

The social structure invoked by the friar in these lines, like the
physical relationship implied in his description of the village as
below the manor ("adoun"), is strictly hierarchical. The lord, at
the top of the social ladder, is responsible for the actions of the
villagers, whom Friar John treats as the lord's possessions:

160

Thomas lives in "youre village" and "youre toun," he pointedly remarks. Furthermore, according to Friar John, the lord must see to it that the friar not be treated as though he were merely a "povre . . . page." With these lines the friar seeks to reinsinuate himself into the social framework that earlier he had ignored, during his attempt to establish brotherly relations of mercantile equality with Thomas. Now for the first time the friar prudently and with great show—complete with the biblical authority of Matthew 23.7-8—rejects the title *maister* (Skeat, p. 340; Williams, "Chaucer," p. 509; Havely, p. 146):

> "Now, maister," quod this lord, "I yow biseke—"
> "No maister, sire," quod he, "but servitour,
> Thogh I have had in scole that honour.
> God liketh nat that 'Raby' men us calle,
> Neither in market ne in youre large halle."
>
> (Lines 2184-88)

The title has in fact proven very useful "in market," where the deference it brings from such villagers as Thomas can easily be translated into large donations. But here in the lord's "large halle" Friar John judges it more productive to withdraw into the feudal hierarchy in which the clergy serve the nobility in teaching and prayer and thus deserve their protection, especially from the insults of socially inferior churls.[13]

While Friar John works to reestablish himself in the feudal hierarchy, he also seeks to reestablish the hierarchical structure of the Church, which he had earlier abused in his competitive aggression against other religious groups. To the lord the friar depicts Thomas's gift not as an insult to a single friar but as a threat aimed at the whole convent of friars:

> "And yet ne greveth me nothyng so soore,
> As that this olde cherl with lokkes hoore
> Blasphemed hath oure hooly covent eke."
>
> (Lines 2181-83)

In fact, the friar continues, the insult strikes at the whole order of mendicant friars; finally, by a logical extension ("*per consequens*"), he holds Thomas guilty of attempting to rupture the fabric of the Church as a whole, in all of its degrees:

> "Sire," quod this frere, "an odious meschief
> This day bityd is to myn ordre and me,
> And so, *per consequens*, to ech degree
> Of hooly chirche—God amende it soone!"
>
> (Lines 2190-93)

Although he is not at all perturbed by this apparent threat to the order of the Church, the lord seems perfectly willing to amend this so-called assault on the social hierarchy of Church and State, if only Friar John will tell him more specifically what form the threat has taken. The tale's second great comic deflation (the first, of course, being Thomas's gift itself) occurs when the friar finally tells the lord what we already know, that the insult is merely a fart, delivered not as an act of defiance to the feudal hierarchy of Church and State but only as what Thomas judges to be an equivalent exchange between himself and his market partner, as Friar John kneels at his bedside groping in a private place for this private gift.[14]

The lord does not respond immediately to this revelation. He does not seem eager to humiliate the friar. Indeed, especially when he is measured against the angry Thomas and the raging friar, the lord appears remarkably cool and friendly, if somewhat distant. A sense of leisure, detachment, and studied amusement marks the lord's social status just as surely as the unseemly "bisy"-ness (line 1940) of the friar (Barney, pp. 27-28) and the churlish gift of Thomas mark theirs. But in his own genteel way the lord has already begun the transition from deference to impatience to rejection by subtly reversing roles with his longtime confessor. While the friar is busy withdrawing from his brotherly relations with Thomas to what he takes to be the protection of the feudal hierarchy, the lord, by agreeing to amend the insult, has begun to play the role of the confessor. In this role the lord becomes more dominant and distanced from the friar even as Friar John's wounded pride compels him to inflate the consequences of Thomas's insult without naming it.

The confessor's duty, as Friar John well knows, is to urge the sinner to reveal his sins so that they can be amended in sacramental confession. Earlier the friar-confessor had urged Thomas to "shewe to me al thy confessioun" (line 2093) so that his sinful ire could be "amended" (line 1833). But in this passage it is the lord who three times urges the furious friar to tell his story of grief. The first occurrence, which specifically associates the telling with amendment, has been cited: "Sit doun anon, and tel me what youre grief is, / And it shal been amended, if I may" (lines 2174-75). A few lines later the lord repeats the request, this time in response to the friar's newfound modesty in objecting to the title *maister*: "'No fors,' quod he, 'but tel me al youre grief'" (line 2189). Finally, the lord pointedly reminds his petitioner that their relationship depends upon the friar, not the lord, being the confessor:

> "Sire," quod the lord, "ye woot what is to doone.
> Distempre yow noght; ye be my confessour;
> Ye been the salt of the erthe and the savour.
> For Goddes love, youre pacience ye holde!
> Tel me youre grief. . . ."
>
> (Lines 2194-98)

The friar, experienced in the cure of souls, should know "what is to doone." As the friar had earlier told Thomas's wife, a good confessor should "grope tendrely a conscience / In shrift" (lines 1817-18). The word "tendrely" alludes to the traditional representation of sinners as wounded patients in need of a cure brought by a spiritual physician, or "leche" as Friar John calls it (lines 1892, 1956), who must gently direct the penitent to reveal his wounds in confession and thus be cured (Tentler, pp. 82-94). Up to this point the lord has been gentle enough, but he now sternly reminds the friar that he risks losing his position as confessor if he falls further into "distempre," a term which still had medical associations in Chaucer's time (see Havely, pp. 146-47). The lord's reference to the friar as the "salt of the erthe" in part compliments the apostolic mission of friars, but it also serves as a warning to friars who fail to fulfill their function as confessors and preachers: if they become useless, they can be thrown out, like salt that has lost its flavor. As Christ says to his apostles in the Sermon on the Mount: "You are the salt of the earth; but if salt goes flat, how can its flavor be restored? It is then good for nothing except to be thrown out and trampled on by man" (Matthew 5.13). By citing the gospel, the lord has not only replaced the friar as confessor but also begun to usurp the friar's other major role, preacher and glosser of texts; in this case he reinterprets one of the very texts used by friars to justify their high claims to continuing the apostolic mission (Szittya, *Tradition*, p. 241).

Unable to function in the lord's court as preacher or confessor, the very roles that originally accounted for his easy entrance to the nobleman's house, Friar John has thus already lost considerable ground because of his rage against Thomas. When he finally reveals to his new confessor the source of his grief, he sinks much further in the lord's esteem, finally becoming for the court as a whole—as well as for Chaucer's courtly audience—an object of ridicule, helpless to say a word in his own defense.

"Is ther oght elles?" (line 2203), the lord's wife asks when the friar finally reveals that the insult, which he has represented as a threat against the social and spiritual hierarchy, had been no more than a fart. The lady dismisses Thomas's act as behavior typical of an ill-bred churl, harmless enough (at least to one far removed from churls in the social hierarchy) to be passed off with the mildest of imprecations: "I seye a cherl hath doon a cherles dede. / What shold I seye? God lat hym nevere thee!" (lines 2206-07). The friar, however, whose close familiarity with churls has just been epitomized by his groping of Thomas's private parts, flatly rejects the lady's casual approach to the harm Thomas has caused him, swearing vengeance against "this false blasphemour":

> "Madame," quod he, "by God, I shal nat lye,
> But I on oother wyse may be wreke,
> I shal disclaundre hym over al ther I speke,
> This false blasphemour that charged me
> To parte that wol nat departed be
> To every man yliche, with meschaunce!"
>
> (Lines 2210-15)

As with his earlier fateful remark about the worth of a "ferthyng . . . parted in twelve" (line 1967), the friar here draws attention to the very detail that will lead to further humiliation—his final humiliation, in fact, for these turn out to be the friar's last words in the tale.

In preparing the friar to receive his gift, Thomas had dwelt in particular on the hypocrite's "false dissymulacioun" (line 2123) concerning the brotherhood of friars and their lay brothers. As was noted earlier, the friar walks alone, operating entirely independently and for himself. Thomas mocks the friar's self-interest masking as fraternity through the terms of his gift, which emphasize with pseudo-solemnity the necessity of the gift's being shared equally by all the brothers in Friar John's convent. "Ye sey me thus, how that I am youre brother?" Thomas asks (line 2126), pointedly alluding to the friar's repeated use of the epithet:

> "Now wel," quod he, "and somwhat shal I yive
> Unto youre hooly covent whil I lyve;
> And in thyn hand thou shalt it have anon,
> On this condicion, and oother noon,
> That thou departe it so, my deere brother,
> That every frere have also muche as oother.
> This shaltou swere on thy professioun,
> Withouten fraude or cavillacioun."
>
> (Lines 2129-36)

Both the contractual language and the promise to deliver the gift into the friar's hand mock the mercantile terms of the agreement that has up to now defined this brotherhood, as does Thomas's insistence that the gift be precisely divided among all thirteen friars. This language promises a material, calculable, "resonable" gift, precisely the kind of charity Friar John seeks and understands.

In dwelling on Thomas's terms in his complaint to the nobles, the friar misses the point of the mockery. For the literal-minded friar, Thomas's so-called blasphemy has less to do with the insulting spiritual implications of the scatological gift itself than with the logical problem of equally dividing a fart thirteen ways. Thus the friar confuses physical and metaphysical insults, bypassing the meaning of the gift in favor of glossing its terms (Adams, p. 130). Seen from this point of view, the fart becomes a problem for scholars, but it is also a problem particularly suited to the commercial bent of the friar. After all, in a profit economy commodities must have a precise value. By raising the issue of what Thomas's fart is worth the friar releases the final comic chaos that brings him down.

The transformation of a fart into a problem of rational calculation is what finally triggers the lord's extraordinary reaction: "The lord sat stille as he were in a traunce, / And in his herte he rolled up and doun" (lines 2216-17). Following the friar's own lead, the lord completely ignores the insulting fart itself and therefore can ignore for now, at least, the need to avenge the insult. All questions of correction or "amendment," the lord implies with a mock seriousness similar to Thomas's, must be delayed until the prior legal question of the proper implementation of the terms of Thomas's agreement can be resolved. The delay turns out to be all but endless, as the whole court joins in the game of trying to determine the precise value of one-thirteenth of a fart.

By speaking not to the friar but to himself, the lord indicates that he has already in some sense dismissed Friar John from his attention, if not from his hall. He marvels at the ingenuity of "this cherl" who devised the "probleme" so "shrewedly" (see Havely, p. 144) that even the learned friar cannot solve it:

> "How hadde this cherl ymaginacioun
> To shewe swich a probleme to the frere?
> Nevere erst er now herde I of swich mateere."
>
> (Lines 2218-20)

"Swich mateere" is one of those wonderful Chaucerian phrases that points in several directions at once. First, the phrase reminds us that Thomas's joke depends on his conviction that the friar is interested only in material things, "swich mateere" as can be divided, hoarded, and spent. The friar's automatic transformation of an insubstantial fart—it "Nis but of eir reverberacioun" (line 2234)—into a commodity to be divided, transported, and delivered points up the utter materiality of his perspective (Adams, p. 128).

In addition, the "mateere" that causes the lord to wonder has to do with the matter of degree. The friar, in treating Thomas's terms as a contract—or text to be glossed—has already unwittingly elevated Thomas to the status of a scholar. The lord here confirms (at least for the moment) and dwells gleefully on Thomas's supposed new status when he attributes to "this cherl" the "ymaginacioun" to devise a logical "probleme" much like the "inpossibles" imposed by masters on their students (Pearcy, pp. 322-25). In confirming Thomas's new condition the lord also asserts his own authority as a "maister," using the language of the schools freely—"demonstration," "inpossible," "probleme," "question," and, of course, "ars-metrike"—to mock the friar's problem.

Finally, the problem itself, as posed by the friar and reinterpreted by the lord, concerns "swich mateere" to make any lord (and any churl for that matter) marvel. The problem of "part[ing] that wol nat departed be" (line 2214) not only elevates Thomas and his gift, but it also diminishes the value of one distinguishing characteristic of friars—the fraternal ideal of communal sharing—which in effect eliminates the matter of degree among the brotherhood (P. Olson, *CT*, p. 233; Szittya, *Tradition*, pp. 126-28). The lord marvels three times within a few lines at the supposed equality among friars, which would make the division of Thomas's insubstantial fart such a difficult problem:

> "Who sholde make a demonstracion
> That every man sholde have yliche his part
> As of the soun or savour of a fart?"
>
> (Lines 2224-26)

The joke in this first reference is not only that the lord himself has begun to part the fart, distinguishing even its "soun" and its "savour," but also that each of these three parts must be divided precisely among the thirteen members of the convent. Two lines later the lord marvels again at the difficulties imposed by the need to divide the indivisible equally among the friars, here stressing the presumably impossible nature of the problem:

> "Who evere herde of swich a thyng er now?
> To every man ylike? Tel me how.
> It is an inpossible; it may nat be."
>
> (Lines 2229-31)

In his third reference the lord presents the ridiculous picture of an insubstantial fart whose worth "wasteth" away before it can be divided among thirteen very substantial friars:

> "The rumblynge of a fart, and every soun,
> Nis but of eir reverberacioun,
> And evere it wasteth litel and litel awey.
> Ther is no man kan deemen, by my fey,
> If that it were departed equally."
>
> (Lines 2233-37)

Now it certainly might be that in drawing so much attention to the equality among friars, the lord is merely expressing doubt that friars actually lived up to the ideal of sharing all gifts with their brothers, keeping nothing for themselves in imitation of Christ's poverty.[15] But it also seems that the lord is poking fun at the fraternal ideal itself, which by eliminating status and degree eliminates the hierarchical order on which depends the lord's position in relation to both friars and churls. Finally, the lord seems to mock the cash economy as a whole, which, unlike the feudal gift economy, depends upon a kind of "ars-metrike," the determining of a market value in all exchanges. That is, the lord is perhaps amused not only at the idea that "every man ylike" must receive an equal share of Thomas's gift but also that it falls to the commodity-oriented friar to calculate the value of the fart.

It is important to recognize that by siding with Thomas in his dispute with the friar, the lord is not suggesting a reordering or elimination of the social hierarchy but is rather reconfirming his own status as a lord and Thomas's as a useful churl who has punished a transgressor. While the friar repeatedly had called Thomas by name in an effort to establish brotherly relations, the lord never refers to Thomas by name but only by his status as a churl. Yet each time the lord repeats and expands upon the problem of dividing the fart, he mentally addresses the churlish Thomas with growing respect. Thomas is at first "this cherl" (line 2218), then a "nyce cherl" (line 2232) and a "nice, proude cherl" (line 2227), "nyce" meaning not "foolish" but rather the opposite, "sophisticated" or "elegant," as today a solution in mathematics might be called "nice" by fellow mathematicians (Havely, pp. 147-48). Finally, the lord ends with an accolade to Thomas: "What, lo, *my* cherl, lo, yet how shrewedly / Unto *my* confessour to-day he spak" (lines 2238-39; italics mine). The lord's identification with Thomas is based firmly on feudal relations. In fact, by referring to Thomas finally as "my cherl," the lord confirms the hierarchical social structure put forward by the friar when he arrived at the court, that the feudal lord owns and is responsible for the actions of those living in "his" village.

What has changed is the friar's place in that structure. No longer the welcome confessor to the rich and powerful, Friar John is in effect given a status similar to Thomas's. It is "my confessour" and "my cherl"—and the lord is now fully in control of both, as he orders the one to eat his dinner and the other to go play (line 2241). The squire who finally solves the problem of dividing a fart, effectively isolating each thirteenth of a fart by means of his ingenious use of a twelve-spoked cartwheel, is, appropriately, the lord's "kervere." The interloping friar—who worries about farthings being carved up among religious groups and who describes prayers as commodities efficiently produced in order to deliver precise results—is at least put in his place, if not altogether closed out of a reestablished feudal world in which lords rule by giving gown cloths to their squires and allowing their churls to play at being masters.

If such a comically satisfying story could be reduced to pithy morals, one of them might read like the one so incongruously attached by the friar to his sermon on anger:

> "Beth war, therfore, with lordes how ye pleye.
> Syngeth *Placebo* and 'I shal, if I kan,'
> But if it be unto a povre man.
> To a povre man men sholde his vices telle,
> But nat to a lord, thogh he sholde go to helle."
>
> (Lines 2074-78)

The lord of the tale, though far more composed and judicious than the "irous" (line 2079) lords of Friar John's terrifying exempla, nevertheless has his limits, and his patience with this interloping, pretentious friar who invades his village and his home is at an end. The friar's independent status, his freedom to "walke allone" in the houses of the rich and the middle class, has been sharply but comically checked.

LORDS, CHURLS, AND FRIARS

NOTES

[1]For Chaucer's portrait of summoners, see GP (I.623-68) and FrPro (III.1280-85, 1321-74). On the office and reputation of summoners, see Haselmayer, pp. 43-57; Woodcock, pp. 45-49, 69-70; P. Olson, *CT*, pp. 183-201; and Bowden, pp. 262-73.

[2]Kean notes Chaucer's creation in the tale of an internal audience similar to his own courtly audience (2:89-90). Williams judges that Chaucer's attitude closely accorded with that of the secular clergy in its dispute with the friars, noting that it is "no wonder, for the secular clergy must have dominated the thinking of the upper class, governmental circles in which Chaucer moved" ("Chaucer," p. 513). See also Manly, *Light*, pp. 120-21.

[3]For a succinct statement of the ways in which feudal practice restricted independent trading and selling, see Postan, p. 239.

[4]See ShipT (VII.29) and *MED*, s.v. *god man* phr. and n., 2(a). On Thomas's status as burgher, see Birney, p. 111 and n. 15.

[5]Havely notes that ME *werker* could have a broader general meaning, i.e., "doer" (p. 142). Nevertheless, the friar does seem to literalize the term. It is frequently repeated in the tale in conjunction with the more particular word "labour," with the references to the friar's ability to "deliver" souls from purgatory to heaven, and with the general tendency of the friar to treat prayers as commodities. The term *deliver* does, of course, have a particular spiritual referent in Christ's deliverance of the just souls in the Harrowing of Hell. In the friar's parlance, however, its meaning leans toward literal delivery, with a strong emphasis on the speed with which souls will travel to heaven because of the friars' efficient "mass production."

[6]On the "commodification" of religion in the tale, see the brief but useful remarks of Knight, pp. 106-07, and the less temperate analysis of Aers, pp. 38-45. Aers provides no evidence for his identification of the friar's practices with the whole of "orthodox" medieval religious practice.

[7]The phrase was aptly coined by John Crafton at the 1987 Chaucer Institute. On the rise of "arithmetical piety" in the late Middle Ages, see Oakley, p. 118; see also Wood-Legh for an analysis of the tendency to quantify

and commodify masses in records concerning the establishment of chantries in the later Middle Ages (pp. 307-13).

[8]For a brief description of the interests of merchant societies and market guilds, see Postan, pp. 233-51. See also J. Fleming, who notes that confraternities could function both as examples of spiritual idealism and as "trade guilds . . . and insurance programs" ("SumPro," p. 102).

[9]On gown cloths as feudal rewards, see Skeat, vol. 5, p. 341. On the feudal gift economy, see Little, pp. 3-14, and Duby, pp. 48-72. N. Brown, among others, has written of the particular dualism that leads to money being viewed as simultaneously attractive and repulsive (pp. 234-304). That the connection between money and excrement was as familiar in the Middle Ages as it is in our post-Freudian society is made evident by Little, p. 34 and n. 86, and J. Fleming, "Antifraternalism," pp. 698-99.

[10]According to Hanning, the squire's name Jankyn means "little John," thus emphasizing the parallels between these two beggars and glossers of difficult "texts" ("Roasting," p. 13).

[11]J. Fleming notes the frequency with which friars were criticized as "penetrantes domos" ("Antifraternalism," p. 693). Langland names the last friar who appears in *Piers Plowman* "Sire Penetrans Domos"; see Szittya, *Tradition*, pp. 3-10, 58-61. In the antifraternal literature the "house" penetrated is usually identified with the individual soul or conscience, which Friar John also unsuccessfully attempts to penetrate in his effort to "grope" (line 1817) Thomas's conscience in confession. Friars were also regularly criticized for their close ties to the wealthy and the powerful. See GP (I.246-51), and the characterization of Fals Semblant in *Rom* 6482-6520. See also Williams, "Chaucer," pp. 507-09.

[12]An exception is the brief remark by Knight, p. 107.

[13]See Little, pp. 197-98, on feudalism and the idea of spiritual service.

[14]On the several meanings of ME *grope*, see Havely, p. 139.

[15]On the history of the ideal of apostolic poverty and communal sharing, see Lambert, and Little, pp. 148-50, 160-65.

HE FALCON'S COMPLAINT
IN THE SQUIRE'S TALE

Charles A. Owen, Jr.

The falcon in The Squire's Tale develops an idiom in her complaint that is unique in Chaucer's poetry. It represents the culmination of a series of experiments that extends throughout the poet's career. This series begins with the Black Knight's effort in *The Book of the Duchess* and includes Dido in *The House of Fame* and *The Legend of Good Women*, both Troilus and Criseyde, Venus, Dorigen, and the poet's own "slant" complaints to the dead allegorical figure Pity and to his empty purse.

The closest analogues to the falcon's complaint are those of Mars and Anelida.[1] In both these instances the complaint brings the poem to an end, by design in the first but not in *Anelida and Arcite*, where, as in The Squire's Tale, the complaint seems to have exhausted the poet's creative energies. With a gesture toward what he had originally planned in continuation Chaucer seems to have aborted his efforts, leaving the poems as further examples of his penchant for unfinished work.[2]

We have good evidence that he gave some thought to both form and content in the complaint. In The Complaint of Mars, for instance, after 154 lines of narrative in rime royal Chaucer invents a new and more elaborate rhyme scheme for the introductory stanza and for the five sections of three stanzas each that constitute the complaint. Chaucer develops this new nine-line pattern by the simple expedient of doubling the a-rhymes in rime royal. In the introductory stanza we get a critical statement on the subject matter appropriate to the genre:

> The ordre of compleynt requireth skylfully
> That yf a wight shal pleyne pitously,
> Ther mot be cause wherfore that men pleyne;
> Or men may deme he pleyneth folily
> And causeles; alas, that am not I.
> Wherfore the ground and cause of al my peyne,
> So as my troubled wit may hit atteyne,
> I wol reherse; not for to have redresse,
> But to declare my ground of hevynesse.
>
> (Lines 155-63)[3]

This important if somewhat awkward critical comment emphasizes the balance between cause and expression, between content and form, and makes clear the archetypal motivation for the genre in its therapeutic value rather than in any practical expectation of "redresse." Each of the five sections of the complaint that follows treats some general aspect of the god's distress. They do not make explicit use of Mars's plight as recounted in the narrative section.

In the *Anelida* the complaint draws extensively on the preceding narrative. It also represents Chaucer's most difficult experiment with rhyme. Each half of the complaint starts out using a nine-line pattern derived from that of the Mars, but with only two rhymes.[4] After four repetitions the pattern shifts to a two-rhyme, sixteen-line stanza with three out of every four lines shortened to four beats and having a single rhyme, and with the longer fourth lines rhyming; after eight lines the rhymes reverse. Each half of the complaint then concludes with a return to the nine-line stanza that has internal rhyme on the second and fourth stresses of every line. The incremental quickening of the rhyme accompanies and is intended to reinforce emotional intensification in each half of the complaint. In addition, Anelida's complaint has a proem and a conclusion, with the final line an echo of the first. This elaborate construction was Chaucer's own invention. It draws, of course, on the fixed forms of Chaucer's French contemporaries, but for them the complaint employed a single stanza pattern. The intricate rhyming in French poetry was an end in itself; it tended not to reflect meaning or emotion (Owen, "Rymyng," pp. 533-34).

The falcon's lament in The Squire's Tale differs from its analogues in two very important respects. It does not set itself off in metrical form from the rest of The Squire's Tale but continues in the pentameter couplets standard in the majority of *The Canterbury Tales*. The lament furthermore combines the functions of narrative and complaint. To some extent the narrative elements determine the form. Only in a single forty-line passage, where the narrative is recounting the critical moment—the moment when the falcon granted the tercelet her love and he expressed his gratitude—does the idiom reach full definition. What form there is emerges gradually, develops under the pressure of emotional intensity, and then tends to fade, recalled by occasional elements but not again fully coalescing.

The first words spoken by the falcon actually belie her despair. They come as she awakens from her swoon and responds to Canacee's sympathy, forming what one critic has called the exordium to the lament.[5] But they show a calmness, a logical control, surprising from one whose only previous utterance has been piteous shrieks:

> "That pitee renneth soone in gentil herte,
> Feelynge his similitude in peynes smerte,
> Is preved alday, as men may it see,
> As wel by werk as by auctoritee;
> For gentil herte kitheth gentillesse."

> (V.479-83)

175

Only in one respect do we have a foreshadowing of what is to come—in the concentration of the simile she chooses to illustrate one of her two reasons for confessing her "harm" (line 494), namely to forewarn others, "As by the whelp chasted is the leon" (line 491). Here the suffering of the innocent beast whose punishment will chasten the lion suggests the bitter pain her confession will entail. The simile, however, applies more accurately to the experience behind the complaint: the complaint is self-imposed; the agony she suffered was inflicted unjustly by another. These meanings will emerge, moreover, only for those with some previous knowledge of this lion-taming technique— beating a dog in the lion's presence.

The narrative and the lament begin in the same line, "Ther I was bred—allas, that ilke day!" (line 499). We get in this juxtaposition a first example of the effort throughout the lament to see the whole experience, and in a sense all of experience, at once. Over her birth and breeding the falcon wants us to see the shadow of the future. Her young untroubled life finds expression in the reinforced negative, "I nyste nat what was adversitee" (line 502). The narrative continues in the single line "Tho dwelte a tercelet me faste by" (line 504). Immediately there are five lines on the perfidy underlying his gentle behavior, five lines with four repetitions of "under" (lines 505-09), followed by the multi-leveled figure "So depe in greyn he dyed his coloures" (line 511). The image suggests the painting of a surface, cosmetics, and rhetoric, but it refers explicitly to a process in the wool industry by which wool is colored so that it will not fade. Both the positives and the negatives are strongly expressed, for the falcon cannot believe herself to have been easily deceived.

Meanwhile, the story and the complaint have progressed hand in hand. We know that the tercelet has become the falcon's suitor and done all the things expected of him to win the love of his lady. We also know her cause of complaint: the treason, the falseness, the feigning that lay under the gentle surfaces of courtship. It brings to her mind the image of a serpent lurking under flowers for the opportunity to bite, and she calls him "this god of loves ypocryte" (line 514) as she remembers all the proper ways he sought to woo her.

The next forty lines (lines 518-57) present the heart of the complaint with no grammatical break.[6] Beginning and ending with striking biblical images, they recount the moment when the falcon granted the tercelet her love and he kneeled before her in gratitude. These lines not only include the entire affair—her concern for honor and reputation, the wholeheartedness of her love, his passion for her, her joy in his professions of love, the depth of what she has found to be his perfidy, and the way his duplicity has colored her memories of the whole relationship—but these forty lines go back through all history to the first man as the falcon searches for anything remotely parallel to the bitterness of her experience.

The images at beginning and end derive from the Gospels. The first comes from Christ's denunciation of the scribes and Pharisees, "hypocrites! for ye are like unto whited sepulchres, which indeed appear beautiful outward, but are within full of dead men's bones and of all uncleanness" (Matthew 23.27):

> "As in a toumbe is al the faire above,
> And under is the corps, swich as ye woot,
> Swich was this ypocrite, bothe coold and hoot.
> And in this wise he served his entente
> That, save the feend, noon wiste what he mente,
> Til he so longe hadde wopen and compleyned. . . ."
>
> (Lines 518-23)

The further repetition of "under" and the image of a serpent-hypocrite hiding in a flower bed, which precede the forty lines, give way to the more powerful figure of a beautiful tomb with a corpse rotting beneath it. As an introduction to the moment of greatest fulfillment, this picture casts a shadow over the forty lines and the rest of the lament. Especially strong are the falcon's ironic fear for her lover's death (line 527), the way death twists

177

her heart at anything troubling him (line 566), and "the peyne of deeth" she suffers at his impending departure (line 582). The images of the tomb and the hot and cold lover who is in essence a corpse express her disgust, the revulsion that now fills her senses at the very thought of his love.

Two lines in the center of the forty-line section epitomize the falcon's sense of how she has been deluded: "But sooth is seyd, goon sithen many a day, / 'A trewe wight and a theef thenken nat oon'" (lines 536-37). The proverbial expression gives a respite from the tangled complexity of personal story, emotional commitment, and mankind's history present in the thirty-eight surrounding lines and indeed in the whole complaint. At the same time the proverb presents a vision that holds for all times and all spaces, a vision of the distance between the thought processes of good and evil. It relates to the images on either side: the fiend that alone knew what the tercelet meant (line 522) and the fiend that by implication the tercelet became, for lack of any human figure with whom to compare him in the whole history of God's creation (lines 538-57). This identification with the devil, suggested as early as the hidden-serpent image (line 512), becomes finally explicit in the return to proverbial wisdom just before the falcon's account of her betrayal: "'Therfore bihoveth hire a ful long spoon / That shal ete with a feend,' thus herde I seye" (lines 602-03).

At the end of the forty lines, as she searches history for a parallel and dismisses Jason, Paris, and Lameth, the falcon finds in a second gospel reference the ultimate metaphor for what she has experienced:

> "Ne nevere, syn the firste man was born,
> Ne koude man, by twenty thousand part,
> Countrefete the sophymes of his art,
> Ne were worthy unbokelen his galoche,
> Ther doubleness or feynyng sholde approche,
> Ne so koude thonke a wight as he dide me!"

> (Lines 552-57)

Behind this powerful obliquity is John the Baptist's expression of his own unworthiness as compared to Him for whom John is harbinger (present in all four Gospels): "I indeed baptize you with water, but one mightier than I cometh, the latchet of whose shoes I am not worthy to unloose" (Luke 3.16; cf. Matthew 3.11, Mark 1.7, John 1.27). The allusion to John's statement concludes a series of seven negatives with an epitome of negativity. The phrase "Ne were worthy unbokelen" points to the worthiness of the Son of God, but the idea is reversed in the next line to a measure of infamy.

The syntax of the forty-line section is worth noting. Three coordinating conjunctions link the tomb image at the beginning (line 521) and the thief image in the middle (lines 536, 538) to the rest of the passage. Most of the other coordinating conjunctions are set deep within the subordinations that dominate the forty lines. The first movement goes as follows:

> "And in this wise he served . . .
> That, . . . noon wiste . . .
> Til he so longe . . .
> . . . .
> Til that myn herte, . . .
> . . . .
> Graunted . . . , upon this condicioun,
> That everemoore myn honour and renoun
> Were saved, bothe privee and apert;
> This is to seyn, that after his desert,
> I yaf hym al myn herte and al my thoght—
> God woot and he, that ootherwise noght—
> And took his herte in chaunge of myn for ay."
> (Lines 521-23, 525, 529-35)

The strength of the meaning reveals itself in the position of the parenthetical and strikingly elliptical "God woot and he, that ootherwise noght." The "ootherwise" means that none of this would have happened if he had not agreed to her condition stated four lines earlier. The second movement starts out with the kind of *whan*-clause that opens *The Canterbury Tales*. "Saugh" (line 538) is the only main verb in the "whan" section, and the "anon" conclusion has only the single verb "fil" (line 544). All the rest is subordinate in a *that*-clause dependent itself on a series of four adverbial "so"s that modify, in turn, two adjectives in adverbial phrases, a preposition introducing an adverbial phrase, and a past participle.

Subordination is of the essence for the meaning of this complaint. Nothing in the falcon's experience is simple or what it originally seemed to be. References to doubleness (lines 543, 556), feigning (lines 510, 524, 556), and seeming (lines 505, 547) repeat themselves through the passage and are reinforced by verbs such as "wrapped" (line 507), "dyed" (line 511), "hit" (line 512), "kepeth in semblaunt" (line 516), and "countrefete" (line 554); by nouns such as "treson" (line 506), "ypocryte (-crite)" (lines 514, 520), "malice" (line 526), and "sophymes" (line 554); and by the oft-repeated preposition "under." The falcon's memories of her love affair have become an obsession that dominates her consciousness and brings everything she knows, her whole experience of life and death, into a subordinate relationship.

The complaint continues after its forty-line nexus with a sixteen-line section based on the lovers' time of happiness:

> "His manere was an hevene for to see
> Til any womman, were she never so wys,
> So peynted he and kembde at point-devys
> As wel his wordes as his contenaunce."

(Lines 558-61)

The image recalls the "coloures" of the wool dyed in grain, but this time the primary level of meaning after the more general "peynted" becomes cosmetic, with the combing "at point-devys" a daring extension of the metaphor for what the tercelet does with words. The sixteen lines include the image of death twisting the falcon's heart at the slightest sign of anything causing her lover "smerte" (lines 564-66); the line "Kepynge the boundes of my worshipe evere" (line 571) recalls the "oothcrwise nought" and, along with the word "reson" (line 570), represents the only sign of a limit of the extent to which she will make her will the "instrument" of his (line 568). The falcon ends this section with the certainty that in the future she will never love anyone as she did the tercelet.

She no longer has to put so much emphasis on his perfidy to convey the whole experience. The images of painting and combing and the implication of the word "demed" when she speaks of the truth in his heart (line 563) are sufficient. The subordinations drop off in importance as well. There are, in fact, four main clauses connected by the conjunctions "and" (lines 562, 567) and "ne" (line 572). Only in the second of these clauses (lines 562-66) do we find the kind of subordination present in the forty lines. Here the main clause, intensified by "so," has a subordinate *that*-clause, which moves into a condition modified by a concessive clause and then by another condition. The final line with the delayed main verb of the *that*-clause produces two further subordinations: "Me thoughte I felte deeth myn herte twiste" (line 566).

The next section of the complaint (lines 574-620) deals with the separation of the lovers, caused as in The Franklin's Tale by the knightly obligations of the man. His "honour" (line 592) compels what she expects to be a temporary "twynn[ing]" (line 577). The verb suggests how close she had felt their association to be, an association that had lasted, we learn in the first line, more than two years. The mutual sorrow each shows at parting receives the constant commentary of her present knowledge. She "supposed" (line 575), "wende" (line 585), "thoughte" (line 588) only good of him. She finally comes to the actual parting: "I knowe what is the peyne of deeth therby; / Swich harm I felte for he ne myghte bileve" (lines 582-83). She tries to hide her sorrow from him and make the best of it; her last words to him are, "Lo, I am youres al; / Beth swich as I to yow have been and shal" (lines 597-98). Do her final words and the death image she uses to convey her grief at what was supposed to be a short separation contain a premonition of his later conduct? Did she sense at the end of those more than two years, however subliminally, that he did not fully return her love?

Her treatment of his parting words is symptomatic of what is happening in this whole passage:

> "What he answerde, it nedeth noght reherce;
> Who kan sey bet than he, who kan do werse?
> Whan he hath al wel seyd, thanne hath he doon."
>
> (Lines 599-601)

The emotions of the lament have given way in part to the stark facts of the narrative. Form corresponding once again to meaning, connections are more distant. Occasionally we get subordinations (lines 584-87, 588-94, 610-20), but the verbs are for the most part independent (twenty-seven verbs in forty-seven lines), and the sentences are sometimes paratactically connected, occasionally by the connective adverbs "so" (lines 584, 604), "therfore" (line 602), and "thus" (line 603).

Toward the end of the complaint lament reestablishes itself in proverbial sayings that relate to a series of previous passages and prepare for a final, striking simile. The connections are to some extent tangential, but they reflect the kind of richness and indirection present in the imagery of death and colors. The series includes the serpent hiding under the flowers (line 512); the falcon's sense that only the fiend could know what her lover meant (line 522); the saying "A trewe wight and a theef thenken nat oon" (line 537, the mid-point of the forty lines); the proverb about needing a long spoon to eat with the devil (lines 602-03); and the text the falcon thinks her lover had in mind when he arrived at his destination: "That 'alle thyng, repeirynge to his kynde, / Gladeth hymself'; thus seyn men, as I gesse" (lines 608-09). The sense of something different in kind from her own

182

fidelity, with which she has been in close contact at her peril, unites these passages. But here a significant change occurs in the complaint. The emphasis in the final proverbial saying on "men" and "kynde" in lines 608-09 prepares for the transitional line to the caged-bird simile: "Men loven of propre kynde newefangelnesse" (line 610). The falcon uses male humans who are like caged birds to probe the character of her tercelet lover.[7] In doing so, she subtly moderates the difference she sees between his conduct and her own fidelity. What she had previously presented as a snakelike, deadly, fiendish betrayal she now sees as different in kind from her behavior but natural for male creatures:

> "So newefangel been they of hire mete,
> And loven novelries of propre kynde,
> No gentillesse of blood ne may hem bynde."

(Lines 618-20)

This saying and the caged-bird simile prepare for the surprising conclusion the narrator plans for this strand of his interlaced romance:

> How that this faucon gat hire love ageyn
> Repentant, as the storie telleth us,
> By mediacion of Cambalus. . . .

(Lines 654-56)

A short nine-line passage brings the falcon's narrative and complaint to an end (lines 621-29). In a sense, the values have been reversed. The narrative records the tercelet's sudden love for the kite. But first, in a concessive clause, the falcon remembers the tercelet's good qualities, this time without derogation. The whole experience is again present. The falcon's passion has largely spent itself. After a single line (627) condemning the tercelet's action as false, she expresses her despair: "Thus hath the kyte my love in hire servyse, / And I am lorn withouten

183

remedie!" (lines 628-29). Then she swoons.

The falcon's complaint stands out as *sui generis* in The Squire's Tale, in *The Canterbury Tales*, and in Chaucer's work as a whole. It follows closely upon the narrator's reflections on how important it is to come to the point—the knot of a tale—before the audience's attention wanders. Just as the reflections collapse in the resolution to "condescende" to the knot by making an end of Canacee's early morning walk (lines 407-08), so does the complaint add complexity and another loose end to a tale that to this point has done nothing in the way of resolution or even development. The love affair of falcon and tercelet is, furthermore, a loose end that adds to the disparity of moods already present in the tale.

Within the complaint itself similar disparities occur. The emotional and formal climax in the forty-line passage without syntactical break comes early in the complaint. Even with the proem included, what follows the central passage is twice as long as what precedes it. The end marks a sudden shift in feeling, as the falcon imagines the tercelet's state of mind when on his flight away from her he reached his destination. This conclusion occupies the final twenty-four lines and finds expression mainly in subtle modulations of imagery and language.

Everything in the complaint as well as in its context suggests improvisation. The situation of the falcon, derived as it is from the *Anelida*, absorbed Chaucer's creative energies as he imagined her response to her lover's betrayal. The forty-line passage, with its special syntactical structures, with its images at beginning, middle, and end, and with its range of experience and history, does not derive from any model, nor does it serve as one, not even for the rest of the complaint. It developed as Chaucer sought to express the falcon's intensity of feeling about what she had seen for more than two years as perfect fulfillment and what she now sees as total deception. The structure is subtle enough and sufficiently asymmetrical to escape calling attention to itself. The tomb image, for instance, finds echoes in three other passages, and the thief proverb in the middle is one of a series that includes the serpent-hypocrite under the flowers. But the image of John's humility preaching in the wilderness, unworthy as he claims to unbuckle the "galoche" of Him who is to come, this image has an implicit value but no referents. We continue to hear of death from the falcon and even of concealing colors. But the redemptive power of love remains outside the complaint in the Squire's brief mention of what is to follow, especially in the single word "repentant" (line 655).[8] The falcon's emotional change is tied, rather, to the words "kynde," "newefangel," and "novelries," to the influence of the male nature on conduct, and to the lengthy image of the caged bird.[9] The falcon experiences an emotional purgation through the expression of her suffering, emerging somewhat purified because she has indulged in her bitterness. What she calls at the beginning a confession starts out with a fierce animus against her lover and ends with the recognition that her despair at his sudden fall from grace cannot be assuaged by remembering him as a base deceiver. She thus goes beyond what Mars and Anelida effected in their complaints. She experiences not only the purgation of having expressed her plight but a change in her attitude. She demonstrates that the greatest value in the genre, as the introductory stanza of the Mars suggests, lies not in "redresse," but in declaring "ground of hevynesse" (lines 162-63).

The narrative and the lament conflate. They include at each point the whole story and in the forty-line passage all the falcon's knowledge of history as well. They employ a series of images, to the final one of the caged bird, interrelated, intense, and oblique. To a considerable extent they reflect in the syntax the developing state of mind of the speaker. In the last twenty-four lines they show a change that has been brought about by the complaint itself, by the very articulation of what had originally been mere cries of woe encouraged by the "gentillesse" of the sympathetic listener Canacee.

NOTES

[1]For the relationship with Anel, see Skeat 1:534, n. to Anel 105, and 5:384, n. to SqT F.548. David sees the falcon as a "more believably human character than Anelida," displaying a "moral and sententious streak." He emphasizes the humor that results from turning Anelida and Arcite into birds, noting that Chaucer is an innovator, the direction of his poetry "determined within and not by the accident of his reading" ("Recycling," pp. 109-15). The relationship of the Mars to the falcon's complaint is to be seen through Anel. Mars's complaint is actually reported by a bird and comes at the end of a narrative poem. It also has the expression "Seint John to borowe" (Mars 9; see SqT V.596). For a discussion of Mars's complaint, see Owen, "Problem," pp. 434-35.

[2]As Pearsall argues, "It is hard to see how Chaucer could have returned to the world of the first part of the Tale after this." He finds the falcon's lament "an effective combination of tenderness and bitterness, which at one or two points . . . strikes as keenly to the heart as the tale of another departure and betrayal in *Troilus and Criseyde*" (*CT*, p. 142). For a different view of the falcon, see Göller.

[3]The relationship between rime royal and the Mars stanza is an interesting one. In rime royal the quickening of rhyme in the two couplets at the end is balanced by the three b-rhymes in the middle. The stanza is unobtrusive and versatile. The Mars stanza, by its doubling of the a-rhymes, strengthens the beginning. Now there are four a-rhymes, three b-rhymes, and two c-rhymes, and three couplets at the end instead of the two in rime royal. Just as the completed alternating quatrain modulates to the two couplets in rime royal, the two tercets in the Mars stanza modulate to three couplets. The four and four have in a sense been replaced by the six and six. For a fuller discussion of rime royal, see Owen, "Rymyng," pp. 543-54.

[4]The Anel stanza substitutes for the final couplet of the Mars stanza a return to the a- and b-rhymes: aabaabbab. The effect is of a stanza with interlaced rhymes that turns back on itself rather than settling for three couplets at the end. A nine-line stanza with only two rhymes puts emphasis on technique, on rhymes for their own sake. For a full discussion of metrical form in the complaint of Anelida, see Owen, "Rymyng," pp. 536-38.

THE FALCON'S COMPLAINT IN THE SQUIRE'S TALE

[5]Berger, though he speaks of the "flatulence and redundance of the falcon's lament," is the one critic who has commented on its rhetoric: "Taken by itself, the lament is a finely structured piece of rhetoric complete with exordium (478-94). The courtly matter is introduced and concluded by brief sorties into birdland (499-504, 611-29). The conclusion is approached by a turn in which birds supply the comparison to men: 'Men loven of propre kynde newefangelnesse / As briddes doon that men in cages fede' (610-11)" (p. 92).

[6]Modern punctuation obscures the grammatical continuity of the forty lines. *The Riverside Chaucer* has periods at the end of lines 520, 535, and 537, wherever the absence of subordination permits (p. 175). Other modern editions do the same (see Robinson, Donaldson, Baugh, and Fisher). They all break the following sixteen-line passage at lines 561, 566, and 571. Skeat has a period at line 522 before the first "til" rather than at line 520, where "and" is reinforced by "in this wise." Blake not only has periods where the others do but indents at line 538, where Hengwrt has a paraph (Hengwrt also has paraphs at lines 499 and 574).

[7]The caged-bird image comes to Chaucer originally from Boethius and the *Roman de la Rose*. In addition to Chaucer's translation of the image in Bo, he composed two poetic versions, in MancT and SqT. According to Göller, the falcon treats her lover like a caged bird. Peterson argues that the Squire blunders in reversing the value of the luxuries of the cage and the natural life in the woods as presented originally in Boethius. See also Haller, "SqT."

[8]"Repentant" receives metrical emphasis in a run-on with caesura.

[9]The caged-bird simile provides important evidence for the dating of SqT, which modern critics insist on ignoring. The "milk"/"silk" rhyme in the SqT version (lines 613-14) derives from the cat image in MancT (lines 175-82), the second of the three similes that show the impossibility of "destreyning" natural impulse. What accounts for its presence in SqT is its association in MancT with the caged-bird image, and not any likelihood that men would see milk as tempting food for a bird. This association was pointed out by Koeppel in 1892 (pp. 261-62) and referred to by Robinson (p. 764, n. to MancT, lines 163 ff.), where it is listed without mention of Koeppel as proposing a "chronological theory." Koeppel's point is fully set forth in Owen ("Development"), who also points out that the bird in SqT exemplifies men's "newefangelnesse" as if on the suggestion of MancT IX.187-95, esp. line 193. The

vivid line "Yet right anon as that his dore is uppe" (V.615), introducing the imagined escape of the bird (not in Boethius, Jean de Meun, or MancT, though perhaps based on Chaucer's mistranslation of Boethius's "arto saliens tecto") finds no echo in MancT as we might expect it to if MancT were the later work. That the two passages influenced each other can hardly be doubted, for we have in addition the repeated reference to worm-eating that is original to Chaucer. No reference to Koeppel's point appears in *The Riverside Chaucer* or in David's discussion of the date of SqT ("Recycling," p. 109). David speculates that SqT antedates the conception of CT—extremely unlikely if it is later than MancT.

ND PAVE IT AL OF SILVER AND OF GOLD": THE HUMANE ARTISTRY OF THE CANON'S YEOMAN'S TALE

David Raybin

Thirty years ago Charles Muscatine lifted The Canon's Yeoman's Tale from the obscure position to which most readers had relegated it. The traditional view held the tale to be an arcane and perhaps even autobiographical tract on alchemy.[1] In a tentative argument that has provided the forum for much that has been written since, Muscatine argued for the significance of "religious overtones" that lend a symbolic meaning to the text (*Chaucer*, p. 216). The heart of his idea is that when alchemists lose "al that evere they hadde" (line 876), their loss "is more than money and clothing and a fresh complexion. It is also, perhaps, the spiritual tradition that a community of men takes with it along the way, and that gives purpose and direction to the journey" (p. 221). Muscatine also suggested a relationship between this tale and The Second Nun's Tale that precedes it: "There is perhaps something more than coincidence in the contrast between St. Cecilia, unharmed in her bath of flames, conquering fire through faith, and the blackened, sweating believers in earth, whose fire blows up in their faces" (p. 216).

Although scholars have not abandoned the question of determining Chaucer's attitude towards alchemy,[2] Muscatine's general emphasis on spirituality and his casual reference to Cecile as "curiously anticipat[ing] the Yeoman's teaching" (p. 216) have dominated criticism of the tale for the past twenty years.[3] This change in approach has both illuminated important thematic questions that link the two tales and opened up The Canon's Yeoman's Tale to much-needed analysis. Too often, though, the analysis has been unidirectional, reading the moral vision projected in The Canon's Yeoman's Tale as the degraded inverse of the orthodox view that The Second Nun's Tale is seen to present. The Second Nun's Tale, such a view suggests, offers Chaucer's own ideal of the highest religious path, while The Canon's Yeoman's Tale illustrates a wayward variant from that path. Chaucer's central religious concern is the heavenly afterlife; he constructs an earthly digression such as that of The Canon's Yeoman's Tale precisely so that he may show it to be self-consuming and faulty.

I find this reading tautological—the earth-centered perspective Chaucer offers in The Canon's Yeoman's Tale is misguided because Chaucer is not earth-centered—and therefore I do not accept it. That Cecile's path in The Second Nun's Tale is straight and that the path explored in The Canon's Yeoman's Tale is earthbound and slippery are undeniable points. What may be questioned is the prevalent view that the moral vision presented in The Canon's Yeoman's Tale, indeed in *The Canterbury Tales* as a whole, privileges a strict path of orthodox observance. On the contrary, as I will argue in this essay, The Canon's Yeoman's Tale offers an exaltation of artistic striving—that is, human striving in its ultimate expression—that is founded in Chaucer's intense interest in life in *this* world. In the metaphor of the tale this striving becomes the philosopher's search for his elixir. Like Muscatine, I examine the tale for "the spiritual tradition that a community of men takes with it along the way." I depart from Muscatine in that I am not convinced that Chaucer's alchemists lose that communal spiritual tradition. Chaucer's interest in people, and not just saints, encompasses the philosophers of the *prima pars* and even the swindler of the *pars secunda* as the poet enunciates a spiritual view more tolerant and comprehensive than the single-mindedness on which The Second Nun's Tale seems to focus.[4]

This reading is grounded in the tale's structure. As I will show, the Canon's Yeoman's Prologue displays a formal and thematic presentation that is identical to that in the Canon's Yeoman's episode (prologue and tale) seen as a unit. The prologue thus provides a clear model of how the tale's four parts join to create a coherent whole. The first part of The Canon's Yeoman's Tale glorifies distinctively human paths, in all their wandering, variety, and multiplicity. The principal characters in the *prima pars* believe in their capacity to achieve a kind of transcendent goal—the transmutation of baser metals into gold—and they devote their lives to the pursuit of that ultimate success. The tale's second part, with its intense look at a more sordid aspect of human nature, modifies this vision to offer a grim picture of what our lives might be like were we to deny the capacity of the human mind (as represented by the alchemist-artist) to reach beyond the shallow boundaries of mundane existence. The tale's conclusion meditates upon the dichotomous world views of the *prima pars* and *pars secunda*. It exalts the worldly, and therein inherently limited, accomplishment of the alchemist even as it suggests how we others must act if we are to follow the artist's lead and make good use of our time-bound and earth-bound existence.

PROLOGUE

Like many of the prologues in *The Canterbury Tales*, the prologue to The Canon's Yeoman's Tale offers clues as to how the tale proper is to be read. Its four-part structure—introduction, praise of canon, condemnation of canon, summarizing conclusion—matches that of the tale. The prologue opens with a verse paragraph (VIII.554-92) that plays an introductory and transitional role in its immediate context equivalent to that which the prologue itself fills in the larger context of the tale. Through its directly asserted contrast to what has just happened in The Second Nun's Tale, the passage suggests the complementary relationship of the adjacent tales. "The lyf of Seinte Cecile," both the spiritual story of her life and that ephemeral, otherworldly life itself, has been "ended" (line 554). St. Cecile had been so far removed from the life of this world that she did not perspire during her twenty-four hours in a cauldron: "She sat al coold and feelede no wo. / It made hire nat a drope for to sweete" (lines 521-22). Now she is dead. The titular characters of the Yeoman's tale are not only alive but distinctly of this world. Their horses and they themselves are imbued with a sweat that becomes a mark of their physicality. Nor is this fact presented as in any way distasteful: as the general narrator insists and as the vigor of the description confirms, "it was joye for to seen hym swete!" (line 579). When we find in The Second Nun's Tale such concepts as "good cheere" (line 304), "blisse above" (line 281), and especially "joye" (lines 161, 189), they refer not to this world but to translation into the next. The Canon's Yeoman's Tale neither denies nor confirms the heavenly pleasures that the previous tale has asserted, but instead proposes a complementary and joyously world-centered fascination of its own.

As the prologue progresses (lines 593-626) we learn more precisely whence these earthly joys arise. Prefiguring the tantalizing presentation of scientists at work in the *prima pars*, the Yeoman remarks of his master, "Ye wolde wondre how wel and craftily / He koude werke, and that in sondry wise" (lines 603-04), cautions us that "He is a man of heigh discrecioun; / I warne yow wel, he is a passyng man" (lines 613-14), and then advances to his boldest assertion of all:

"AND PAVE IT AL OF SILVER AND OF GOLD"

"I seye, my lord kan swich subtilitee—

. . . .

That al this ground on which we been ridyng,
Til that we come to Caunterbury toun,
He koude al clene turnen up-so-doun,
And pave it al of silver and of gold."

(Lines 620, 623-26)

On a literal level these lines are of course untrue. The philosopher has been unsuccessful in his search for the "elixer" (line
863), the possession of which would permit the construction of a
precious pavement. But in a figurative way the lines describe
exactly what the Yeoman's master accomplishes, and indeed
what the *prima pars* will do as poetry. Turning the world and
values of The Second Nun's Tale upside-down, the Canon creates for himself and his co-workers, and Chaucer will create for
us, the vision of a pavement "al of silver and of gold," of an in-
credibly beautiful and even lyrical human environment founded
on the earthy matter of alchemy, the most mysterious of the arts.
As the prologue ends, the Yeoman imagines himself to be asking
vainly for the power "To tellen al that longeth to that art!" (line
716). To a large extent the *prima pars* will demonstrate just such
a power, becoming in itself a metaphorical examination of the
artistic process. The creations of artists do not in fact transcend
the real, but at their best they permit us momentarily to believe
that they have done so. As he is presented in the second section of
the prologue and throughout the *prima pars*, the Yeoman's Canon
can be likened to a consummate human artist—a failure in divine
terms, to be sure, but not for that without merit. He lives in the
knowledge, however false, that in the future he will succeed in
creating something new, transcendent, beyond the more commonly human: gold. We may read the *prima pars* for its vision
of the artist at work, casting for eternal truths among the solid
and intransient matter of the world.[5]

Brought sharply back to pragmatic concerns by the Host,
who asks about the mundane necessities of dress and housing,

the Yeoman in the next section of the prologue (lines 627-83) abandons artistic/scientific processes to explore the sordid practicalities of the alchemist's life. In a series of confessions that parallel the exposé of deceit in the *pars secunda*, the Yeoman offers first the bold philosophical statement that "whan a man hath overgreet a wit, / Ful oft hym happeth to mysusen it" (lines 648-49) and then hints at the types of misuse that can follow when the artist gropes for a conclusion beyond human competence. The *pars secunda* will focus on the limitations of the mortal frame, on the day-to-day actuality of the human struggle among the temptations and treacheries of practical life. The central theme of the *prima pars*, the illusory power of art, will receive only secondary attention in this section. The Canon as he is here presented in the third section of the prologue appears not as an alchemist, an artist, but like the canon of the *pars secunda* as a trickster, a con-artist. As the *pars secunda* develops, we will learn of the consequences when one abandons the search for artistic transcendence, leaving the tools of the alchemist's creation to the machinations of a figure part human and part devil. The text will explore what remains to those who abuse artistic power, the power to create and to believe in the sublimity of one's creations; the second canon, perverting this power, relies not on wisdom but on cunning.

In the final section of the prologue (lines 684-719) the Canon slips away, fearful that "his pryvetee" (line 701)—the concrete and distasteful realities of his worldly life—will be exposed, that his carefully wrought creation will be analyzed and destroyed. The Yeoman curses his fleeing master, "Syn he is goon, the foule feend hym quelle!" (line 705); but then he suddenly philosophizes, focusing particularly on the relationship, often considered in *The Canterbury Tales*, between "game" and "ernest." The ensuing meditation matches the conclusion to The Canon's Yeoman's Tale (lines 1388-1481). In each meditation the concrete details of the preceding sections fade into the background as the major themes of those sections come into focus:

"He that me broghte first unto that game,
Er that he dye, sorwe have he and shame!
For it is ernest to me, by my feith;
That feele I wel, what so any man seith.
And yet, for al my smert and al my grief,
For al my sorwe, labour, and meschief,
I koude nevere leve it in no wise.
Now wolde God my wit myghte suffise
To tellen al that longeth to that art!
But nathelees yow wol I tellen part.
Syn that my lord is goon, I wol nat spare;
Swich thyng as that I knowe, I wol declare."

(Lines 708-19)

Here, in tentative outline, the Canon's Yeoman explores the fundamental connections between art ("that game") of which one may speak only with God's assistance, and life ("al my smert and al my grief, / . . . al my sorwe, labour, and meschief") of which even a person unaccommodated by poetic vision may "tellen part."

PRIMA PARS

Toward the close of the *prima pars* a pot filled with metals explodes, its contents scattering violently to pierce through walls, sink into the ground, and even leap to the ceiling. Those observing the scene react in a variety of ways:

Somme seyde it was long on the fir makyng;
Somme seyde nay, it was on the blowyng—

. . . .
"Straw!" quod the thridde, "ye been lewed and nyce.
It was nat tempred as it oghte be."
"Nay," quod the fourthe, "stynt and herkne me.
By cause oure fir ne was nat maad of beech,
That is the cause and oother noon, so thee'ch!"

(Lines 922-23, 925-29)

The conflict seems finally to be resolved by the Canon's summary explanation, "I am right siker that the pot was crased" (line 934), only to resurface some twenty lines later, as "Another seyde the fir was over-hoot" (line 955). The narrator, caught up in his own confusion and fears, is reduced to proclaiming a doctrine of human inadequacy and contradiction that in its imagery and word-play equates alchemists with their alchemy:

> But, be it hoot or coold, I dar seye this,
> That we concluden everemoore amys.
> We faille of that which that we wolden have,
> And in oure madnesse everemoore we rave.
> And whan we been togidres everichoon,
> Every man semeth a Salomon.
>
> (Lines 956-61)

Our logical conclusions, like our scientific experiments, are inadequate, leading inevitably to failure. Our speech is no more than madness, our seeming wisdom as illusory as the alchemist's false gold:

> But al thyng which that shineth as the gold
> Nis nat gold, as that I have herd told;
> Ne every appul that is fair at eye
> Ne is nat good, what so men clappe or crye.
> Right so, lo, fareth it amonges us:
> He that semeth the wiseste, by Jhesus,
> Is moost fool, whan it cometh to the preef;
> And he that semeth trewest is a theef.
>
> (Lines 962-69)

There are no human absolutes. Our truths are but covers for thievery. Or so the Yeoman, in his confusion, explains the alchemical calamity.

The narrator in the *prima pars* repeatedly asserts the futility, even the cursedness, of the alchemist's search, insisting that the Canon's science is a perversion of the ultimate wisdom at which a self-proclaimed "lewed man" (line 787) like the Yeoman can gaze only from afar. Yet his own fascination with the alchemical processes, paralleling that of the other observers, belies his fatalistic conclusions. His inability to break from his participatory role, to observe dispassionately the scientific activity, highlights the tremendous intellectual excitement of that activity and finally suggests the inadequacy of the Yeoman's subjective interpretation.[6]

Unlike the Yeoman, whose confused narrative shows him caught up in his own concerns and contradictions, the Chaucerian voice that underlies the tale does not condemn the philosophers who strive for something greater. Rather, it rejoices in them, pulling us into their world until we, now like the Yeoman, discover that we have become strangely one with those searching for a knowledge beyond their ken. We may note in particular the intense humanness associated with the different participants' inadequate responses to an intellectual and artistic achievement they do not fully understand. Even if they are none of them right, insofar as "Every man semeth a Salomon" they are all of them equal in their various opinions, and thus equal also with us. With their illusory wisdom, playfully mocked in the text, they seem (at least momentarily and to themselves) something more glorious than what they are. We go beyond a simple condemnation of Adam, Eve, and their progeny for eating of the fruit—for surely this is the significance of the Yeoman's reference to the fair apple that is not good (lines 964-65)—to an exploration and even enjoyment of what it is in the human condition that renders such eating both exciting and inevitable, what it is that makes us seek to transcend.

The *prima pars*, I am suggesting, is a story about artistry, a humane artistry that in refusing to accept the limitations of the mortal frame explores the ultimate limits of the beauty that can be created within that frame. To get at how this artistry works, one needs to consider briefly the extraordinary and unexpected lyricism that transforms lists of alchemical materials (what Muscatine blandly calls "a solid, unspiritual mass of 'realism'" [p. 219]) into what at least a few readers have found to be among the most compelling poetry in *The Canterbury Tales*. Jane Hilberry has recently explored "the appealing qualities of [the] alchemical language" of the *prima pars*, noting among many other instances

> the riming of five-syllable words, such as "citrinacioun" and "fermentacioun" . . . the shifting series of sounds in lines 806-08, from the liquid "l"s of "Unslekked lym, chalk, and gleyre of an ey" to the "s"s in "Poudres diverse, asshes, donge, pisse, and cley," to the crisp "k" and "t"s of "Cered pokkets, sal peter, vitriole" . . . [the frequent occurrence of] participles formed from verbs that describe technical processes [such that] the repetition of their common ending begins to sound throughout the verse: "enlutyng," "sublymyng," "amalgamyng," "calcenyng," "rubifiying," "enbibyng," "encorporyng," "cementyng"—all . . . within fifty lines of each other . . . [and] nouns ending with "-cio(u)n"—"proporcion," "ascencioun," "calcinacioun," "albificacioun," "citrinacioun," "fermentacioun"—[which] appear six times in sixty-three lines, and another three times in the Yeoman's reprise in lines 849-55. (P. 440)

The result is indeed, in Hilberry's phrase, "a highly wrought, quasi-musical language" (p. 440) that one would do well to read aloud. As in the later literary styles of Shakespeare and Dickens, the lyrical power is overwhelming.

The appeal of the language entices a reader into the tale's technical subject. As Hilberry puts it, the "equation between the content of the lines and their verse form suggests how technical language can be poetic, can in fact *become* poetry" (pp. 441-42). But what *is* the subject of this technical language? Beakers, chemicals, and chemical operations, certainly, and in extraordinarily great number and variety, but it is something more subtle, too. In his faulty "erthen pot[s]" (line 761; see also lines 791, 934) the Canon strives to sublimate gold and silver from the "bones," (line 759), "unslekked lym, chalk," "asshes, donge, pisse, and cley" (lines 806-07) that are the matter for his experimentation. With a success that is more obvious, Chaucer takes the same earthly, ultimately human, material and transforms it into the sustainable whole that is the world of *The Canterbury Tales*. The alchemist's and the poet's methods and goals are much the same. Both are caught up in the physicality and abundance of earthly, human things. Both mimic the divine creation of corporeal substance from chalk, earth, ash, and clay, and then go a step further to attempt the creation of a transcendent beauty from these elements and with them the bones, dung, "mannes heer," and piss that are not simply the dregs but are also the substance of the human body:

> Oure lampes brennyng bothe nyght and day,
> To brynge aboute oure purpos, if we may;
> Oure fourneys eek of calcinacioun,
> And of watres albificacioun;
> Unslekked lym, chalk, and gleyre of an ey,
> Poudres diverse, asshes, donge, pisse, and cley,
> Cered pokkets, sal peter, vitriole,
> And diverse fires maad of wode and cole;
> Sal tartre, alkaly, and sal preparat,
> And combust materes and coagulat;
> Cley maad with hors or mannes heer, and oille
> Of tartre, alum glas, berme, wort, and argoille,
> Resalgar, and oure materes enbibyng,
> And eek of oure materes encorporyng,
> And of oure silver citrinacioun,
> Oure cementyng and fermentacioun,
> Oure yngottes, testes, and many mo.

(Lines 802-18)

Both artists, alchemist and poet, draw their audiences into a fascination with the poetic wonders of a newly imagined world and hence, in a curious way, make yeomen of us all.

What is most important, then, about the philosophers' alternative explanations for the exploding pot is not simply that they are inadequate, for of course they are inadequate: these investigators try to make human sense of phenomena that transcend human comprehension. To achieve the creation of precious metal they would need heavenly assistance, as the tale's Boethian conclusion makes evident (lines 1467-71), and this they do not receive. What is significant here is that the responses are diverse, as numerous as the observers.[7] In *The Canterbury Tales* variety is a consistent indicator of the fallible, and thus human, presence. It exists in the multiple pilgrims of the General Prologue; in the conflicting and inadequately understood prayers and interpretations of The Knight's Tale; in the alternate concluding morals and questions of the Nun's Priest's, Manciple's, and Franklin's tales; in the parallel yet always different marriages, schemes, and cuckoldings of the fabliaux; in the seventeen tragic profiles of The Monk's Tale; in the contrasting paths and related spiritual messages of the four rime royal tales; in the variously inaccurate responses to superhuman phenomena in The Squire's Tale (as well as in The Canon's Yeoman's Tale); and, indeed, in the minutely described sins and mortifications that extend to the end of The Parson's Tale. Diversity, as measured by the insufficiency implicit in a multiplicity of responses to a single extraordinary event, lies at the heart of what The Canon's Yeoman's Tale (here representative of *The Canterbury Tales* as a whole) projects as characteristic of the human.

As interpreters of the failed experiment, the Canon of the *prima pars* and his fellow philosophers search for meaning in what they have encountered. They seek to find something other, and higher, than bones, dung, hair, piss, and clay—some explanatory spirit, some soul, some gold in the metaphor of the tale—that may come from those very elements of which they themselves are composed. What they do find, as we discover, are the symbols of their own humanity.

PARS SECUNDA

The *prima pars* is generally read as a pseudo-autobiography, an extension of the introduction of the Canon and Yeoman that begins in the prologue. Following Muscatine (*Chaucer*, p. 214; see also Herz, p. 233), Jackson J. Campbell, for example, remarks that "*Prima Pars* should really be considered part of the prologue, since the Yeoman begins no tale proper until line 972, and there is clear continuity between the personal revelations of the prologue and those of the *Prima Pars*" (p. 173). Along with this presumed psychological realism most readers note physical realism as well—in the depiction of the alchemists at work and in the lists of elements and equipment—which renders The Canon's Yeoman's Tale the most material of the Canterbury tales. As I have just argued, however, the presentation of the material world in the *prima pars* goes beyond the realistic to open an unusual door into the world of the creative imagination. In showing us the labors of the Canon and his co-workers, using the alchemists and alchemy as figures for artists and poetry, Chaucer shows us also how artists struggle to formulate from the materials of their trade—words, colors, sounds, metaphors, the sculptor's stone—something higher and more beautiful.

The *pars secunda* inverts this relationship of the immaterial to the material. Transforming the vigorous artistic wit of the *prima pars* into petty cleverness and cheap scheming, the *pars secunda* discloses, with no small degree of cynicism, how human intervention and ingenuity actually do cause things to become other than what they seem. As in the prologue, where the Yeoman's initial idealistic description of his master's powers is followed by disclosure of the grubby material realities of his and the Canon's life, so too the portrayal of dreamy-minded philosophers at work in the *prima pars* introduces the more sordid depiction of a master con-man hard at his work of material deception. From a text that explores art through a metaphor of materiality we move to a tale that refocuses the metaphor, as the second canon's gulling of a priest displays the alchemical arts employed for decidedly material purposes. Here, indeed, an alchemist is successful in transmuting his baser materials into gold, "fourty pound . . . / Of nobles fette" (lines 1364-65), to be precise.[8]

In one sense the leveling of art to life in the *pars secunda* produces a uniform baseness, the natural result when poetic vision is lost, when the metaphoric reality of the artist's gold-and-silver pavement is denied. The second canon's scam is presented in abundant and clear detail, with the Yeoman's repeated interruptions of his narrative emphasizing the cursedness that underlies a rather simple operation:

> And while he bisy was, this feendly wrecche,
> This false chanoun—the foule feend hym fecche!—
> Out of his bosom took a bechen cole. . . .
>
> (Lines 1158-60)[9]

When artistry is abused, when the truth-seeker enticed by his dreams has been replaced by the con-man enticing his mark, the more devilish instincts have free range. In the *pars secunda* of The Canon's Yeoman's Tale, as John Gardner puts it, "things get confusing for blear-eyed fallen man" ("Signs," p. 207).

The participants themselves, canon and priest, are developed vaguely, and the undefined quality of their characterizations implies unpleasantness. The priest enjoys, for example, a seemingly inappropriate relationship with the "wyf" with whom he dwells. Except as it indicates his shady character, it is irrelevant to the story that the priest is "so plesaunt and so servysable / Unto the wyf" (lines 1014-15). That the landlady is mentioned at all suggests indiscretion. The adjectives that offer more exact revelation of the priest's character—"sely" (line 1076), "unhappy" (line 1084), "sotted" (line 1341)—are uniformly contemptuous. What most clearly marks the priest is his desire to be something other than what his religious estate demands: his quick interest in the illicit manufacture of gold is the perverse extension of his involvement with his landlady.

The canon is more slippery and darker still: "he is heere and there; / He is so variaunt, he abit nowhere" (lines 1174-75). Is he the devil, as is suggested by his ability to

"AND PAVE IT AL OF SILVER AND OF GOLD"

infecte al a toun,
Thogh it as greet were as was Nynyvee,
Rome, Alisaundre, Troye, and othere three

(Lines 973-75)

or is he simply a human who is excessively devious and malevolent? Whether the repeated appellation of "feend[ly]" (lines 984, 1071, 1158, 1303) is meant as literal statement or as hyperbole (as suggested by the narrator's hope that "the foule feend hym fecche!" [line 1159]), the emphasis on the protagonist's wickedness is absolute and definitive.[10] What defines the priest is his foolish presumption that he has been chosen to receive easy, unlimited, and immoral gain; the canon, for his part, is identified by his single-minded excursion into fraud. Like the forty solid pounds of gold, the canon's sly machinations—described by the narrator in their smallest workings—are firmly rooted in tangible detail, even as his own character is elusive and shady. No dreams illuminate the *pars secunda*; one sees only deceit, ugliness, ignorance, and perversion. The idea of happiness is displayed in the priest's rejoicing in his good fortune, but this joy (none might be "gladder" than the priest [lines 1341-42]) is both illusory and misdirected. Much is distorted here, and nothing is straightforwardly positive.

The *prima pars* illustrates a shining splendor in the human aspiration to knowledge; the *pars secunda* displays in coarser terms the human inability to rise above the material, to move beyond original sin. Thus while there is a good deal in the imagery of the *pars secunda* to support Muscatine, who compares it to Dante's Hell (*Chaucer*, p. 221), or Glending Olson, who suggests that "Chaucer had the *Purgatorio* in mind, in some way, as he shaped Fragment VIII" ("Chaucer," p. 230), there is also reason for seeing in the misty movement of the *pars secunda* a commentary on human behavior in *this* world. While the slippery, earthy path of the *pars secunda* lacks a gold-and-silver pavement, its portrayal of the darker side of human nature nonetheless develops a dangerous interest of its own. The sting embodied by

203

the story line is what initially pulls in a reader's attention, as it plays skillfully on the common fascination with scheming and deception. What ultimately binds a reader, however, is not the mechanical working out of the scam; it is the harsher perception that all people partake in the twisted and contradictory motivations (only marginally more pronounced in canon and priest) that produce the scam and permit its success. Behind one's recognition of the sleazy cynicism of canon and priest lies the deeper understanding that those dark qualities are shared by all people, that all people will work to obtain the gold of their desires, that in the absence of higher goals we are all prone to obey our lowest instincts.

One is not "attracted," in the normal sense of the word, to the naturalistic portrayal of the canon's supreme and confident gall. Indeed, one of the most striking qualities of the *pars secunda* is that the different characters, the various settings, and even the narration itself are grossly repulsive. Nonetheless, as in the Pardoner's Prologue, the narrator's excessive emphasis on repulsion is itself compelling, and the story he tells is frighteningly believable. For example, the smooth hypocrisy in the canon's repeated references to God and Christ (lines 1046, 1064, 1122, 1327, 1361, 1372) becomes credible—and exemplary in its perversity—when the very ordinariness of the adopted tone allows the blasphemous remarks to slide past the priest's eager ears. In a sense, the narrator's careful instruction of his audience into the minute details of the canon's tools and methods (lines 1158-71, 1224-35, 1263-82, 1308-25) makes a reader complicit with the "falsnesse," "feendly[ness]," and "doublenesse" of this "roote of alle cursednesse" (lines 1300-04). To follow the intricacies of the canon's threefold temptation a reader must attend closely to the scam's operation. In a peculiar way, moreover, one's contempt for the priest's stupidity leads one to join in the laughter of the initiate when, for example, the canon's feigned pity draws his mark away from the perversely emphasized "crosselet" (carried by the unholy canon in "his bosom" [lines 1117-18]) so that the master may work his secret artifice:

"AND PAVE IT AL OF SILVER AND OF GOLD"

"Now lat me medle therwith but a while,
For of yow have I pitee, by Seint Gile!
Ye been right hoot; I se wel how ye swete.
Have heere a clooth, and wipe awey the wete."

(Lines 1184-87)

The casual allusions to "Seint Gile" (an obvious pun on "guile"),
to sweat (suggesting here the priest's loss of composure in contrast to the canon's own coolness), and to the ambiguous term for
the action, "medle" (denoting "interfere" as well as "stir" or "mix
in" [see Haskell, "Oath," p. 222]) reflect both the language of
common speech and the classic scheming of the superior intellect
that openly mocks its puny target. As one imagines the canon
aware of his cursedness and the priest blind to himself as he is to
his deceiver, the reader as observer becomes strangely allied with
the dominant, fiendish mind.

The description of the priest's delight in his good fortune is
constructed entirely of clichés:

Was nevere brid gladder agayn the day,
Ne nyghtyngale, in the sesoun of May,
Was nevere noon that luste bet to synge;
Ne lady lustier in carolynge,
Or for to speke of love and wommanhede,
Ne knyght in armes to doon an hardy dede,
To stonden in grace of his lady deere,
Than hadde this preest this soory craft to leere.

(Lines 1342-49)

The clichés denote a conventional response, but here the May-
time commonplaces are misplaced. The priest is not an adoles-
cent lover; his object is not romantic love but crass, material
gain. Nonetheless, one joins uncomfortably in the canon's cool
disdain for his easy mark. Like the pleasure of youthful love-
longing, the priest's joy seems momentarily all-consuming, is
centered in this world, and may ultimately lead to despair. No
sympathy is evinced by the inhuman, irrevocably fiendish canon,

205

but only a heart as closed as that devilish figure's would not feel some pity for the priest who has succumbed entirely to a misplaced joy.

The ambivalence underlying our response to the ugliness of the *pars secunda* relates closely to the Yeoman's own uncertain voice: the inconsistencies in his commentary and his apparent compulsion to condemn everything he associates with his alchemical experiences have encouraged many readers to explore the intricacies of his character. Noting that "here as elsewhere, Chaucer's focus is on human beings," Gardner comments on these contradictory motives in the Yeoman-narrator: "in renouncing his old way of life he renounces a foolish and hopeless pursuit, but he renounces, too, a man with whom he has much in common, and, at the same time, an aspect of himself" ("*Canon's*," p. 17). As readers of the *pars secunda* we are asked to note our own dark fascination with deceptive tricks wrought for gain, to divine from this depiction of dissipation a compelling illustration of the slippery path that might be any human life. Like the canon, we may err intentionally; like the priest, we may naively permit ourselves to be drawn into error; and like the Yeoman-narrator, we may misunderstand our experiences and responses and be drawn erringly into the stories we tell. In the *pars secunda* the unmitigated corruption of the nonbelieving alchemist's life surfaces as an emblem of the tendency to corruption that threatens each of our lives. When the creative artist is absent, and with him the entrancing beauty of the *prima pars*, what remains of our humanity is frighteningly dark.

MEDITATION

The closing ninety-four lines of The Canon's Yeoman's Tale have puzzled critics for many years. Judith Scherer Herz, in a typical reading, characterizes them as "set in so radically different a key from all the preceding that one doubts if the same character is speaking them" (p. 236).[11] The concluding meditation serves the tale well, however: it compresses into a short space the various moral and philosophical strands that compose The Canon's Yeoman's Tale, and thus, like the Prologue, it unifies the different parts of the narrative. The meditation reintroduces almost every theme suggested in the tale and relates these themes to a complex vision of the human spirit.

Let us recall first the strands, that is, some of the major themes that enter the narrative of The Canon's Yeoman's Tale and together constitute the common matter for scholars examining the tale. These themes include the diverse and dichotomous subjects of "debaat" that distinguish *prima pars* and *pars secunda*: art and the material, belief and cynicism, clarity and mistiness, exploration and concealment, expense and thrift, joyful game and sorrowful earnest, glorious failure and sordid success, light and darkness, material loss and gain, the human and the superhuman, the search for knowledge and the exploitation of ignorance, reduction and multiplication, science and its limits, spiritual gain and loss, transformation and solidity, truth and falsity, vision and blindness, and words and deeds. The depth and breadth of these divisions is astounding, but therein lies the significance of The Canon's Yeoman's Tale in the larger scheme of *The Canterbury Tales*; therein lies the all-encompassing nature of Chaucer's forgiving vision for a fallible humanity.

For what holds these many threads together, offering the tale its "purpose and direction," is the artist's struggle to overcome the innate disparity between the divine perfection of the gold for which we search and our own human limitations: "Bitwixe men and gold ther is debaat" (line 1389). The idea that such a gap may be bridged is central to the epilogue; it is the metaphoric equivalent to the alchemists' long-sought elixir. Like alchemists we try to understand this distance between our flawed selves and our golden goals and thus to close it, but our very humanity precludes the accomplishment of that endeavor. The narrator offers the truism that

> whoso maketh God his adversarie,
> As for to werken any thyng in contrarie
> Of his wil, certes, never shal he thryve. . . .
>
> (Lines 1476-78)

The real difficulty, however, lies in daring to imagine ourselves capable of so knowing God's will that we may always follow the chosen path. As the tale indicates, making powerful use of the second person, we

> been as boold as is Bayard the blynde,
> That blondreth forth and peril casteth noon.
> He is as boold to renne agayn a stoon
> As for to goon bisides in the weye.
> So faren ye that multiplie, I seye.
>
> (Lines 1413-17)

Just as all individuals have the capacity to multiply (figuratively in all our endeavors, literally according to the biblical injunction), so like Bayard we are blind and blunder. In The Knight's Tale Arcite complains that

> "We faren as he that dronke is as a mous.
> A dronke man woot wel he hath an hous,
> But he noot which the righte wey is thider,
> And to a dronke man the wey is slider.
> And certes, in this world so faren we. . . ."
>
> (I.1261-65)

The "slider" path is the typically human path, an earthly path at an opposite extreme from the kind of heavenly route trodden by St. Cecile. It is the path of the drunken Miller, whose tale transports the company and *The Canterbury Tales* from the Knight's idealism (so like that of the *prima pars*) to the fabliau world that informs also the *pars secunda*. Alchemy, we learn at the beginning of the *prima pars*, is a "slidynge science" (line 732). In the prologue the Yeoman suggests that

". . . that science is so fer us biforn,
We mowen nat, although we hadden it sworn,
It overtake, it slit awey so faste."

(Lines 680-82)

Occasionally we achieve some significant goal (running against a stone is in a peculiar way exactly what the alchemists were attempting); more often we are blocked or go off-track. In neither case do we know with certainty which has occurred.

True philosophers, the golden among us, the chosen of God, may have knowledge of eternal truths, but they "speken so mystily / In this craft that men kan nat come therby" (lines 1394-95). The line between the initiate and the ignorant is uncrossable. There is no possible transfer of knowledge. The divinely initiated, those who, tautologically, "th'entencioun and speche / Of philosophres understonde kan" (lines 1443-44), the Platos and Arnalduses of Villanova, may speak among themselves of the different names for the stone that symbolizes their knowledge, but they cannot break their hermeneutic circle: not only are "The philosophres sworn . . . everychoon / That they sholden discovere it unto noon" (lines 1464-65), but Christ himself "wol nat that it discovered bee" (line 1468). For the rest of us, the ensemble of humanity, even questioning signals limitation; to search is itself to demonstrate one's ignorance and incapacity: "Lat no man bisye hym this art for to seche, / . . . / And if he do, he is a lewed man" (lines 1442, 1445).

Is this a sad conclusion? Is it Chaucer's message in The Canon's Yeoman's Tale that we ought sorrowfully to accept, or passionately to complain, that

God of hevene

Ne wil nat that the philosophres nevene
How that a man shal come unto this stoon . . . ?

(Lines 1472-74)

Is Chaucer conceding that we ought not strive for perfection?

I think not. The narrator counsels us to "lete it goon" (line 1475), pragmatically to accept the Christian precept that to be human is not necessarily to be damned, that "God [will] sende every trewe man boote of his bale!" (line 1481). In his despair the Yeoman-narrator may have lacked the fortitude to continue in his profession, but that does not make the Canon-alchemist's answers entirely or unforgivably wrong. In Chaucer's world there is space for disagreement and debate, room for the whole variety of human responses. Although we may not be as saintly as Cecile, neither are we, as is St. Cecile, dead to the world. We cannot so transmute the heavenly as to live it here on earth, but as we work and read we may learn much from the humane artistry of those—failed alchemists though they may be—who know how best to "multiplie terme" (line 1479) of this our earthly life. We may with good reason admire that poet who "kan swich subtilitee" (line 620),

> "That al this ground on which we been ridyng,
> Til that we come to Caunterbury toun,
> He koude al clene turnen up-so-doun,
> And pave it al of silver and of gold."

(Lines 623-26)

NOTES

[1]Among early explorations of Chaucer's knowledge of or attitude towards alchemy are Damon, Aiken, and Baum.

[2]See Rosenberg, "Alchemist," and Grennen, "Mass," along with Schuler's examination of the Renaissance view of Chaucer as alchemist; Finkelstein's study of Chaucer's use of Arabic alchemical terminology; and Duncan's exploration of the literary sources for Chaucer's presentation of the alchemist.

[3]Grennen, "Wedding"; Rosenberg, "Tales"; Olmert, pp. 71-72; Whittock, pp. 252-53; Haskell, "Oath," pp. 225-26; Howard, pp. 304-05; David, *Strum-*

pet, p. 234; Kolve, "*SNT*," p. 139 (in part a dissent); Allen and Moritz, p. 144; Gardner, "Signs," pp. 201-07; Campbell, p. 178; G. Olson, "Chaucer"; Cooper, pp. 188-95; and Dean, pp. 749-52, are among those who note the various connections linking the moral messages of the two tales of Fragment VIII. The present reading treats SNT only marginally, joining those readers (esp. Harwood, Hilberry, and Lawler [pp. 125-46]) who have looked for CYT's own unity and artistry.

[4]Hamilton argues convincingly from historical evidence that a medieval audience would know that the Canon was patterned as "a Canon Regular of St. Augustine" (p. 103), "apostate from his Order" (p. 107). Such a turning away from the religious life for the freedom and seductive attractions of this world seems to me to be emblematic of the tale.

[5]The connection between the Canon and the creative artist has been suggested by Traversi, p. 208, and Hanning, who calls the tale "an audacious comparison of alchemy and his [Chaucer's] own art" ("Theme," p. 36).

[6]In interpreting the *prima pars*, perhaps the key question involves determining the extent to which the Yeoman's response is to be accepted at face value. Dramatic critics (see Baldwin, "Canons"; Campbell; Gardner, "*Canon's*"; Harrington; Reidy; and Ryan) typically search for ironies that undercut a narrator's argument (though R. Cook argues at some length for "a steady development in the Yeoman . . . which reveals him to be a morally attractive person whose reform is likely to be permanent" [p. 30]); but here even most nondramatic readers find reason to question the narrative voice. Pearsall notes that CYT, more than any other tale, is an "experiment by Chaucer in the art of the dramatic monologue, and one in which, initially at any rate, he was seeking to grant a greater degree of autonomy to the speaker" (*CT*, p. 105). Lawton argues similarly that this is the only one of CT regarding which one may appropriately "speak of [a] narratorial *persona*" (p. 103). C. David Benson, who calls the Yeoman's "dramatic voice nothing more . . . than a brilliant narrative device" ("*CT*," p. 99), grants the *prima pars* unique status as "the only explicitly autobiographical tale . . . in the entire *Canterbury Tales*" (p. 98).

[7]Dean's reading is somewhat the reverse of mine. He proposes that "while the alchemists may constitute a brotherhood of sorts, it scarcely represents a true fellowship. When the alchemical work fails miserably . . . the

DAVID RAYBIN

conventicle of scientists too explodes as everyone present offers a different explanation of what went wrong" (p. 750).

[8]The apparent inversion of the hierarchical relation of life and art ought not surprise; already the opening lines of CYPro have begun a careful preparation for it. The bursting of the Canon and his Yeoman upon the scene immediately breaks the framed narrative of the Canterbury pilgrimage, disrupting its tale-telling contest and ignoring the ostensibly religious object. The Canon's haste in overtaking the company is motivated not by the mixture of spiritual concern and delight in game stressed in GP but only by his desire "To riden in this myrie compaignye" (VIII.586), a somewhat lax purpose confirmed by the Yeoman's comment that his master "to ryden with yow is ful fayn / For his desport; he loveth daliaunce" (lines 591-92; see also lines 597-98), and then validated by the company's rapid acceptance of these late arrivals. Has Chaucer anticipated Cervantes in allowing ostensibly real life— in the form of an observer delighted by the antics of a set of literary characters—to violate the frame of his book? The presumably distinct realms of art and life, always problematic in *The Canterbury Tales*, have here been homogenized. See Dean for a similar suggestion that the "boundaries between fiction and life are blurred in the Canon's Yeoman's Tale" (p. 752).

[9]Among other such narrative interruptions emphasizing the scam's cursedness are lines 1188-89, 1224-27, 1258-60, 1271-75, and 1319-20.

[10]The canon's fiendishness is central to the critical discussions of Muscatine, *Chaucer*; Olmert; Rosenberg, "Alchemist"; and Traversi, among others. Dean, pp. 751-52, reads the hellish references with subtlety and insight.

[11]Muscatine, *Chaucer*, pp. 214-15, joins the prologue and *prima pars* but sets these lines apart as a separate section with its own narrative voice. Pearsall, portraying a Chaucer who "steps outside the Yeoman's character, and delivers . . . a verdict on the nature of alchemy," agrees (*CT*, p. 112). Harwood proclaims the lines "both detachable and detached" (p. 346). Harrington dissents, calling "the final section of the poem . . . a natural conclusion for the total narrative" (p. 96), but hardly supports the assertion, a strategy also adopted by Whittock, pp. 274-76. Grenberg reads backwards, interpreting the tale in terms of its Boethian ending rather than as it progresses. Most scholarly interpretations simply ignore the lines.

# MEMOIR OF CHAUCER'S INSTITUTE

C. David Benson

In 1987 I spent my summer vacation as the Director of an NEH-supported institute for college teachers entitled "Chaucer's Canterbury Tales: Medieval Contexts and Modern Responses." The following is an attempt to describe something of the effort and delight of those six weeks, both as a memorial of what we accomplished and in the hope that it may be of interest to those thinking of planning or attending other such institutes.

Howell Chickering of Amherst first convened a group of English medievalists from Massachusetts and Connecticut to talk about the possibility of holding a Chaucer Institute in New England. The working group also included Anthony Farnham and Carolyn Collette from Mount Holyoke College, Vincent DiMarco and Arlyn Diamond from the University of Massachusetts at Amherst, Rosemarie McGerr from Yale, and Charles Owen and myself from the University of Connecticut. Although I wrote the final grant with Chic Chickering and Charles Owen, everyone contributed to its ideas, proving that, as with the King James Bible, committees can sometimes produce good things.

We had much help throughout. The planning and running of the institute would have been impossible without the intelligence, generosity, and hard work of two University of Connecticut doctoral students, Jane Tolimieri and Steven Shelburne.

A central focus in designing the institute was our fear that the poetry of Geoffrey Chaucer was beginning to fall out of the standard American undergraduate curriculum. Many English majors are no longer required to take a course in Chaucer, even though he has traditionally been grouped with Shakespeare and Milton as one of the three great poets in our language. When Chaucer is taught at all, the emphasis tends to be on a few familiar works, often read in translation. Even for highly educated people, English literature seldom begins earlier than Shakespeare, and for many readers, who would enjoy him if given a chance, Chaucer is only a name.

Although Chaucer is the most accessible of medieval poets, the apparent difficulties of his language intimidate many college instructors into presenting him only in modern English. We thought that an institute might help to revivify the teaching of Chaucer by emphasizing the ease and delight of reading his poetry in the original. We also wanted to expose our participants (many of whom would come from small and remote colleges and would, thus, be limited in their contact with other medievalists) to a wide variety of current academic approaches to Chaucer. In a familiar paradox, while Chaucer is under threat in the classroom, Chaucer scholarship and criticism are flourishing. We hoped to close the gap between the two. We also wanted to show that individual Canterbury tales might make useful contributions to a number of different courses in which they are usually not included, from women's studies to narrative theory.

The work of the Chaucer Institute was divided into two main sessions. The first and more important part involved small discussion groups that met every weekday morning from 10:00 to 12:30. Our thirty participants were divided into three units of ten, each of which was led by one of our full-time faculty:

Charles Owen, Linda Georgianna of the University of California at Irvine, and myself. We changed leaders of the groups each week and, to the dismay of some, reconstituted the groups themselves after three weeks. Over the course of the institute we discussed all of *The Canterbury Tales*. The simultaneous reading of the same tale in all three sections united the participants. At the 11:00 coffee break a member from one group would often seek out a friend from another to discover what had been talked about, and the discussion after the break would sometimes begin, "In Group II, they say. . . ."

The Canterbury Tales are usually read in one of the several orders in which they appear in published editions, sequences that represent decisions by fifteenth-century scribes and modern scholars more than a definitive plan of Chaucer's. We thought we might see the tales afresh and discover new relationships if we considered them by genre, a practice followed by several recent critical books on Chaucer. Our introductory work was The Nun's Priest's Tale, whose witty variety of styles and narrative stances well represents the complex achievement of the collection as a whole. The second week we read romances: The Knight's Tale, Sir Thopas (and Melibee), The Squire's Tale, and The Franklin's Tale. The third week was given to the fabliaux: the tales of the Miller, Reeve, Cook, Shipman, and Merchant. The neglected religious tales occupied us during the next week: the poems assigned to the Clerk, Man of Law, Prioress, Second Nun, and Monk. Because the diversity of *The Canterbury Tales* resists neat division by genre, we called our fifth week "Three Portraits" and read the tales of the Pardoner (along with that of the Physician), the Wife of Bath, and the Canon's Yeoman. In our last week we got to those tales that did not fit elsewhere (the tales of the Manciple, Friar, Summoner, and Parson), and then we returned to a second reading of The Nun's Priest's Tale. Participants, faculty, and visitors all gave special praise to the discussion groups.

One reason for the success of the groups was Charles Owen's suggestion that we begin each session with a participant reading a brief passage from the tale of the day and then commenting on it for five to ten minutes. This simple device emphasized reading Chaucer aloud in Middle English, moved us immediately into the text, and made the participants the principal speakers. These opening statements did not control or conclude discussion but inspired new, often contradictory ideas from the others. Such cooperative work should be the ideal of any seminar and indeed of all intellectual discourse, but I had never before seen a group of academics work together so productively. The organizing principle of most conferences, which are the usual public forums for the exchange of scholarly ideas, is the individual self-assertion of written papers. Too often the result is a struggle between fixed positions rather than genuine exploration. At the Chaucer Institute I was continually amazed at the willingness of the participants to listen and to build on the insights of others. Again and again the groups produced results together that would have been impossible for any one of us to achieve individually. I soon discovered that my function as presider was not to lecture but to ask questions and to act as one of the group.

Because all the thirty participants had taught Chaucer before (sometimes for many years), they possessed an authority denied to even the brightest graduate student. The participants were not there just to be taught; they already knew. The work of the groups, therefore, was less instruction than a kind of deconstruction. Each of us already had a command of Chaucer and of Chaucer scholarship; what we wanted was a way of seeing the poet anew. In teaching, one inevitably begins to use certain paths to move through a work: favorite passages, comparisons, and ideas that bring the work under control and make it possible to present the poetry to students. The risk is that by so doing we tame the power of even the greatest works and make them dull. The Chaucer Institute forced us off well-worn paths into the complexity and challenge of the text itself. We asked questions and accepted uncertainties, trying to get beyond the familiar ideas we had brought with us. In contrast to other kinds of classroom work, there was no need for us to come to any final resolution. Each of us came with an interpretation of Chaucer, and each, after that interpretation had been put to the test of competing views and reexamined, would later be able to reconstruct a new and richer understanding for himself or herself. Once I adapted to this kind of open discussion, it was the most fun I have had in twenty years of teaching.

Three or four days a week we reassembled after lunch for the second part of the institute: talks or panels that presented a variety of contemporary scholarly approaches to Chaucer. All the original planners of the institute took part in these sessions: Vincent DiMarco spoke on medieval romance, Rosemarie McGerr on Chaucer's Retraction, and Chic Chickering, complete with funny ties, a puppet, and unpunctuated texts, on ways of teaching Chaucer. Carolyn Collette and Arlyn Diamond joined Linda Georgianna on a panel about recent critical theory, a subject whose attractions and dangers were a submerged but persistent issue throughout the institute. Our last talk, a magisterial survey of medieval ideas about language by Anthony Farnham, was a wonderful tonic for the exhaustion felt by everyone during the final week. As one of the participants said to me when it was over, "Imagine going to a talk to wake up!"

Our two principal visiting faculty members contributed much. Derek Pearsall of Harvard, who was with us for the first two weeks, spoke on a variety of central topics (from medieval iconography to the history of Chaucerian scholarship) and set a tone of intellectual and personal generosity that lasted throughout the six weeks. Pearsall also uttered the phrase that became the unofficial motto of the institute and best characterized our way of reading Chaucer: "the maximization of fun." Charles Muscatine came from the University of California at Berkeley to spend the fourth week with us, during which he challenged the religious reading of Chaucer's work and discussed the poet's style and comedy. Muscatine's obvious excitement at what we were doing was flattering to us all. Both Pearsall and Muscatine gave full days to the institute, from mornings in which they joined the small groups to a pair of memorable evenings during which each man proved that an eminent Chaucerian could also be a croquet shark.

We also had a number of distinguished one-day visitors: Larry Benson of Harvard, who explored the unexpected prudery of Chaucer's language; John Fleming of Princeton, who wittily defended moral interpretations of the poet; and Alan Gaylord of Dartmouth, who gave a virtuoso reading of The Miller's Tale. In addition to questions and discussion from the participants after these talks, there was also good humor, including a memorable recitation at the end of Derek Pearsall's stay from a newly discovered Hokum Manuscript (named for the institute dorm, Holcomb Hall) entitled "A Muddle English Valediction: Requiring Mourning."

During the afternoon lectures and panels we tried to offer a number of contrasting approaches to Chaucer without affixing the institute seal of approval on any one in particular. Even with six weeks, there was so little time to cover the many ways of interpreting Chaucer that all we could hope to do was introduce a range of possibilities that participants might want to follow up later. The one party line that was common during the institute was an admirable reluctance to employ the wooly concept that has infected Chaucer scholarship like crabgrass—irony. Irony came to be referred to as "the *i*-word," and its occasional use was greeted with the shock and embarrassment produced by any breach of good taste and decorum.

In addition to being a member of one of the morning discussion groups, each participant also belonged to a small bibliography group and a performance group. Each of the ten bibliography groups collaborated on an extensive annotated survey of recent criticism about one of the major tales, which was distributed before discussion of that tale. The performance groups also met on their own to practice reading aloud a tale of their choosing, which was then recorded at the campus radio station for later classroom use. During this time it was common to turn a corner of the campus in the late afternoon and find two or three participants under a tree or on a bench giving their all in performing a fabliau or religious tale. Although some of the participants were nervous at the beginning of the institute about reading Chaucer aloud, the daily recitation of passages in the discussion groups and the recordings brought out many unsuspected hams. Popular demand forced the group doing The Nun's Priest's Tale to give a general performance, at which we were delighted to discover that one of our most brilliant participants could convincingly impersonate the foolish Chaunticleer and one of our most saintly the devilish fox, Daun Russell.

Despite all these demanding activities, the participants kept asking for more. Although some complained with good reason that the official schedule made for too long a day, there were always a few (and frequently more) who would go over to the faculty club with the speaker of the afternoon and continue talking about Chaucer over a few beers, often until dinner time. Moreover, the participants themselves organized a series of evening sessions during which they read and discussed works in progress; some of these proved to be early versions of the essays appearing in this volume. The prize for overachievement among these extraordinarily hardworking people would have to go to the group that stayed up most of one night in the last week reading The Parson's Tale aloud. They claimed to enjoy it. On the badges provided for the participants by the office that coordinates conferences at the University of Connecticut, the title of our endeavor came out as "Chaucer's Institute." There were times when we fondly imagined that the poet might have been willing to accept the designation.

I had worried that Storrs, which is so rural that it does not even have a single store whose name is a pun, might be too sleepy a location for an institute. As it turned out, it was a perfect place because the group was forced to come together and entertain itself as I do not think would have happened at a larger, more diverse site. Nevertheless, our trips to libraries and museums in New Haven, New York, and Cambridge, where we were able to examine original medieval manuscripts and art, provided a welcome change of scene. The geniality of the group throughout the six weeks was remarkable. We seldom got on one another's nerves but became better friends as the weeks went on, a spirit that culminated in the emotion and pride of the farewell banquet.

The only bad part of the institute was the need to turn away so many good people. That we had one hundred completed applications for thirty places, and that, judging from their credentials, at least ninety of the hundred would have made excellent participants, suggests that others elsewhere should organize new Chaucer Institutes. The thirty teachers we chose, who, as it happened, were fifteen men and fifteen women from throughout the United States, including Hawaii and Puerto Rico, were an impressive group. Although many hard things are said about American higher education these days, and with some justification, it was inspiring to see the quality and dedication of our participants, who manage to keep alive a love of good literature in our far from hospitable society.

I am not sure that the institute came to any revolutionary new ways of understanding Chaucer (nor was that our intention); but reading the tales by genre revealed fresh relationships, reading all the tales made us appreciate some that are usually neglected, and reading the tales with one another made each of us look closely at certain passages previously ignored. Perhaps most important of all, the institute helped us to scrape off the rust of discouragement that teaching so often produces and reminded us what a privilege it is to spend one's life reading great poetry.

The work of the 1987 Chaucer Institute is not over. Many participants have told me that they are now writing and thinking about Chaucer as never before. In addition to the essays in this volume, new articles written by participants have been appearing in scholarly journals. A month-long NEH-sponsored institute for high-school teachers at Northern State University in June-July 1989 was directed by two participants and featured many of the scholars invited to the original Chaucer Institute. A lively weekend conference on Chaucer for high-school teachers, which stressed reading the poet in his original language, was organized at Eastern Illinois University in April 1988 and staffed by several participants. The conference was repeated at Rosary College in April 1989. At the 1988 International Congress on Medieval Studies at Kalamazoo, Michigan, two special sessions organized by the Chaucer Institute attempted to get away from the usual conference format and instead recreate the sharp and friendly diversity of opinion that characterized our summer. Another special session was organized in 1989. Yet the ultimate measure of our accomplishment will be taken in the classroom. Our students will tell us how successful we are in passing along to them the excitement and delight we all found in reading Chaucer during his Institute.

APPENDIX:

HE PORTRAYALS OF

FORTUNE IN THE TALES OF

THE MONK'S TALE

(Abstract)

Peter C. Braeger

It is a common complaint about The Monk's Tale that there is
insufficient variety in its seventeen tragic stories of the unfortunate falls of great men and women. Nevertheless, critics have
begun to notice some kinds of variety in Chaucer's treatment of
Fortune in these tales. Edmund M. Socola finds in the stories a
gradual movement from a portrayal of an abstract Fortune in the
tales from Hercules through Ugolino to a portrayal of Fortune as
a "personal and individualized being" in the tales from Nero
through Croesus (p. 164). William C. Strange finds a tension
throughout The Monk's Tale between Fortune as a servant of
God and Fortune as a force that is "passionate," "fickle," and
"pagan"—two views of Fortune that come together in the final
tale of Croesus (pp. 169-70). Neither of these critics, however,
explores the connections between each of Chaucer's descriptions
of Fortune and the individual tragic narrative that includes it.

The words and phrases Chaucer uses to characterize Fortune
in The Monk's Tale are largely conventional, found, in particular, in Boethius's *De consolatione Philosophiae* and the *Roman*

de la Rose. It is striking, however, that Fortune is never described in the same way twice in the course of The Monk's Tale. Fortune, we are told, can "list to flee" (VII.1995); "may noon angel dere" (tale of Lucifer, line 2001); can "list to glose" (Hercules, line 2140); can "caste [one] doun," "forsake" one, and then "bereth away . . . richesse" (Belshazzar, lines 2189, 2241-42); can have "in hire hony galle" and can make one "falle / To wrecchednesse" (Cenobia, lines 2347, 2349-50); can hold "so hye in magestee" (Peter of Spain, line 2376); can "hir wheel governe and gye" (Peter of Cyprus, line 2397); can "briddes . . . putte in swich a cage" and "carf" one away from "heigh estaat" (Ugolino of Pisa, lines 2414, 2457); can "lough, and [have] a game" (Nero, line 2550); can kiss "likerously, and [lead one] up and doun" (Holofernes, lines 2556-57); can enhance "in pride" (Antiochus, line 2583); can make one "the heir of hire honour" and then turn "sys . . . into aas" (Alexander, lines 2643, 2661); can serve as "freend" or "foo" (Julius Caesar, line 2723); can make one "gape" "on the galwes" and "assaille / With unwar strook" (Croesus, lines 2734, 2763-64); can, moreover, think (line 2522) and fail (line 2765).

Overall, the word "Fortune" appears in the tale more than thirty times, yet it is never placed in the same verbal context. Even what Socola groups together as the "abstract" portrayals of Fortune (pp. 166-67) are essentially different—and have different kinds of relationships with the narratives that include them—because in each tale Chaucer uses different words.

In some instances, the words, phrases, and metaphors used to describe Fortune are suited to the tone and character of the individual narrative that includes them. In the story of Holofernes, for example, "Fortune ay kiste" him "So likerously, and ladde hym up and doun / Til that his heed was of, er that he wiste" (lines 2556-58). This characterization of Fortune is appropriate in a story about a man who is killed by a woman whom he brought into his tent one night.

Sometimes the words used to describe Fortune relate to the

particular story in more subtle ways. In the story of the fall of Julius Caesar, for example, Fortune is described in terms that suggest the military world: "Fortune weex his adversarie" (line 2678); she "was first freend, and sitthe foo" (line 2723); and, finally, Fortune should be kept forever "in awayt" (line 2725), a phrase that means "under surveillance" and carries the suggestion that she is preparing a military ambush.

In the beginning of the tale of Croesus we learn that first Fortune was favorable to him. When he was about to be burned to death, "Fortune hym sente / Swich hap that he escaped thurgh the rayn" (lines 2737-38). Later he dreams of sitting in a tree and being washed by Jupiter and dried by Phoebus (lines 2744-46). He assumes that this dream portends even more good fortune. But when his daughter explains the meaning of the dream, Croesus learns that the symbolism of the rain has changed: being washed by Jupiter refers to the rain that will wash Croesus's corpse after he has been hanged on the gallows. At the end of the tale the rain image appears again, this time in a general comment about Fortune's instability: "For whan men trusteth hire, thanne wol she faille, / And covere hire brighte face with a clowde" (lines 2765-66). The metaphors that link Fortune to rain thus relate the details to the plot: Croesus's escape from death by means of the rain and his subsequent dream about the rain and the sun. Moreover, the metaphors for Fortune in this narrative highlight her inscrutability. In each case Fortune is associated with the movement from sun to rain, but, for the human beings who trust in her, this sometimes leads to good fortune, sometimes to bad fortune. Her movement is as ordinary, and as unalterable, as the weather.

This essay, then, will explore some of the descriptions of Fortune that Chaucer employs in The Monk's Tale, focusing not so much on overall patterns that unify the tale as a performance from the Monk as on how the descriptions of Fortune contribute in different ways to the tone, structure, and character of the individual stories. There will be some examination of the words used to describe Fortune in the sources and analogues for Chaucer's stories, that is, in Boethius, the *Roman de la Rose*, Boccaccio's *De casibus virorum illustrium*, and perhaps even Lydgate's *Fall of Princes*, in order to demonstrate what is conventional and what is special about Chaucer's connections between various aspects of Fortune and the stories of men and women who fall from greatness.

[Professor Braeger's projected essay was not completed before his death in 1988.—Eds.]

WORKS CITED

All quotations from *The Canterbury Tales* are taken from *The Riverside Chaucer*, 3rd ed., general editor Larry D. Benson (Boston: Houghton Mifflin Company, 1987). Contributors to the *Riverside* edition who are cited in the text are listed individually below. Abbreviations of individual tales cited in the Notes are those of this edition.

Adams, John F. "The Structure of Irony in *The Summoner's Tale*." *Essays in Criticism* 12 (1962): 126-32.

Aers, David. *Chaucer*. Atlantic Highlands, N. J.: Humanities Press International, 1986.

Aiken, Pauline. "Vincent of Beauvais and Chaucer's Knowledge of Alchemy." *Studies in Philology* 41 (1944): 371-89.

Alford, John A. "The Wife of Bath Versus the Clerk of Oxford." *The Chaucer Review* 21 (1986): 108-32.

Allen, Judson Boyce. "The Old Way and the Parson's Way: An Ironic Reading of the *Parson's Tale*." *Journal of Medieval and Renaissance Studies* 3 (1973): 255-71.

Allen, Judson Boyce, and Theresa Anne Moritz. *A Distinction of Stories*. Columbus: Ohio State University Press, 1981.

WORKS CITED

Andreas, James R. "Festive Liminality in Chaucerian Comedy."
Chaucer Newsletter 1 (1979): 3-6.

Aubailly, Jean-Claude, ed. *Deux jeux de Carnaval.* Textes Lit-
téraires Français. Paris and Geneva: Librairie Droz, 1978.

Baird, Joseph L. "Law and the *Reeve's Tale.*" *Neuphilologische
Mitteilungen* 70 (1969): 679-83.

Bakhtin, Mikhail. *Rabelais and His World.* Translated by Hélène
Iswolsky. Cambridge: MIT Press, 1968.

Baldwin, Ralph. *The Unity of the Canterbury Tales.* Anglistica, 5.
Copenhagen: Rosenkilde and Bagger, 1955.

————. "The Yeoman's Canons: A Conjecture." *JEGP* 61
(1962): 232-43.

Barkan, Leonard. *The Gods Made Flesh: Metamorphosis and the
Pursuit of Paganism.* New Haven: Yale University Press, 1986.

Barney, Stephen. "Suddenness and Process in Chaucer." *The
Chaucer Review* 16 (1981): 18-37.

Bartholomaeus Anglicus. *On the Properties of Things: John
Trevisa's Translation of Bartholomaeus Anglicus' De pro-
prietatibus rerum: A Critical Text.* Edited by M. C. Seymour
et al. 2 vols. Oxford: The Clarendon Press, 1974.

Baugh, Albert C., ed. *Chaucer's Major Poetry.* New York:
Appleton-Century-Crofts, 1963.

Baum, Paull Franklin. "The *Canon's Yeoman's Tale.*" *Modern
Language Notes* 40 (1925): 152-54.

Bennett, J. A. W. *Chaucer at Oxford and Cambridge.* Oxford:
The Clarendon Press, 1974.

Benson, C. David. "The *Canterbury Tales*: Personal drama or experiments in poetic variety?" In *The Cambridge Chaucer Companion*. Edited by Piero Boitani and Jill Mann. Cambridge: Cambridge University Press, 1986. Pp. 93-108.

———. *Chaucer's Drama of Style: Poetic Variety and Contrast in the Canterbury Tales*. Chapel Hill: The University of North Carolina Press, 1986.

Benson, Larry D. "Explanatory Notes: *The Canterbury Tales*." In *The Riverside Chaucer*. Pp. 795 97.

Benson, Larry D., and Theodore M. Andersson, eds. *The Literary Context of Chaucer's Fabliaux: Texts and Translations*. New York: Bobbs-Merrill, 1971.

Berger, Harry, Jr. "The F-Fragment of the *Canterbury Tales*." *The Chaucer Review* 1 (1966): 88-102; 135-56.

Bernardus Silvestris. *Cosmographia*. Translated by Winthrop Wetherbee. New York: Columbia University Press, 1986.

Birney, Earle. "Structural Irony within the *Summoner's Tale*." In *Essays on Chaucerian Irony*. Edited by Beryl Rowland. Toronto: University of Toronto Press, 1985. Pp. 109-23.

Blake, N. F., ed. *The Canterbury Tales by Geoffrey Chaucer, Edited from the Hengwrt Manuscript*. London: Edward Arnold, 1980.

Blodgett, E. D. "Chaucerian *Pryvetee* and the Opposition to Time." *Speculum* 51 (1976): 477-93.

Bloomfield, Morton W. "The *Friar's Tale* as a Liminal Tale." *The Chaucer Review* 17 (1983): 286-91.

Boklund, Karin M. "On the Spatial and Cultural Characteristics of Courtly Romance." *Semiotica* 20 (1977): 1-37.

Bowden, Muriel. *A Commentary on the General Prologue to the Canterbury Tales*. 1948. 2nd ed. London: Macmillan, 1967.

Brewer, Derek. "The Reeve's Tale." In *Chaucer's Frame Tales: The Physical and the Metaphysical*. Edited by Joerg O. Fichte. Cambridge: D. S. Brewer, 1987. Pp. 67-81.

Brown, Norman O. *Life Against Death: The Psychoanalytical Meaning of History*. Middletown, Conn.: Wesleyan University Press, 1959.

Brown, Peter. "The Containment of Symkyn: The Function of Space in the *Reeve's Tale*." *The Chaucer Review* 14 (1980): 225-36.

Burlin, Robert B. *Chaucerian Fiction*. Princeton: Princeton University Press, 1977.

Burnley, David. *A Guide to Chaucer's Language*. London: Macmillan, 1983.

Burrow, John A. *The Ages of Man*. Oxford: Oxford University Press, 1986.

Caie, Graham D. "The Significance of the Early Chaucer Manuscript Glosses (with Special Reference to the *Wife of Bath's Prologue*)." *The Chaucer Review* 10 (1976): 350-60.

Campbell, Jackson J. "The Canon's Yeoman as Imperfect Paradigm." *The Chaucer Review* 17 (1982): 171-81.

Caro Baroja, Julio. *El carnaval*. Madrid: Taurus, 1965.

Carruthers, Mary. "Letter and Gloss in the Friar's and Summoner's Tales." *Journal of Narrative Technique* 2 (1972): 208-14.

————. "The Wife of Bath and the Painting of Lions." *PMLA* 94 (1979): 209-22.

WORKS CITED

The Christmas Prince, An Account of the St. John's College Revels Held at Oxford, 1607-8. Edited by Frederick Boas and W. W. Greg. Malone Society Reprints. London: Oxford University Press, 1932.

Clark, Peter. *The English Alehouse: A Social History 1200-1830.* London and New York: Longman, 1983.

Clark, Roy Peter. "Doubting Thomas in Chaucer's *Summoner's Tale.*" *The Chaucer Review* 11 (1976): 164-78.

————. "Wit and Witsunday in Chaucer's *Summoner's Tale.*" *Annuale Mediaevale* 17 (1976): 48-57.

Cline, Ruth Huff. "Four Chaucer Saints." *Modern Language Notes* 60 (1945): 480-82.

Coffman, George. "Old Age from Horace to Chaucer." *Speculum* 9 (1934): 273-77.

Colgrave, Bertram, ed. and trans. *Two Lives of Saint Cuthbert.* New York: Greenwood, 1969.

Cook, Jon. "Carnival and *The Canterbury Tales*: 'Only Equals May Laugh' (Herzen)." In *Medieval Literature: Criticism, Ideology & History.* Edited by David Aers. New York: St. Martin's Press, 1986. Pp. 169-91.

Cook, Robert. "The Canon's Yeoman and His Tale." *The Chaucer Review* 22 (1987): 28-40.

Cooper, Helen. *The Structure of the Canterbury Tales.* Athens: The University of Georgia Press, 1983.

Copland, Murray. "*The Reeve's Tale*: Harlotrie or Sermonyng?" *Medium Ævum* 31 (1962): 14-32.

Cowen, J. M. "The Miller's Tale, line 3325: 'Merry Maid and Gallant Groom'?" In *Medieval English Studies Presented to George Kane.* Edited by E. D. Kennedy, R. Waldron, and J. S. Wittig. Totowa, N. J.: D. S. Brewer, 1988. Pp. 147-52.

Cowgill, Bruce Kent. "The *Knight's Tale* and the Hundred Years' War." *Philological Quarterly* 54 (1975): 670-79.

Craik, T. W. *The Comic Tales of Chaucer.* London: Methuen, 1958.

Crane, Susan. "Alison's Incapacity and Poetic Instability in the Wife of Bath's Tale." *PMLA* 102 (1987): 20-28.

Curtius, Ernst Robert. *European Literature and the Latin Middle Ages.* Translated by Willard R. Trask. New York: Harper & Row, 1953.

Damon, S. Foster. "Chaucer and Alchemy." *PMLA* 39 (1924): 782-88.

Dante Alighieri. *The Divine Comedy.* Edited and translated by Charles S. Singleton. 3 vols. Bollingen Series, 80. Princeton: Princeton University Press, 1973.

David, Alfred. "Recycling *Anelida and Arcite*: Chaucer as a Source for Chaucer." *Studies in the Age of Chaucer* 1984; Proceedings 1:105-15.

—————. *The Strumpet Muse: Art and Morals in Chaucer's Poetry.* Bloomington: Indiana University Press, 1976.

Dean, James. "Dismantling the Canterbury Book." *PMLA* 100 (1985): 746-62.

Delany, Sheila. "Rewriting Woman Good: Gender and the Anxiety of Influence in Two Late-Medieval Texts." In *Chaucer in the Eighties.* Edited by Julian N. Wasserman and Robert J. Blanch. Syracuse: Syracuse University Press, 1986. Pp. 75-92.

————. *Writing Women*. New York: Schocken Books, 1983.

Delasanta, Rodney. "Penance and Poetry in the *Canterbury Tales*." *PMLA* 93 (1978): 240-47.

Diamond, Arlyn. "Chaucer's Women and Women's Chaucer." In *The Authority of Experience*. Edited by Arlyn Diamond and Lee R. Edwards. Amherst: University of Massachusetts Press, 1977. Pp. 60-83, 282-84.

DiMarco, Vincent J. "Explanatory Notes: The Knight's Tale." In *The Riverside Chaucer*. Pp. 826-41.

Donaldson, E. T. *Chaucer's Poetry: An Anthology for the Modern Reader*. 2nd ed. New York: Ronald Press, 1975.

Dove, Mary. *The Perfect Age of Man's Life*. Cambridge: Cambridge University Press, 1986.

Dryden, John. "Preface to Fables Ancient and Modern." In *Prefaces & Prologues to Famous Books*. Edited by Charles W. Eliot. Harvard Classics Series, 39. New York: P. F. Collier & Son, 1909. Pp. 160-83.

Du Boulay, F. R. H. "The Historical Chaucer." In *Geoffrey Chaucer*. Edited by Derek Brewer. Athens: Ohio University Press, 1975. Pp. 33-57.

Duby, Georges. *The Early Growth of the European Economy: Warriors and Peasants from the Seventh to the Twelfth Century*. Translated by H. B. Clark. Ithaca: Cornell University Press, 1974.

Ducange, Charles du Fresne. *Glossarium et mediae infimae latinitatis*. Supplement by D. P. Carpentier. Edited by G. A. L. Herschel. 10 vols. Niort: L. Favre, 1883-87.

WORKS CITED

Duncan, Edgar H. "The Literature of Alchemy and Chaucer's Canon's Yeoman's Tale: Framework, Theme, and Characters." *Speculum* 43 (1968): 633-56.

Eadmer. *Life of Oswald.* In *The Historians of the Church of York and Its Archbishops.* Edited by James Raine. Rolls Series, no. 71, vol. 2 (London, 1886). Pp. 1-6.

Eagleton, Terry. *Literary Theory: An Introduction.* Minneapolis: University of Minnesota Press, 1983.

Elbow, Peter. *Oppositions in Chaucer.* Middletown, Conn.: Wesleyan University Press, 1973.

Elliott, R. W. V. "The Pardoner's Sermon and Its *Exemplum.*" In *Twentieth Century Interpretations of the Pardoner's Tale: A Collection of Critical Essays.* Edited by Dewey R. Faulkner. Englewood Cliffs, N. J.: Prentice-Hall, 1973. Pp. 23-32.

Erickson, Carolly. *The Medieval Vision: Essays in History and Perception.* London and New York: Oxford University Press, 1976.

Ferrante, Joan M. *Woman as Image in Medieval Literature: From the Twelfth Century to Dante.* New York: Columbia University Press, 1975.

Ferster, Judith. *Chaucer on Interpretation.* Cambridge: Cambridge University Press, 1985.

————. "Interpretation and Imitation in Chaucer's Franklin's Tale." In *Medieval Literature: Criticism, Ideology & History.* Edited by David Aers. New York: St. Martin's Press, 1986. Pp. 148-68.

Finke, Laurie A. "'To Knytte up al this Feeste': The Parson's Rhetoric and the Ending of the *Canterbury Tales.*" *Leeds Studies in English* 15 (1984): 95-107.

WORKS CITED

Finkelstein, Dorothee. "The Code of Chaucer's 'Secree of Secrees.' Arabic Alchemical Terminology in *The Canon's Yeoman's Tale.*" *Archiv für das Studium der Neueren Sprachen und Literaturen* 207 (1970-71): 260-76.

Finlayson, John. "The Satiric Mode and the *Parson's Tale.*" *The Chaucer Review* 6 (1971): 94-116.

Finucane, Donald C. *Miracles and Pilgrims: Popular Beliefs in Medieval England.* Totowa, N. J.: Rowman and Littlefield, 1977.

Fiorenza, Elisabeth Schussler. *In Memory of Her.* New York: Crossroad Press, 1986.

Fisher, John H., ed. *The Complete Poetry and Prose of Geoffrey Chaucer.* 2nd ed. New York: Holt, Rinehart and Winston, 1989.

Fleming, John V. "Anticlerical Satire as Theological Essay: Chaucer's Summoner's Tale." *Thalia* 6 (1983): 5-22.

————. "The Antifraternalism of the *Summoner's Tale.*" *JEGP* 65 (1966): 688-700.

————. "The Summoner's Prologue: An Iconographic Adjustment." *The Chaucer Review* 2 (1967): 95-107.

Fleming, Martha H. "'Glosynge Is a Glorious Thing, Certyn': A Reconsideration of *The Summoner's Tale.*" In *The Late Middle Ages.* Edited by Peter Cocazella. Binghamton, N. Y.: Center for Medieval and Early Renaissance Studies, 1984. Pp. 89-101.

Forehand, Brooks. "Old Age and Chaucer's Reeve." *PMLA* 69 (1954): 984-89.

Fradenburg, Louise O. "The Wife of Bath's Passing Fancy." *Studies in the Age of Chaucer* 8 (1986): 31-58.

Frank, Robert Worth, Jr. "The *Reeve's Tale* and the Comedy of Limitation." In *Directions in Literary Criticism: Contemporary Approaches to Literature*. Edited by Stanley Weintraub and Philip Young. University Park: The Pennsylvania State University Press, 1973. Pp. 53-69.

Fritz, Donald W. "Reflections in a Golden Florin: Chaucer's Narcissistic Pardoner." *The Chaucer Review* 21 (1987): 338-59.

Gaignebet, Claude. "Le combat de Carnaval et de Careme de P. Bruegel (1559)." *Annales: Economies, Sociétés, Civilisations* 27/2 (March-April 1972): 313-45.

Gallacher, Patrick. "The *Summoner's Tale* and Medieval Attitudes Towards Sickness." *The Chaucer Review* 21 (1986): 200-12.

Ganim, John M. "Bakhtin, Chaucer, Carnival, Lent." *Studies in the Age of Chaucer* 1986; Proceedings 2:59-71.

————. "Carnival Voices and the Envoy to the *Clerk's Tale*." *The Chaucer Review* 22 (1987): 112-27.

Gardner, John. "The *Canon's Yeoman's Prologue and Tale*: An Interpretation." *Philological Quarterly* 46 (1967): 1-17.

————. "Signs, Symbols, and Cancellations." In *Signs and Symbols in Chaucer's Poetry*. Edited by John P. Hermann and John J. Burke, Jr. University: The University of Alabama Press, 1981. Pp. 195-207.

Gaylord, Alan T. "*Sentence* and *Solaas* in Fragment VII of the *Canterbury Tales*: Harry Bailly as Horseback Editor." *PMLA* 82 (1967): 226-35.

Gerould, Gordon Hall. *Chaucerian Essays*. Princeton: Princeton University Press, 1952.

Göller, Karl Heinz. "Chaucer's Squire's Tale: 'The Knotte of the Tale'." In *Chaucer und Seine Zeit*. Edited by Arno Esch. Tübingen: Max Niemeyer Verlag, 1968. Pp. 173-74.

Gottfried, Barbara. "Conflict and Relationship, Sovereignty and Survival: Parables of Power in the *Wife of Bath's Prologue*." *The Chaucer Review* 19 (1985): 202-24.

Greene, Gayle, and Coppelia Kahn. "Feminist Scholarship and the Social Construction of Women." In *Making a Difference: Feminist Literary Criticism*. Edited by Gayle Greene and Coppelia Kahn. New York: Methuen, 1985. Pp. 1-36.

Grenberg, Bruce L. "The *Canon's Yeoman's Tale*: Boethian Wisdom and the Alchemists." *The Chaucer Review* 1 (1966): 37-54.

Grennen, Joseph E. "The Canon's Yeoman's Alchemical 'Mass'." *Studies in Philology* 62 (1965): 546-60.

————. "Saint Cecilia's 'Chemical Wedding': The Unity of the *Canterbury Tales*, Fragment VIII." *JEGP* 65 (1966): 466-81.

Hackwood, F. W. *Inns, Ales, and Drinking Customs of Old England*. London: Unwin, 1909.

Hagen, Susan K. "The Wife of Bath, The Lion, and the Critics." In *The Worlds of Medieval Women: Creativity, Influence, Imagination*. Edited by Constance H. Berman, Charles W. Connell, and Judith Rice Rothschild. Morgantown: West Virginia University Press, 1985. Pp. 130-38.

Haller, Robert S. "Chaucer's *Squire's Tale* and the Uses of Rhetoric." *Modern Philology* 62 (1965): 285-95.

————. "*The Knight's Tale* and the Epic Tradition." *The Chaucer Review* 1 (1966): 67-84.

Halverson, John. "Aspects of Order in the *Knight's Tale.*" *Studies in Philology* 57 (1960): 606-21.

—————. "Chaucer's Pardoner and the Progress of Criticism." *The Chaucer Review* 4 (1970): 184-202.

Hamilton, Marie P. "The Clerical Status of Chaucer's Alchemist." *Speculum* 16 (1941): 103-08.

Hanning, Robert W. "Roasting a Friar, Mis-Taking a Wife, and Other Acts of Textual Harrassment in Chaucer's Canterbury Tales." *Studies in the Age of Chaucer* 7 (1985): 3-22.

—————. "The Theme of Art and Life in Chaucer's Poetry." In *Geoffrey Chaucer.* Edited by George D. Economou. New York: McGraw-Hill Book Company, 1975. Pp. 15-36.

Harrington, David V. "The Narrator of the *Canon's Yeoman's Tale.*" *Annuale Mediaevale* 9 (1968): 85-97.

Harwood, Britton J. "Chaucer and the Silence of History: Situating the Canon's Yeoman's Tale." *PMLA* 102 (1987): 338-50.

Haselmayer, Louis A. "The Apparitor and Chaucer's Summoner." *Speculum* 12 (1937): 43-57.

Haskell, Ann. S. "The St. Giles Oath in the *Canon's Yeoman's Tale.*" *The Chaucer Review* 7 (1973): 221-26.

—————. "St. Simon in the Summoner's Tale." *The Chaucer Review* 5 (1971): 218-24.

Havely, Nicholas R. *Geoffrey Chaucer: The Friar's, Summoner's and Pardoner's Tales from the Canterbury Tales.* London: University of London Press, 1975.

Heffernan, Carol Falvo. "A Reconsideration of the Cask Figure in the *Reeve's Prologue.*" *The Chaucer Review* 15 (1980): 37-43.

WORKS CITED

Heist, William W. "Folklore Study and Chaucer's Fabliau-Like Tales." *Papers of the Michigan Academy of Science, Arts and Letters* 36 (1952): 251-58.

Herz, Judith Scherer. "*The Canon's Yeoman's Prologue* and *Tale.*" *Modern Philology* 58 (1961): 231-37.

Hilary, Christine Ryan. "Explanatory Notes: The Pardoner; The Pardoner's Introduction, Prologue, and Tale." In *The Riverside Chaucer*. Pp. 823-24, 904-10.

Hilberry, Jane. "'And in Oure Madnesse Everemoore We Rave': Technical Language in the *Canon's Yeoman's Tale.*" *The Chaucer Review* 21 (1987): 435-43.

Hornsby, Joseph A. "Was Chaucer Educated at the Inns of Court?" *The Chaucer Review* 22 (1988): 255-68.

Houle, Peter J. *The English Morality and Related Drama: A Bibliographical Survey*. Hamden, Conn.: Archon Books, 1972.

Howard, Donald R. *The Idea of the Canterbury Tales*. Berkeley: University of California Press, 1976.

Jacques de Baisieux. *Li Dis de le vescie a prestre*. In *The Literary Context of Chaucer's Fabliaux: Texts and Translations*. Edited by Larry D. Benson and Theodore M. Andersson. Indianapolis: Bobbs-Merrill, 1971. Pp. 344-59.

Joseph, Gerhard. "Chaucerian 'Game'-'Earnest' and the 'Argument of Herbergage' in the *Canterbury Tales.*" *The Chaucer Review* 5 (1970): 83-96.

Jusserand, J. J. *English Wayfaring Life in the Middle Ages*. London: Benn, 1889.

Kaiser, W. *Praisers of Folly: Erasmus, Rabelais, Shakespeare*. Cambridge, Mass.: Harvard University Press, 1963.

WORKS CITED

Kean, Patricia M. *Chaucer and the Making of Middle English Poetry*. 2 vols. London: Routledge and Kegan Paul, 1972.

Kern, Edith. *The Absolute Comic*. New York: Columbia University Press, 1980.

Klene, Jean, C. S. C. "Chaucer's Contributions to a Popular Topos: The World Upside-Down." *Viator* 11 (1980): 321-34.

Knapp, Peggy. "Alisoun Weaves a Text." *Philological Quarterly* 65 (1986): 387-401.

Knight, Stephen. *Geoffrey Chaucer*. London: Blackwell, 1986.

Koeppel, E. "Chauceriana." *Anglia* 14 (1892): 227-67.

Kolodny, Annette. "A Map for Reading: Gender and the Interpretation of Literary Texts." In *The New Feminist Criticism*. Edited by Elaine Showalter. New York: Pantheon Books, Inc., 1983.

Kolve, V. A. *Chaucer and the Imagery of Narrative: The First Five Canterbury Tales*. Stanford: Stanford University Press, 1984.

—————. "Chaucer's *Second Nun's Tale* and the Iconography of Saint Cecilia." *New Perspectives in Chaucer Criticism*. Edited by Donald M. Rose. Norman, Okla.: Pilgrim Books, 1981. Pp. 37-74.

Ladner, Gerhart B. "*Homo Viator*: Mediaeval Ideas on Alienation and Order." *Speculum* 42 (1967): 233-59.

Lambert, M. D. *Franciscan Poverty: The Doctrine of the Absolute Poverty of Christ and the Apostles in the Franciscan Order, 1210-1323*. London: S. P. C. K., 1961.

WORKS CITED

Lancashire, Ian. "Moses, Elijah, and the Back Parts of God: Satiric Scatology in Chaucer's *Summoner's Tale*." *Mosaic* 14 (1981): 17-30.

———. "Sexual Innuendo in the *Reeve's Tale*." *The Chaucer Review* 6 (1972): 159-70.

Langland, William. *Piers Plowman: An Edition of the C-text*. Edited by Derek Pearsall. Berkeley: University of California Press, 1979.

———. *The Vision of Piers Plowman: A Complete Edition of the B-Text*. Edited by A. V. C. Schmidt. London: J. M. Dent, 1978.

Larwood, Jacob, and John Camden. *The History of Signboards from Earliest Times to the Present Day*. London: John Camden Hotten, 1866.

Lawler, Traugott. *The One and the Many in the Canterbury Tales*. Hamden, Conn.: Archon Books, 1980.

Lawton, David. *Chaucer's Narrators*. Cambridge: D. S. Brewer, 1985.

Le Goff, Jacques. *The Birth of Purgatory*. Translated by Arthur Goldhammer. Chicago and London: University of Chicago Press, 1984.

Leitch, L. M. "Sentence and Solaas: The Function of the Hosts in the *Canterbury Tales*." *The Chaucer Review* 17 (1982): 5-20.

Levitan, Alan. "The Parody of Pentecost in Chaucer's *Summoner's Tale*." *University of Toronto Quarterly* 40 (1971): 236-46.

Levy, Bernard S. "Biblical Parody in the *Summoner's Tale*." *Tennessee Studies in Literature* 11 (1966): 45-60.

Leyerle, John. "Chaucer's Windy Eagle." *University of Toronto Quarterly* 40 (1971): 247-65.

————. "The Rose-Wheel Design and Dante's *Paradiso.*" *University of Toronto Quarterly* 46 (1977): 280-308.

Lindahl, Carl. *Ernest Games: Folkloric Patterns in the Canterbury Tales.* Bloomington: Indiana University Press, 1987.

Little, Lester K. *Religious Poverty and the Profit Economy in Medieval Europe.* Ithaca: Cornell University Press, 1978.

Lowes, J. L. "Chaucer and the Seven Deadly Sins." *PMLA* 23 (1915): 237-371.

Lozinski, Grégoire, ed. *La Bataille de Caresme et de Charnage.* Bibliothèque de l'Ecole des Hautes Etudes, 262. Paris: Librarie Honoré Champion, 1933.

Lucas, Angela M. *Women in the Middle Ages: Religion, Marriage and Letters.* Brighton, England: Harvester, 1983.

Lumiansky, R. M. *Of Sondry Folk: The Dramatic Principle in the Canterbury Tales.* Austin: University of Texas Press, 1955.

Lydgate, John. *The Fall of Princes.* Edited by Henry Bergen. 4 vols. Washington, D. C.: Carnegie Institute, 1923-27.

MacLaine, A. H. "Chaucer's Wine-Cask Image: Word Play in *The Reeve's Prologue.*" *Medium Ævum* 31 (1962): 129-31.

Malvern, Marjorie M. "'Who peyntede the leon, tel me who?': Rhetorical and Didactic Roles Played by an Aesopic Fable in the *Wife of Bath's Prologue.*" *Studies in Philology* (1983): 238-52.

Manly, John M. *Some New Light on Chaucer.* New York: Holt, 1926.

————. "Tales of the Homeward Journey." *Studies in Philology* 28 (1931): 613-17.

Manly, John M., and Edith Rickert, eds. *The Text of the Canterbury Tales.* 8 vols. Chicago: University of Chicago Press, 1940.

Mann, Jill. *Chaucer and Medieval Estates Satire: The Literature of Social Classes and the* General Prologue *to the* Canterbury Tales. Cambridge: Cambridge University Press, 1973.

Manzoni, Luigi, ed. *Libro di Carnevale dei secoli XV et XVI.* Bologna: G. Ramagnoli, 1881.

McAlindon, T. "Cosmology, Contrariety and the *Knight's Tale.*" *Medium Ævum* 55 (1986): 41-57.

Merrill, Thomas F. "Wrath and Rhetoric in 'The Summoner's Tale'." *Texas Studies in Language and Literature* 4 (1962): 341-50.

Meyerhoff, Hans. *Time in Literature.* Berkeley: University of California Press, 1957.

Mitchell, Charles. "The Moral Superiority of Chaucer's Pardoner." *College English* 27 (1966): 437-44.

Morse, Charlotte C. "The Exemplary Griselda." *Studies in the Age of Chaucer* 7 (1985): 51-86.

Muscatine, Charles. *Chaucer and the French Tradition.* Berkeley: University of California Press, 1957.

————. "Form, Texture and Meaning in Chaucer's *Knight's Tale.*" *PMLA* 65 (1950): 911-29.

————. *The Old French Fabliaux.* New Haven and London: Yale University Press, 1986.

Myers, A. R. *London in the Age of Chaucer.* Norman: University of Oklahoma Press, 1972.

Nashe, Thomas. *The Works of Thomas Nashe.* Edited by R. B. McKerrow. Revised by F. P. Wilson. 5 vols. Oxford: Blackwell, 1958.

Nichols, John, ed. *The Progresses and Public Processions of Queen Elizabeth.* 3 vols. London: John Nichols and Son, 1823.

Oakley, Francis. *The Western Church in the Late Middle Ages.* Ithaca: Cornell University Press, 1979.

O'Donnell, James J. *Augustine.* Twayne's World Authors Series. Boston: Twayne Publishers, 1985.

Olmert, K. Michael. "*The Canon's Yeoman's Tale*: An Interpretation." *Annuale Mediaevale* 8 (1967): 70-94.

Olson, Glending. "Chaucer, Dante, and the Structure of Fragment VIII (G) of the *Canterbury Tales.*" *The Chaucer Review* 16 (1982): 222-36.

————. "The *Reeve's Tale* as a Fabliau." *Modern Language Quarterly* 35 (1974): 219-30.

Olson, Paul A. *The* Canterbury Tales *and the Good Society.* Princeton: Princeton University Press, 1986.

————. "The *Reeve's Tale*: Chaucer's *Measure for Measure.*" *Studies in Philology* 59 (1962): 1-17.

Oursel, Raymond. *Les Pèlerins du moyen âge.* Paris: Fayard, 1963.

Ovid. *Metamorphoses.* Translated by Mary M. Innes. London: Penguin, 1955.

Owen, Charles A., Jr. "The Development of the *Canterbury Tales*." *Journal of English and Germanic Philology* 57 (1958): 449-78.

—————. "'Thy Drasty Rymyng . . .'." *Studies in Philology* 63 (1966): 533-64.

—————. *Pilgrimage and Storytelling in The Canterbury Tales: The Dialectic of "Ernest" and "Game."* Norman: University of Oklahoma Press, 1977.

—————. "The Problem of Free Will in Chaucer's Narratives." *Philological Quarterly* 46 (1967): 433-56.

The Owl and the Nightingale, Cleanness, St. Erkenwald. Translated by Brian Stone. 2nd ed. London: Penguin, 1988.

Owst, Gerald R. *Literature and the Pulpit in Medieval England.* 2nd ed. Oxford: Blackwell, 1961.

Page, Barbara. "Concerning the Host." *The Chaucer Review* 4 (1969): 1-13.

The Parlement of the Thre Ages. Edited by M. Y. Offord. EETS, o.s. 246. London: Oxford University Press, 1959.

Patterson, Lee W. "'For the Wyves Love of Bath': Feminine Rhetoric and Poetic Resolution in the *Roman de la Rose* and the *Canterbury Tales*." *Speculum* 58 (1983): 656-95.

—————. "The 'Parson's Tale' and the Quitting of the 'Canterbury Tales'." *Traditio* 34 (1978): 331-80.

—————. "'What Man Artow?': Authorial Self-Definition in The Tale of Sir Thopas and The Tale of Melibee." *Studies in the Age of Chaucer* 11 (1989): 117-75.

Payne, F. Anne. *Chaucer and Menippean Satire.* Madison: University of Wisconsin Press, 1981.

Payne, Robert O. *Geoffrey Chaucer*. 2nd ed. Twayne's World Authors Series. Boston: Twayne Publishers, 1986.

Pearcy, Roy J. "Chaucer's 'An Impossible' ('Summoner's Tale' III, 2231)." *Notes and Queries*, n.s. 14 (1967): 322-25.

Pearsall, Derek. *The Canterbury Tales*. London: George Allen & Unwin, 1985.

————. "The *Canterbury Tales* II: Comedy." In *The Cambridge Chaucer Companion*. Edited by Piero Boitani and Jill Mann. Cambridge: Cambridge University Press, 1986. Pp. 125-42.

————. "Chaucer's Pardoner: The Death of a Salesman." *The Chaucer Review* 17 (1983): 358-65.

Peck, Russell A. "St. Paul and *The Canterbury Tales*." *Mediaevalia* 7 (1981): 91-131.

Peterson, Joyce. "The Finished Fragment: A Reassessment of the *Squire's Tale*." *The Chaucer Review* 5 (1970): 62-74.

Pison, Thomas. "Liminality in the *Canterbury Tales*." *Genre* 10 (1977): 157-71.

Postan, M. M. *The Medieval Economy and Society: An Economic History of Britain in the Middle Ages*. London: Weidenfeld and Nicolson, 1972.

Reidy, John. "Chaucer's Canon and the Unity of *The Canon's Yeoman's Tale*." *PMLA* 80 (1965): 31-37.

Rendle, William. *The Inns of Old Southwark*. London: Longman, Green, 1880.

Richardson, Cynthia C. "The Function of the Host in *The Canterbury Tales*." *Texas Studies in Language and Literature* 12 (1970): 325-44.

WORKS CITED

Richardson, Janette. "Explanatory Notes: The Summoner's Prologue and Tale." In *The Riverside Chaucer*. Pp. 876-79.

—————. "Friar and Summoner: The Art of Balance." *The
Chaucer Review* 9 (1975): 227-36.

Robertson, D. W., Jr. *A Preface to Chaucer: Studies in Medieval
Perspectives*. Princeton: Princeton University Press, 1962.

—————, ed. and trans. *Saint Augustine, On Christian Doctrine*.
New York: Liberal Arts, 1958.

Robinson, F. N., ed. *The Works of Geoffrey Chaucer*. 2nd ed.
Boston: Houghton Mifflin Company, 1957.

Rolle, Richard. *The Form of Living* In *English Writings of Richard
Rolle, Hermit of Hampole*. Edited by Hope Emily Allen. Oxford: The Clarendon Press, 1931. Pp. 82-119.

Root, Robert Kilburn. "The Manciple's Prologue." *Modern Language Notes* 44 (1929): 493-96.

Rosenberg, Bruce A. "The Contrary Tales of the Second Nun and
the Canon's Yeoman." *The Chaucer Review* 2 (1968): 278-91.

—————. "Swindling Alchemist, Antichrist." *The Centennial
Review* 6/4 (1962): 566-80.

Rowland, Beryl. *Blind Beasts: Chaucer's Animal World*. Kent,
Oh. : The Kent State University Press, 1971.

—————. "Chaucer's Dame Alys: Critics in Blunderland?" *Neuphilologische Mitteilungen* 2 (1972): 381-95.

—————. "On the Timely Death of the Wife of Bath's Fourth
Husband." *Archiv für das Studium der Neueren Sprachen und
Literaturen* 209 (1973): 273-82.

Ruether, Rosemary Radford. *Sexism and God-Talk.* Boston: Beacon, 1983.

Ruiz, Juan. *The Book of True Love.* Bilingual Edition. Old Spanish edited by Anthony N. Zahareas. Translation by Saralyn R. Daly. University Park: The Pennsylvania State University Press, 1978.

Ruggiers, Paul G. *The Art of the Canterbury Tales.* Madison: University of Wisconsin Press, 1967.

Ryan, Lawrence V. "The Canon's Yeoman's Desperate Confession." *The Chaucer Review* 8 (1974): 297-310.

Sandler, Lucy Freeman. *The Psalter of Robert de Lisle in the British Library.* London: Harvey Miller, 1983.

Sands, Donald B. "The Non-Comic, Non-Tragic Wife: Chaucer's Dame Alys as Sociopath." *The Chaucer Review* 12 (1977): 171-82.

Scattergood, V. J. "Perkyn Revelour and the *Cook's Tale.*" *The Chaucer Review* 19 (1984): 14-23.

Scheps, Walter. "'Up Roos Oure Hoost, and Was Oure Aller Cok': Harry Bailly's Tale-Telling Competition." *The Chaucer Review* 10 (1975): 113-28.

Schibanoff, Susan. "The New Reader and Female Textuality in Two Early Commentaries on Chaucer." *Studies in the Age of Chaucer* 10 (1988): 71-108.

Schuler, Robert M. "The Renaissance Chaucer as Alchemist." *Viator* 15 (1984): 305-33.

Sears, Elizabeth. *The Ages of Man: Medieval Interpretations of the Life Cycle.* Princeton: Princeton University Press, 1986.

WORKS CITED

Sedgewick, G. G. "The Progress of Chaucer's Pardoner, 1880-1940." *Modern Language Quarterly* 1 (1940): 431-58.

Shakespeare, William. *The Riverside Shakespeare*. Edited by G. Blakemore Evans et al. Boston: Houghton Mifflin Company, 1974.

Showalter, Elaine. "Women's Time, Women's Space: Writing the History of Feminist Criticism." In *Feminist Issues in Literary Scholarship*. Edited by Shari Benstock. Bloomington: Indiana University Press, 1987. Pp. 30-44.

Siegel, Marsha. "What the Debate Is and Why It Founders in Fragment A of *The Canterbury Tales*." *Studies in Philology* 82 (1985): 1-24.

Skeat, Walter W., ed. *The Complete Works of Geoffrey Chaucer*. 6 vols. 2nd ed. Oxford: The Clarendon Press, 1900.

Smallwood, T. M. "The Interpretation of *Somer Soneday*." *Medium Ævum* 42 (1973): 238-45.

Socola, Edward M. "Chaucer's Development of Fortune in the 'Monk's Tale'." *Journal of English and Germanic Philology* 49 (1950): 159-71.

Somer Soneday. In *Historical Poems of the XIVth and XVth Centuries*. Edited by Rossell Hope Robbins. New York: Columbia University Press, 1959. Pp. 98-102.

Spearing, A. C., and J. E. Spearing, eds. *The Reeve's Prologue and Tale with the Cook's Prologue and the Fragment of His Tale*. Cambridge: Cambridge University Press, 1979.

Stallybrass, Peter, and Allon White. *The Politics and Poetics of Transgression*. Ithaca: Cornell University Press, 1986.

Stanbury, Sara. "Space and Visual Hermeneutics in the *Gawain-Poet.*" *The Chaucer Review* 21 (1987): 476-89.

Stevens, Martin, and Kathleen Falvey. "Substance, Accident, and Transformations: A Reading of the *Pardoner's Tale.*" *The Chaucer Review* 17 (1982): 142-58.

Storm, Melvin. "The Pardoner's Invitation: Quaestor's Bag or Becket's Shrine?" *PMLA* 97 (1982): 810-18.

Strange, William C. "The *Monk's Tale*: A Generous View." *The Chaucer Review* 1 (1967): 167-80.

Szittya, Penn R. *The Antifraternal Tradition in Medieval Literature.* Princeton: Princeton University Press, 1986.

————. "The Friar as False Apostle: Antifraternal Exegesis and the *Summoner's Tale.*" *Studies in Philology* 71 (1974): 19-46.

The Tale of Beryn. Edited by F. J. Furnivall and H. B. Wilson. EETS, e.s. 105. London: Kegan Paul, Trench, Trübner, 1909.

Taylor, John. *Jacke-a-Lent, his beginning and entertainment.* In *Works of John Taylor, the Water-Poet.* 1630. London: The Spenser Society, 1869.

Tentler, Thomas N. *Sin and Confession on the Eve of the Reformation.* Princeton: Princeton University Press, 1977.

Tkacz, Catherine Brown. "Chaucer's Beard-Making." *The Chaucer Review* 18 (1983): 127-36.

Traversi, Derek. *The Canterbury Tales, A Reading.* Newark: University of Delaware Press, 1983.

Trevelyan, George Macaulay. *England in the Age of Wycliffe.* 2nd ed. London: Longmans, Green, 1909.

WORKS CITED

Tripp, Raymond. *The Meridian Handbook of Classical Mythology*. New York: New American Library, 1970.

Tristram, Philippa. *Figures of Life and Death in Medieval English Literature*. New York: New York University Press, 1976.

Tupper, Frederick. "Chaucer and the Seven Deadly Sins." *PMLA* 29 (1914): 93-128.

—————. "The Pardoner's Tavern." *Journal of English and Germanic Philology* 13 (1914): 553-65.

—————. "The Quarrels of the Canterbury Pilgrims." *Journal of English and Germanic Philology* 14 (1915): 256-70.

—————. "Chaucer's Sinners and Sins." *Journal of English and Germanic Philology* 15 (1916): 56-106.

Turner, Victor. *The Ritual Process: Structure and Anti-Structure*. Ithaca: Cornell University Press, 1969.

—————. *Dramas, Fields, and Metaphors: Symbolic Action in Human Society*. Ithaca: Cornell University Press, 1974.

—————. "Pilgrimage and Communitas." *Studia Missionalia* 23 (1974): 305-27.

Turner, Victor, and Edith Turner. *Image and Pilgrimage in Christian Culture: Anthropological Perspectives*. New York: Columbia University Press, 1978.

Utley, Francis Lee. *The Crooked Rib*. Columbus: The Ohio State University Press, 1944.

Vasta, Edward. "How Chaucer's Reeve Succeeds." *Criticism* 25 (1983): 1-12.

Weissman, Hope Phyllis. "Antifeminism and Chaucer's Characterization of Women." In *Geoffrey Chaucer*. Edited by George D. Economou. New York: McGraw-Hill Book Company, 1975. Pp. 93-110.

Wenzel, Siegfried. "Chaucer and the Language of Contemporary Preaching." *Studies in Philology* 73 (1976): 138-61.

—————. "Chaucer's *Parson's Tale*: 'Every Tales Strengthe'." In *Europäische Lehrdichtung*. Edited by Hans Gerd Rötzer. Darmstadt: Wissenschaftliche Buchgesellschaft, 1981. Pp. 86-98.

Whiting, Bartlett Jere. *Chaucer's Use of Proverbs*. Cambridge, Mass.: Harvard University Press, 1934.

Whittock, Trevor. *A Reading of the Canterbury Tales*. Cambridge: Cambridge University Press, 1968.

Williams, Arnold. "Chaucer and the Friars." *Speculum* 28 (1953): 499-513.

—————. "The 'Limitour' of Chaucer's Time and His 'Limitacioun'." *Studies in Philology* 57 (1960): 463-78.

Woodcock, Brian L. *Medieval Ecclesiastical Courts in the Diocese of Canterbury*. London: Oxford University Press, 1952.

Wood-Legh, K. L. *Perpetual Chantries in Britain*. Cambridge: Cambridge University Press, 1965.

Woods, William F. "Chivalry and Nature in the *Knight's Tale*." *Philological Quarterly* 66 (1987): 287-301.

Zietlow, Paul N. "In Defense of the Summoner." *The Chaucer Review* 1 (1966): 4-19.

CONTRIBUTORS

C. David Benson (Ph.D. Berkeley), Professor of English and Director of Medieval Studies, University of Connecticut, Storrs, and Director of the 1987 Chaucer Institute, is the author of *Troilus and Criseyde* (1990), *Chaucer's Drama of Style* (1986), and *The History of Troy in Middle English Literature* (1980). He is currently chief editor for the Variorum Edition of *Troilus and Criseyde*.

Peter C. Braeger (Ph.D. Purdue) was Assistant Professor of English and Fine Arts, Loyola College, Baltimore, until his death in 1988. His publications include articles on *Beowulf*, *Cleanness*, Gower, and Richard's *Bestiaire d'Amour*.

Bruce Kent Cowgill (Ph.D. Nebraska-Lincoln), Professor of English, Winona State University, has published on Chaucer in *JEGP*, *Philological Quarterly*, *Journal of Medieval and Renaissance Studies*, and *Mediaevalia*. He also writes much short fiction, and a collection of his outdoor stories, *Raising Hackles on the Hattie's Fork*, has recently been published by Atlantic Monthly Press.

Susanna Greer Fein (Ph.D. Harvard), Assistant Professor of English, Kent State University, and Co-Director of the 1989 NEH-Sponsored Chaucer Institute for High School Teachers, has published on Chaucer, Arthurian literature, and alliterative verse. Her articles have appeared in *The Chaucer Review*, *Modern Philology*, *The Yearbook of Langland Studies*, and *Modern Language Quarterly*.

Linda Georgianna (Ph.D. Columbia), Associate Professor of English, University of California, Irvine, and Co-Director of the 1987 Chaucer Institute, is the author of *The Solitary Self: Individuality in the* Ancrene Wisse (1981) and of numerous articles that have appeared in *Speculum*, *Studies in the Age of Chaucer*, and other journals.

Susan K. Hagen (Ph.D. Virginia), Mary Collett Munger Professor of English, Birmingham-Southern College, is the author of *Allegorical Remembrance* (1990). Her current project is a metacritical study of scholarship on Chaucer's three female pilgrims.

Frederick B. Jonassen (Ph.D. Cornell), Associate Professor of English, University of Puerto Rico at Mayagüez, has served his department as interim director and has published on medieval literature, popular culture, and Shakespeare in *Viator*, *Modern Language Review*, *Folklore*, and *Studies in Philology*.

Charles A. Owen, Jr. (B.Litt. Oxford), Emeritus Professor of English, University of Connecticut, Storrs, and Co-Director of the 1987 Chaucer Institute, has published widely on Chaucer, including *Pilgrimage and Storytelling in the* Canterbury Tales (1977) and *The Design of the* Canterbury Tales (1968).

David Raybin (Ph.D. Columbia), Professor of English, Eastern Illinois University, has published articles on English and French medieval literature and history in *Studies in the Age of Chaucer*, *Viator*, and *Works and Days*, and was a contributing author to *Victor Turner and the Construction of Cultural Criticism* (1990).

CONTRIBUTORS

Jay Ruud (Ph.D. Wisconsin-Milwaukee), Associate Professor of English and Department Chair, Northern State University, and Director of the 1989 NEH-Sponsored Chaucer Institute for High School Teachers, has authored articles on Chaucer's lyric verse, Chaucer's nominalism, and Arthurian legend in *Mediaevalia, Modern Philology, The Chaucer Review*, and other journals.

William F. Woods (Ph.D. Indiana), Associate Professor of English, Wichita State University, writes about medieval literature and the history of rhetoric. His most recent publications include articles in *The Chaucer Review, Philological Quarterly*, and *Studies in Philology*.

CHAUCER INDEX

257

GENERAL INDEX